Language Transfer

THE CAMBRIDGE APPLIED LINGUISTICS SERIES
Series editors: Michael H. Long and Jack C. Richards

This new series presents the finding of recent work in applied linguistics which are of direct relevance to language teaching and learning and of particular interest to applied linguists, researchers, language teachers, and teacher trainers.

In this series:

Language Transfer

Cross-linguistic influence in language learning

Terence Odlin
The Ohio State University

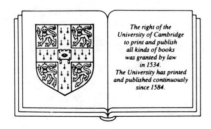

The right of the
University of Cambridge
to print and publish
all kinds of books
was granted by law
in 1534.
The University has printed
and published continuously
since 1584.

Cambridge University Press
Cambridge
New York   New Rochelle
Melbourne   Sydney

Published by the Press Syndicate of the University of Cambridge
The Pitt Building, Trumpington Street, Cambridge CB2 1RP
32 East 57th Street, New York, NY 10022, USA
10 Stamford Road, Oakleigh, Melbourne 3166, Australia

© Cambridge University Press 1989

First published 1989

Printed in the United States of America

Library of Congress Cataloging-in-Publication Data
Odlin, Terence.
Language transfer / Terence Odlin.
p.   cm. – (Cambridge applied linguistics series)
Bibliography: p.
Includes index.
ISBN 0 521 37168 6 hardcover.   ISBN 0 521 37809 5 paperback
1. Language transfer (Language learning)   I. Title.   II. Series.
P118.25.035 1989
418 – dc19   88–30760
                                                                    CIP

British Library Cataloguing in Publication Data
Odlin, Terence
Language transfer. – (The Cambridge applied
linguistics series).
1. Foreign languages. Learning. Role of
native languages.
I. Title
418'.007
ISBN 0 521 37168 6 hardcover
ISBN 0 521 37809 5 paperback

In memory of Walter Odlin
1908–1985

Contents

Series editors' preface

Language transfer has been a central issue in applied linguistics, second language acquisition, and language teaching for at least a century. Within the last few decades, however, its importance in second language learning has been reassessed several times. In the 1950s it was often deemed the most important factor to consider in theories of second language learning as well as in approaches to second language teaching. In the 1960s its importance waned as learners' errors were seen not as evidence of language transfer but rather of "the creative construction process." Some researchers virtually denied the existence of language transfer in their enthusiasm for universalist explanations. In recent years, however, a more balanced perspective has emerged in which the role of transfer is acknowledged and in which transfer is seen to interact with a host of other factors in ways not yet fully understood.

This reassessment of the significance of language transfer is lucidly demonstrated in this new addition to the Cambridge Applied Linguistics Series. In this timely book, Terry Odlin presents a comprehensive and original account of the nature of language transfer and its role in second language acquisition. Dr. Odlin documents the historical development of the concept of language transfer, explores the role of transfer in discourse, semantics, syntax, phonology, and writing systems, and examines the way language transfer interacts with linguistic as well as cultural, social, and personal factors in second language learning and use. In the process, he surveys a large body of literature and examines data from many different languages.

Dr. Odlin's analysis challenges simplistic notions of language transfer and offers instead a convincing account of the process as a phenomenon that is fundamental to research in second language acquisition and applied linguistics. This book will hence be invaluable to students entering the field of second language acquisition, researchers, language teachers, and anyone interested in the fundamental question of how language systems interact during the process of second language acquisition. We are therefore delighted to be able to make Dr. Odlin's research available to a wider audience through the Cambridge Applied Linguistics Series.

Michael H. Long
Jack C. Richards

Preface

The significance of cross-linguistic influences has long been a controversial topic. As this book indicates, the controversy has had a long life not only among second language teachers and researchers, but also among linguists interested in questions of language contact and language change. Although it would be too much to hope that this book will cause such a long-standing controversy to die, the discussion of transfer here may help to set to rest some dubious claims and to point the way toward more productive thinking about cross-linguistic influences. While I have tried hard to avoid the sweeping claims that unfortunately have been frequent in discussions of transfer, I make no secret of my belief that transfer is an extremely important factor in second language acquisition. The available evidence, I feel, warrants that belief. Thus, the focus of this book is on empirical investigations of learners' behavior in many contexts. There is some discussion of the pedagogical implications of certain investigations, but it seems to me that relatively little is known about the best ways to make use of transfer research in the classroom – hopefully, more teachers and teacher trainers will begin to think about what those ways are. There is also some discussion of theoretical work in other areas of linguistics, but I have made efforts to limit that discussion, which could go on interminably, and to limit the jargon that usually accompanies such discussion. Readers familiar with *Government and Binding*, *Schema Theory*, and *Sprachbund* will not find those terms, though they will note allusions to research using those terms. Some background in linguistics will be helpful in reading certain chapters (especially Chapter 7), but the glossary provided should help with some of the terminology that seemed impossible to avoid.

While this book has just one author, there are many people who have helped bring about whatever may be praiseworthy in it. In my graduate work I had the good fortune to take courses with Diana Natalicio, who recognized the seriousness of challenges to contrastive analysis in the 1960s and 1970s but who also recognized that the most extreme – albeit fashionable – criticisms of work on transfer were themselves open to challenges. Some of the more novel ideas in this book owe a great deal to work by Jacquelyn Schachter, Sarah Grey Thomason, and Eric Kellerman, all of whom also provided valuable feedback on a number of my ideas. As this work took shape, Jack Richards provided much encouragement and support – without his interest, this book might never have been finished. Ellen Shaw and Linda Grossman of Cambridge University Press helped in many ways to see the manuscript through the final stages. I would also like to thank several people who made my search for studies of transfer easier by sending me some of their work: Christian Adjemian, David Birdsong, Susan Gass, Lynn Eubank, Marku Filppula, John Hinds, Richard Schmidt, David Singleton, and Lydia White. Many thanks are also due to Lisa Kiser, Alan Brown, and other members of the Department of English at Ohio State who provided valuable comments on earlier drafts of the manuscript. Moreover, I received many forms of assistance from friends and colleagues in the Department of English, the Department of Linguistics, the programs in English as a Second Language, and also from members of the Linguistics Institute of Ireland. In addition, I would like to acknowledge the generous support provided by other units at Ohio State, including the College of Humanities, the Office of Research and Graduate Studies, and the Instructional and Research Computation Center. Finally, I would like to thank my family for their encouragement not only with this project but with much else besides.

1 Introduction

When people hear a speaker with a "foreign accent," they often try to guess the speaker's background. Sometimes racial features and sometimes a style of clothing will help listeners guess correctly, but often the only reliable clue seems to be how the individual talks. In such cases, questions put to the speaker such as "Are you German?" or "Are you Spanish?" suggest an intuition about the nature of language, an awareness, however unconscious, that the native language of a speaker can somehow cause the individual to sound "foreign" in speaking another language.

The detection of foreign accents is just one example of the awareness that people may often have of *cross-linguistic influence*, which is also known as *language transfer*.[1] That awareness is also evident from time to time in opinions that people have about foreign language study. Many believe that the study of one language (e.g., Latin) will make easier the study of a closely related language (e.g., French). Similarly, people often believe that some languages are "easy" in comparison with others. For example, many English-speaking university students see European languages such as French as less difficult than Oriental languages such as Chinese. Since the similarities between English and French seem to be relatively great, French is often considered "easy."

An awareness of language transfer is also evident in the mimicking of foreigners. While the representation of foreigners in ethnic jokes is often crude in more ways than one, stereotypes of the way foreigners talk are sometimes highly developed among actors. The following passage comes from a manual to train English-speaking actors in the use of different foreign accents, in this case a Russian one:

Oh! I very good fellow! why? because I Cossack. I very big Cossack. Yah! I captain of Royal Cossack Guard in Moscow – in old country. Oh! I got fifty – hundred – five hundred Cossack they was under me. I be big mans. And womens, they love me lots. Nastia Alexanderovna – she big ballet dancer in Czar ballet – Countess Irina Balushkovna, she love me. All womens they love

---

1 A more extended definition and also a justification of the term *transfer* appear in Chapter 3 (Section 3.1).

me. And men? Ach! they be 'fraid from me. They hating me. Why? because I
big Cossack. I ride big horse. Drink lots vodka. Oh! I very big mans.
(Herman and Herman 1943:340)

The manual provides a pronunciation guide for this passage so that
actors can make their phonetic mimicry seem plausible, but a number
of grammatical features in the passage also seem to be "typically Russian," such as the absence of an article and a copula in *I very good
fellow*. Another passage in the same manual provides a very different
linguistic – and ethnic – stereotype. While the Irishwoman's speech in
the following passage might be that of a monolingual speaker of English,
it is similar to stereotypical portrayals of Irish-English bilinguals by
modern Irish playwrights:

And what business is it of yours that I be awake or no? Be what right do you
come snooping after me, following me like a black shadow. Are youse never
going to leave me alone? Yous'd be after doing better minding your own
business and letting me for to mind mine. For I have an ache in me long-
suffering heart and lashin's of pain cutting through me brain like a dull knife.
And me eyes is looking at a world that's not of your living. For it's a
revelation I'm after having – a view into the banshee world of devils and
spirits and the dear departed dead now rotting their whitened bones under
the cold, black sod. Ah! sure, now, and it's the likes of you and your friends
that call themselves sane, that disbelieves in what I'm after seeing and
knowing. (Herman and Herman 1943:100)

Analogous to the Russian passage, some of the grammatical features in
the Irishwoman's speech appear to be stereotypically Irish: for example,
the syntactic pattern in *what I'm after seeing and knowing*, which in
standard English would be *what I have seen and known*. While these
portrayals of accents may seem exaggerated, they do typify the use of
special linguistic structures to characterize the speech of bilinguals.[2]

The distinctiveness of foreign accents often seems understandable in
light of cross-linguistic comparisons. For example, Russian does not have
present tense copula forms such as *am* or articles such as *a*, and so
omissions of the copula and indefinite article in *I very good fellow* may
seem to be clearly due to a difference in the grammatical systems of
Russian and English. The comparison of such differences, which is
known technically as **contrastive analysis**, has long been a part of second
language pedagogy, and in the twentieth century contrastive analyses
have become more and more detailed.[3] Since such cross-linguistic comparisons constitute an indispensable basis for the study of transfer, the

---

2 The Irishwoman's speech is a more accurate characterization than what is often
  found in so-called Stage Irish (cf. Bliss 1978; Sullivan 1980).
3 Technical terms that appear in the glossary (see page 165) are indicated by boldface
  at their first occurrence.

discussion of second language research in this book will frequently include contrastive observations.

In light of such everyday abilities as the recognition and mimicry of foreign accents and in light of common beliefs about cross-linguistic similarities and differences, there appears to be a widespread assumption that language transfer is an important characteristic of second language acquisition. It might seem obvious that many characteristics of a learner's linguistic behavior will closely approximate or greatly differ from the actual characteristics of the second language because of similarities and differences predicted by a contrastive analysis. In fact, however, the role of language transfer in second language acquisition has long been a very controversial topic.[4] Some scholars have indeed argued for the importance of transfer; some have gone so far as to consider it the paramount fact of second language acquisition. Yet other scholars have been very skeptical about the importance of transfer. Among linguists and language teachers today, there is still no consensus about the nature or the significance of cross-linguistic influences.

Much of the discussion in the next chapter will review the reasons for the skepticism about transfer, but a brief consideration of one of the most important reasons is appropriate now. As already noted, characteristics of the Russian language seem to explain sentences such as *I very good fellow*. A contrastive explanation, however, seems less than compelling in light of other facts. For example, speakers of Spanish, which, like English, has copula verb forms, frequently omit forms such as *am* and *is* (cf. Section 2.2). Moreover, such errors are found not only among Russian and Spanish speakers but also among speakers of other languages – and also among children learning English as their native language. Thus, while a contrastive analysis might explain a Russian speaker's omission of copula forms, a Spanish-English contrastive analysis would not explain the same error, and a contrastive analysis is irrelevant for monolingual children who make this same error as they acquire English. The pervasiveness of certain types of errors has thus been among the most significant counterarguments against the importance of transfer.

Despite the counterarguments, however, there is a large and growing

---

4 The terms *acquisition* and *learning* will be used interchangeably throughout this work even though much of the writing on second language acquisition (e.g., Krashen 1981) distinguishes between the two terms. I agree with Krashen and others that the outcomes of acquisition can differ depending on the awareness of language that individuals have (cf. Section 8.3). However, I strongly disagree with Krashen's analysis of transfer and with much else in his interpretation of second language acquisition (cf. Sections 2.2, 3.1). Since his characterization of *acquisition* and *learning* is questionable in several respects, I see no reason to use his terminological distinctions (cf. Gregg 1984; Odlin 1986).

body of research that indicates that transfer is indeed a very important factor in second language acquisition. Accordingly, the primary aim of this book is to reconsider the problem of transfer in light of recent second language research. While the research to be reviewed points to the importance of transfer, it also frequently points to the importance of other significant factors in second language acquisition. Thus, even though a comprehensive review of second language research is beyond the scope of this book, there will be frequent discussion of cases in which transfer is either not a significant influence or an influence that interacts with other influences.

There are a number of reasons for language teachers and linguists to consider more closely the problem of transfer. Teaching may become more effective through a consideration of differences between languages and between cultures. An English teacher aware of Spanish-based and Korean-based transfer errors, for example, will be able to pinpoint problems of Spanish-speaking and Korean-speaking ESL students better, and in the process, communicate the very important message to students that their linguistic and cultural background *is* important to the teacher.[5] Also, consideration of the research showing similarities in errors made by learners of different backgrounds will help teachers to see better what may be difficult or easy for anyone learning the language they are teaching.

There are yet other reasons to know about research on transfer. For historical linguists, such knowledge can lead to insights about the relation between language contact and language change. Although languages change for a variety of reasons, the bilingualism that often results from language contact situations can be a major factor. For example, Hiberno-English, the dialect spoken in parts of rural Ireland, does have several of the unusual characteristics of the Irishwoman's speech cited earlier, and a number of those characteristics appear to result from the influence of Irish. Research on transfer is also important for a better understanding of the nature of language acquisition in any context and is thus of interest to anyone curious about what is common to all languages, that is, *language universals*. As Comrie (1984) has noted, second language research can provide a valuable empirical check on the merit of universalist theories, and the issue of transfer is likely to figure prominently in such research.

This book consists of ten chapters. The next two provide an overview of the issues: Chapter 2 is a historical survey of the controversy sur-

---

5 Throughout this book, the term *ESL* (English as a Second Language) will be used even in cases in which *EFL* (English as a Foreign Language) might be more appropriate. While such a terminological distinction can be crucial for those developing syllabi or preparing pedagogical materials, the distinction is less important for researchers studying cross-linguistic influence.

rounding language transfer, and Chapter 3 is a discussion of four types of problems especially important in the investigation of transfer. The next four chapters survey second language research on transfer and universals in relation to linguistic subsystems: discourse (Chapter 4); semantics – including a discussion of morphology (Chapter 5); syntax (Chapter 6); and phonetics, phonology, and writing systems (Chapter 7). Chapter 8 discusses in more detail some aspects of language transfer which structural descriptions cannot always account for, such as the effects of individual variation in second language acquisition. Chapter 9 reviews important currents in the research discussed in earlier chapters, and Chapter 10 considers some of the implications that the research may have for teaching.

Further reading

Most studies of transfer appear in a wide variety of journals, but they sometimes appear in special collections. One of the best collections is edited by Gass and Selinker (1983). A recent book-length study by Ringbom (1987) combines a review of many of the controversies about transfer with a detailed empirical study. Ellis (1985) has written a remarkably comprehensive and judicious survey of research on second language acquisition, including work on transfer. For more discussion of linguistic analyses of the literary treatment of foreign accents, a text by Traugott and Pratt (1980) is useful. Recent introductions to linguistics include texts by Bolinger and Sears (1981) and Fromkin and Rodman (1983).

2 *Earlier thinking on transfer*

Discussions of transfer often begin with the work of American linguists in the 1940s and 1950s. Yet while the work of Charles Fries, Robert Lado, and others was clearly a major catalyst for subsequent research, serious thinking about cross-linguistic influences dates back to a controversy in historical linguistics in the nineteenth century. Accordingly, this chapter begins with a discussion of that controversy among scholars whose primary interests were not second language acquisition or language teaching but rather language classification and language change. The controversy promoted work on language contact that overlaps considerably with more recent studies of second language acquisition. Because the thinking of Fries, Lado, and others prompted much of the growth of research in second language acquisition, their views receive considerable attention, as do the views of some who have been very critical of their work. While this chapter can give only a suggestion of the historical context of the polemics on transfer, it provides important background for some fundamental issues discussed in subsequent chapters.

2.1   Languages (and dialects) in contact

Historical change and language mixing

Language contact situations arise whenever there is a meeting of speakers who do not all share the same language and who need to communicate.[1] When the communicative needs of people go beyond what gestures and other paralinguistic signals can achieve, some use of a second language becomes necessary. The languages learned in contact situations may or may not show some kind of **language mixing**, that is, the merging of characteristics of two or more languages in any verbal communication.

---

1 There are other kinds of language contact besides those discussed in this chapter, as, for example, when a French scholar deciphers a text in ancient Egyptian. Such cases, though, are exceptional in a number of ways.

If mixing does occur, native language influence is only one of the possible forms it can take. Another kind of mixing is in the form of *borrowings* from a second language into the native language (e.g., the use by English speakers of the loanword *croissant* from French to describe a certain kind of pastry), and still another kind is **code-switching**, in which there is a systematic interchange of words, phrases, and sentences of two or more languages (cf. Sections 8.2, 8.3).

People often show some awareness of language mixing, even though they are usually not familiar with terms such as *code-switching* and *transfer* (cf. Chapter 1 and Section 8.3). Among Indians in the Vaupés region of the Amazon rain forest, for example, there is a keen awareness of the mixing that arises in their multilingual villages (Sorenson 1967; Jackson 1974). Such awareness probably reflects a consciousness going far back into prehistory. Whether in the rain forest or elsewhere, humans have often seen themselves as belonging to different social groups, and they have often considered language to be an important distinguisher of their own group from others; it is no accident that the names of languages frequently designate ethnic groups (e.g., *Chinese, Navajo,* and *English*). Accordingly, any introduction of loanwords or other kinds of language mixing may be viewed either as a kind of linguistic intrusion or as a "foreign import," sometimes welcome, sometimes not (cf. Le Page and Tabouret Keller 1985). It is significant that the Indians of the Vaupés do not look upon language mixing favorably; although that attitude is probably not universal, people in many communities do have similarly unfavorable attitudes toward various kinds of mixing. For example, English loanwords in French and other languages have frequently been a target of language purists (cf. Section 8.3).

From antiquity onwards there is a historical record of people associating language contact and mixing with "contamination" (Silvestri 1977; Thomason 1981). Typical of such associations were scholarly discussions in Renaissance Europe about the link between Latin and the vernacular languages related to it. With regard to the origins of French, for example, scholars speculated about how speakers of other languages may have "corrupted" the language brought to Gaul by the Romans (Silvestri 1977). Although some scholarly work before the nineteenth century did make specific claims, most of the discussion about language contact and mixing was rather nebulous. Apart from occasional remarks about loanwords, few discussions included either detailed characterizations of the nature of cross-linguistic influences or specific examples of such influences (Silvestri 1977).

In the nineteenth century, debate about the importance of language contact and mixing intensified. The question of mixing had major implications for two interrelated problems that interested many nineteenth-century linguists: language classification and language change. The steady accumulation of grammars of languages in every part of the world made ever clearer the diversity of human languages and the scientific challenge of classifying them (Robins 1979). Many scholars came to believe that grammar was the soundest basis on which to construct classifications. Aware that lexical borrowings (i.e., loanwords) could often make classification decisions difficult, scholars often expected to find in grammar a linguistic subsystem unaffected by language contact and thus a key to distinguish any language. Müller (1861/1965:75), for example, was well aware of the large number of loanwords from Latin, French, and other languages in English, but considered English grammar to be immune from cross-linguistic influences:

The grammar, the blood and soul of the language, is as pure and unmixed in English as spoken in the British Isles, as it was when spoken on the shores of the German ocean by the Angles, Saxons, and Juts [sic] of the continent.[2]

The beliefs of Müller and others about the uniqueness of grammar were usually related to assumptions about the **tree model** of language change in which languages are viewed as parts of a "family tree." In that model, Latin, for example, is characterized as the "parent" language and French, Spanish, Rumanian, and other Romance tongues as the "daughter" languages.[3] The pattern of change in the tree model is primarily one of *internal development*, in which characteristics of the parent language undergo changes that are systematically manifested in the daughter languages. For example, in French, Spanish, and Rumanian, noun phrases commonly have definite articles, as in the following translations of "the mountain":

French: *le mont*
Spanish: *el monte*
Rumanian: *munte-le*

In Latin there were no articles, but in virtually all of the daughter languages there are definite and indefinite articles. The development of such an innovation in each of the daughter languages suggests the existence of what Whitney (in a slightly different connection) called "forces which are slowly and almost insensibly determining the growth of a language" (1881:25). Like Müller, Whitney took a dim view of the notion of mixing, and their attitude was shared by other scholars aware of the massive evidence of internal change not only in morphology and syntax but also in phonetics and phonology (e.g., Meillet 1948). If internal

2 Despite the racist connotations of this passage, Müller was an outstanding advocate of racial understanding in the nineteenth century.
3 As Robins (1979) observes, such characterizations of historical relationships are metaphoric and only partially revealing. Nevertheless, the family tree metaphor had an enormous impact on thinking about language change.

development could explain so much about language change, were explanations involving language mixture really necessary?

Areal linguistics

In the judgment of many scholars in the nineteenth and twentieth centuries, the answer to this question is affirmative, despite the cogent arguments by Whitney and others. Even while the evidence supporting the tree model of change is strong, there is good evidence supporting a very different model, the **wave model** (cf. Bloomfield 1933; Bailey 1973; Bynon 1977; Zobl 1984). First developed in the nineteenth century, the wave model has long been recognized as a useful complement to the tree model, especially for an understanding of *dialect change*. While characterizations of the wave model have changed over the years, the model still posits that linguistic patterns in one dialect can affect another dialect considerably, especially if the dialects are spoken in adjoining regions. For example, the English spoken in Chicago and that spoken in nearby towns in northern Illinois are similar, but recent changes in pronunciation that have appeared in Chicago make that variety different from other Illinois dialects. The changes seem to be slowly spreading from Chicago into other Illinois towns, largely through contacts between Chicagoans and people in the larger towns (cf. Callary 1975; Chambers and Trudgill 1980).

There is now a considerable body of scholarship pointing to the importance of dialect mixture (e.g., Trudgill 1986). Yet the significance of the wave model is not limited to dialect contact. As most linguists acknowledge, the difference between languages and dialects is often fuzzy, as the linguistic situation in parts of Spanish-speaking Uruguay and Portuguese-speaking Brazil shows. While Spanish and Portuguese are distinct in many ways, they might well be considered two Romance dialects instead of two languages were it not for political facts. On the border between Brazil and Uruguay there have been frequent contacts between people of both nations, and, not surprisingly, the similarity of Spanish and Portuguese has encouraged a great deal of mixing which one might call either dialect mixing or language mixing (Rona 1965).

Even when the differences between two languages are greater than is the case with Spanish and Portuguese, there is a possibility of language mixing. For example, Rumanian and Bulgarian have somewhat different "genetic" classifications (the former is a Romance language and the latter a Slavic language), but centuries of contact between speakers of Rumanian, Bulgarian, and other languages in the Balkans have led to many *areal* (i.e., regional) similarities not due to internal changes (Sandfeld 1930; Joseph 1983a). The definite article, for instance, follows the noun in Rumanian, Bulgarian, and Albanian, as in the following translation equivalents of "the village":

Rumanian: *sat-ul*
Bulgarian: *selo-to*
Albanian: *fshat-i*

As noted earlier, French, Spanish, and Rumanian all have definite articles, but in the Romance languages of Western Europe the definite article precedes the noun, whereas in Rumanian the definite article follows the noun. This divergence of Rumanian from the general Romance pattern can be best explained in terms of areal contact: The position of the article appears to reflect centuries of bilingualism in the border regions between Rumania and Bulgaria.[4]

Pidgins and creoles

The areal similarity of languages in the Balkans is among the best known examples of the long-term effects of language contact, but there is also a great deal of evidence for the importance of language contact in historical change in other areas, such as India (Gumperz and Wilson 1971; Emeneau 1980) and Ethiopia (Leslau 1945, 1952). Not all contact will lead to transfer, however. The importance not only of transfer but of other explanations for contact phenomena became clear as the study of **pidgin** and **creole** languages intensified toward the end of the nineteenth century. In that period Hugo Schuchardt, a German linguist who had noted the likely effects of transfer in certain contact situations in Europe, became interested in the so-called trade languages spawned in Africa, Asia, and elsewhere from encounters between the local inhabitants and Europeans. In some encounters, as in the case of the dealings between European and Chinese merchants on the coast of China, contacts were limited and the trade jargons used had only the status of "marginal languages," which are usually called *pidgins*. In other contact situations, however, the trade languages became more extensively used and often became languages acquired by young children; those languages are usually considered *creoles*.[5] Initially, Schuchardt thought that transfer was

---

4 Explanations about the development of the Rumanian article do not agree in all details, yet whatever the correct explanation is, language contact is probably involved (cf. Joseph 1983a).

5 Todd (1983), Mühlhäusler (1986), and others have argued that it is an oversimplification to equate pidgins with the language of one generation of adults and creoles with the language of children of the subsequent generation. Singler (1988) suggests that the distinction should refer to whether a group has adopted a language as the language of ethnic identification, in which case it is a creole and not a pidgin. If Singler's view is correct, the adoption of a pidgin by children may be a necessary but not a sufficient condition for terming the new language a creole.

a likely explanation for many of the features of pidgins and creoles, and in his earlier articles on the subject he presented cases that he viewed as probable or at least possible instances of transfer: for example, the word order of a Spanish creole in the Philippines and the word order of a Portuguese creole in India (Schuchardt 1883a, b). However, other scholars' arguments and Schuchardt's own investigations of other contact situations led him to speculate about alternative explanations for many characteristics in pidgins, creoles, and other contact languages. In examining the pidginlike English spoken by servants and colonizers in India, Schuchardt (1891/1980) wondered how much the rudimentary structure of the language might be due to attempts by the colonizers to make English more comprehensible by simplifying structures; such attempts have subsequently become known as **Foreigner Talk** (e.g., Ferguson 1975). His growing awareness of the similarities between different trade languages led Schuchardt (1909/1980) to consider various types of **simplification**: the simplification of grammatical features by children learning their native language, the simplification that adults use for the benefit of children, the simplification seen in Foreigner Talk, and the simplification found in the grammars of so many pidgins and creoles (cf. Slobin 1977). As Gilbert (1980) suggests, Schuchardt became more and more aware of apparently *universal* tendencies toward simplicity in situations involving language contact and language acquisition. A similar awareness motivates much of the current research on second language acquisition (cf. Meisel 1983).

In the study of pidgins and creoles in the twentieth century, there has been considerable disagreement about the relative importance of transfer and universals in the creation of contact languages (cf. Andersen 1983a; Muysken and Smith 1986). Explanations based on transfer and those based on universalist notions are not always mutually exclusive, and there are other theoretical positions besides those two (cf. Mühlhäusler 1986). However, universalist and transfer approaches sometimes do conflict, and both approaches have many clear attractions (cf. Section 3.4). Mühlhäusler argues persuasively that *multicausal* explanations are the most satisfactory, but weighing the relative importance of transfer, universals, and other factors in such explanations remains difficult. Most probably, transfer will play a relatively minor role in some situations, but in other cases it will play a major role. Certain pidgins and creoles in New Guinea seem to illustrate the former possibility; perhaps the contact between speakers of many different languages keeps any native-language influence from greatly affecting the newer creoles of the region such as Tok Pisin (Mühlhäusler 1986). On the other hand, the Hawaiian Pidgin English spoken by many Japanese shows unmistakable influences of Japanese word order and other structures, as Nagara (1972) and others have shown (Section 6.1). This, along with other evidence, suggests that when only a small number of languages are spoken in a contact situation, a pidgin will show more transfer effects (cf. Singler 1988).

Borrowing and substratum transfers

Aside from research on pidgins and creoles, scholarship on language contact in general has increased considerably in the nineteenth and twentieth centuries, and with that increase has come much evidence for the importance of cross-linguistic influences. With the growth of this evidence, the diversity of situations in which transfer occurs has also become clearer, as research by Weinreich (1953/1968) and others shows. It should be noted that Weinreich used the term *interference* to cover any case of transfer. Nevertheless, his survey of bilingualism shows that the effects of cross-linguistic influence are not monolithic but instead vary considerably according to the social context of the language contact situation. These effects can often be distinguished through the use of the terms **borrowing transfer** or **substratum transfer** (cf. Thomason and Kaufman 1988). *Borrowing transfer* refers to the influence a second language has on a previously acquired language (which is typically one's native language). For example, borrowing transfer has been amply documented in the case of Young People's Dyirbal (Schmidt 1985). Dyirbal, an Aboriginal language spoken in northeastern Australia, has undergone considerable attrition (i.e., change from the traditional norms) as a result of the younger Aborigines' exposure to English. While not all of the attrition is directly due to English influence, many characteristics of Young People's Dyirbal show clear evidence of transfer. Other cases of attrition with concomitant borrowing transfer include a variety of Swiss Romansh influenced by German (Weinreich 1953/1968), some varieties of Greek influenced by Turkish (Dawkins 1916), and American varieties of Norwegian influenced by English (Haugen 1953).

Substratum transfer is the type of cross-linguistic influence investigated in most studies of second language acquisition; such transfer involves the influence of a source language (typically, the native language of a learner) on the acquisition of a target language, the "second" language regardless of how many languages the learner already knows.[6] Aside from studies of such transfer in the performance of second language students, there are a number of language contact studies showing the importance of native language influence, as in the case of the influence

6 Not all cases of cross-linguistic influence can be neatly classified as borrowing or substratum transfer. In the case of Ethiopia, for example, the evidence suggests a possible occurrence of both kinds of transfer (Thomason and Kaufman 1988). In cases of young children learning two languages simultaneously, cross-linguistic influence can occur (e.g., Taeschner 1983), but such influence differs considerably from typical instances of borrowing or substratum transfer (Sections 8.2, 8.3).

of Irish on the English spoken in Ireland (Henry 1957; Filppula 1986), the influence of Quechua on the Spanish spoken in Peru and Ecuador (Luján, Minaya, and Sankoff 1984; Muysken 1984), and the influence of Arabic and Turkish on the Dutch spoken by immigrant workers in Holland (Jansen, Lalleman, and Muysken 1981).[7] Since the focus of this book is on native language influences, the term *transfer* will hereafter serve as an abbreviation for *substratum transfer*, except where there is an explicit comparison made between borrowing transfer and substratum transfer.

While borrowing transfer and substratum transfer are similar in some ways, their results are often very different. Thomason and Kaufman (1988) argue that such differences reflect differences in social as well as linguistic factors. Borrowing transfer normally begins at the lexical level, since the attrition of the language absorbing the foreign vocabulary normally begins with the onset of strong cultural influences from speakers of another language. The group exerting the influence is often, though not always, a speech community with larger numbers, greater prestige, and more political power. In such cases, words associated with the government, the legal system, the schools, the technology, and the commercial products of the dominant majority are among the first to make their way into the minority language, but massive lexical borrowing may also supplant much of the vocabulary of everyday living. In the case of Young People's Dyirbal, for example, Schmidt found that younger Aborigines were not always aware of the traditional words to describe activities such as cooking and would therefore employ English words instead.[8] When borrowing transfer comes to have such a major effect on lexical semantics, there is often a great deal of cross-linguistic syntactic influence as well. As Schmidt indicates, Dyirbal syntax now shows many influences from English. However, the phonetics and phonology of the native language are less likely to be affected by borrowing transfer. According to Schmidt, the pronunciation of Young People's Dyirbal does not depart drastically from that of older speakers.

Substratum transfer, on the other hand, will normally show a different weighting of cross-linguistic influences. Thomason (1981) suggests that the effects of substratum transfer will be more evident in pronunciation (and also in syntax) than in the lexicon. If pronunciation is the most difficult aspect of a second language to master, as some believe, the influence of native language phonetics and phonology will be more pervasive than the influence of other language subsystems (cf. Section 8.2).

7 In subsequent chapters (especially 6 and 8), there is more extended discussion of these cases.
8 Such behavior may seem to be the same as code-switching, but many studies of switching indicate that such mixing does *not* result from a lack of knowledge of either language in the switch (Section 8.3).

The effects of native language influence may survive the historical acquisition situation, with both pronunciation and syntax in the newly acquired language often providing an enduring testimony of earlier transfer, as is evident in the case of Hiberno-English, the English dialect spoken in many parts of Ireland. Only a small number of people now speak Irish as their native language, while nearly everyone speaks English. However, many monolingual English speakers in Ireland use a pronunciation and grammar that reflect a "substratum" of earlier centuries of widespread Irish-English bilingualism. Some of the clearest examples of this type of transfer involve verb phrases that have parallels in Irish, such as *He's after telling a lie* ("He's told a lie") (cf. Wright 1898; Henry 1957; Bammesberger 1983; Bliss 1984).[9]

The social dimensions of transfer research

Since transfer occurs in a wide variety of social contexts, a thorough understanding of cross-linguistic influence depends very much on a thorough understanding of those contexts. Accordingly, historical research on transfer may serve as a useful cross-check on research in which social factors are not investigated. Because many second language investigations are detailed case studies or experimental studies involving relatively small numbers of individuals, they cannot always suggest the importance of *demographic influences* or other social factors whereas many historical studies can. In the case of Ireland, for example, the widespread adoption of English in the nineteenth century appears to have resulted in much more transfer than might be evident in the English of the relatively small numbers of foreign students at American universities, where so many second language studies are conducted (cf. Section 8.3). Studies of both historical and contemporary cases of wide-scale language contact are also useful for assessing the effects of *formal instruction* on transfer. Some have claimed that transfer will be significant in acquisition affected by formal instruction but will be less so in naturalistic second language acquisition (e.g., Dulay, Burt, and Krashen 1982). That claim is supported by some evidence, but it is probably an oversimplification, as there are studies of language contact in Ecuador, West Africa, and elsewhere indicating that formal education may constrain transfer (Section 8.3). While transfer is primarily a psychological phenomenon, its potential effect on acquisition may be large or small depending on the complex variations of the social settings in which acquisition takes place.

9 In discussions of Hiberno-English there has been little disagreement that transfer is
responsible for constructions such as *He's after telling a lie*. However, some other
constructions may be related to nonstandard usages in British dialects going back to
the seventeenth century (Harris 1984).

2.2   Transfer as a controversy in language teaching

The growth of contrastive studies

Despite the conflicting views on the significance of language contact in historical linguistics, the notion of language transfer remained uncontroversial among language teachers well into the twentieth century. As early as the schools of the ancient world, teachers were writing down contrastive observations about the languages students knew and the languages they wished to learn (Kelly 1969). And as recently as the schools influenced by figures such as Sweet (1899/1972), Jespersen (1912), Palmer (1917), Fries (1945), and other proponents of new (or seemingly new) methods of language teaching, there was a widespread acceptance of the idea that native language influences could greatly affect second language acquisition. Challenges to assumptions about the importance of transfer did not have much impact on the history of language teaching until the late 1960s.

The challenges that arose in that period were largely in reaction to two claims that American scholars had made about transfer in the preceding twenty or so years. The first of those claims was that the existence of cross-linguistic differences made second language acquisition extremely different from first language acquisition. In the foreword to *Linguistics Across Cultures*, a highly influential manual on contrastive analysis by Lado (1957), Fries stated:

Learning a second language ... constitutes a very different task from learning the first language. The basic problems arise not out of any essential difficulty in the features of the new language themselves but primarily out of the special "set" created by the first language habits.

Along with many linguists of his time, Fries subscribed to the behaviorist analysis of linguistic competence as a series of habits (Bloomfield 1933). Native language influence was thus the influence of old habits, some potentially helpful, some potentially harmful (cf. Section 3.1).

The second claim that came to be challenged was that the difficulties of second language acquisition could be determined through contrastive analyses:

We assume that the student who comes in contact with a foreign language will find some features of it quite easy and others extremely difficult. Those elements that are similar to his native language will be simple for him, and those elements that are different will be difficult. The teacher who has made a comparison of the foreign language with the native language of the students will know better what the real learning problems are and can better provide for teaching them. (Lado 1957:2)

While other claims of Fries and Lado have also been disputed, the positions just quoted would serve as major catalysts for research challenging the significance of transfer.

Although Lado and others are sometimes accused of having only been concerned with narrow structural analyses of language, the title of *Linguistics Across Cultures* indicates otherwise. Moreover, Lado stated that "the fundamental assumption" of his book was that

individuals tend to transfer the forms and meanings, and the distribution of forms and meanings of their native language and *culture* [emphasis added] to the foreign language and culture – both productively when attempting to speak the language and to act in the culture, and receptively when attempting to grasp and understand the language and the culture as practiced by the natives. (Lado 1957:2)

The importance of cultural as well as linguistic factors in acquisition was clear to Lado, and he devoted a chapter of his book to suggesting how to compare cultures. Despite this emphasis on culture as well as on language, most contrastive analyses in the 1950s and 1960s concentrated on pronunciation and grammar. However, a discussion by Kaplan (1966) of cultural differences and second language writing proved to be highly influential in subsequent research on second language discourse. Kaplan claimed:

The foreign-student paper is out of focus because the foreign student is employing a rhetoric and a sequence of thought which violate the expectations of the native reader. (1966:4)

The rhetoric and "sequence of thought" reflected, according to Kaplan, the discourse and thought patterns of the student's own culture, and were analogous to the transfer alleged to be so important in second language pronunciation and grammar. Though Lado's analysis only indirectly touched on discourse, Kaplan proposed that contrastive studies were possible beyond the sentence level, and his arguments encouraged the study of what is now frequently termed *contrastive rhetoric* (cf. Sections 4.2, 4.3).

Fries, Lado, and others saw as extremely important the development of materials specifically designed for different groups of students (cf. Fries 1945; Lado 1957). According to Fries (1949:97), "The problems of the Chinese student are very different from those of the Spanish speaker," and the materials for teaching English that he had helped develop some years before reflected that belief. The pedagogical practices advocated by Fries and others encouraged an expansion of contrastive studies for pedagogical purposes. Many books, articles, and graduate theses from 1950 to 1970 reflect the growth of such study (cf. Sajavaara and Lehtonen 1981; Dechert, Brüggemeir, and Futterer 1984). However, another area, empirical studies of transfer, was slower in developing.

Although Lado (1957) and others did recognize the need for such research, it is clear that he believed that the language contact research of Haugen (1953) and Weinreich (1953/1968) provided enough of an empirical demonstration of the importance of transfer to warrant the development of contrastive analyses for language teaching. More research on cross-linguistic influences did eventually appear, though much of it called into question earlier thinking on transfer.

Problems with contrastive analysis

The claims made by Lado and Fries about the predictive power of contrastive analysis and about the relation between first and second language acquisition faced serious challenges by the 1970s. The predictive validity of many contrastive analyses seemed questionable: empirical research was beginning to show that learning difficulties do not always arise from cross-linguistic differences and that difficulties which do arise are not always predicted by contrastive analyses. Moreover, the theoretical significance of transfer seemed dubious to a number of researchers struck by the similarities between first and second language acquisition.[10] Some problems of contrastive analysis will be discussed in this section, and the question of first and second language acquisition will be considered in the next section.

Some differences between languages do not always lead to significant learning difficulties. For example, two verbs in Spanish correspond to different senses of the English verb *know* – *conocer* and *saber*. While this lexical difference poses many problems for English speakers learning Spanish, Spanish speakers learning English seem to have little difficulty in associating two lexical senses with one form (cf. Stockwell, Bowen, and Martin 1965; Lee 1968). Thus the difference between Spanish and English is not in itself enough to allow for accurate predictions of difficulty (cf. Section 3.2).

An even more serious challenge to the validity of contrastive analyses is the occurrence of errors that do not appear to be due to native language influence. For example, a contrastive analysis of Spanish and English would not predict that Spanish speakers would omit forms of the verb *be*, since Spanish has similar grammatical structures.[11] Whatever other

---

10 Criticism of contrastive analysis arose for other reasons in addition to those discussed here, as seen, for example, in the analysis of Lado's claims about testing by Upshur (1962). However, the most serious challenges, those that most influenced arguments against transfer up to the present, have been related to problems of prediction and similarities between first and second language acquisition.

11 Spanish has not one but two verbs equivalent to *be*: *ser* and *estar*. While this contrast causes considerable problems for English speakers learning Spanish, it

errors might arise, one would not predict that Spanish speakers would say *That very simple* instead of *That's very simple* (Peck 1978). Yet a number of studies, including Peck's, have documented the omission of forms of *be* in the speech of Spanish-speaking learners of English (e.g., Butterworth and Hatch 1978; Peck 1978; Schumann 1978; Shapira 1978).

The errors that Spanish-English contrastive analyses fail to predict are not just ones involving *be* forms. Other kinds of errors occur despite clear similarities between English and Spanish in such areas as verb tenses, word order, and prepositional usage (cf. Butterworth and Hatch 1978; Schumann 1978; Andersen 1979). Moreover, in looking at studies of child bilingualism that had been conducted earlier in the twentieth century as well as at more recent ones (e.g., Ronjat 1913; Ravem 1968), scholars noticed that a number of these studies showed only minimal evidence of transfer or any other kind of language mixing (cf. Section 8.2).

Further questioning of the worth of contrastive analysis came from classifications of learners' errors in studies that became known generically as **error analyses** (e.g., Dušková 1969; Richards 1971). Some errors seem to arise not from language transfer but from other sources such as **transfer of training**, that is, the influences that arise from the way a student is taught (cf. Selinker 1972; Stenson 1974; Felix 1981). While some influences from teaching are no doubt beneficial, others can induce errors that might not otherwise occur. For example, Felix notes that question-and-answer drills can produce errors such as the following:

Teacher: Am I your teacher?
Student: Yes, I am your teacher.

As Felix observes, one would not predict such an error from a comparison of pronouns in the student's native language, which was German, and pronouns in English.

Other errors documented in error analysis research seem to arise spontaneously. For example, **overgeneralizations** such as *This program of the Kissinger* (said by a Spanish speaker) often appear to be due to the inappropriate application of a target language rule, here an overextension of an article to a proper noun (Schumann 1978). Since Spanish, like English, does not use articles with personal names such as Kissinger, transfer is not a viable explanation. Similarly, errors such as omitting articles, copulas, and other forms often seem to involve simplification rather than transfer, as Schuchardt had suspected several decades earlier (Section 2.1). For example, the omission by a Spanish speaker of an

---

does not seem to lead to any special problems for Spanish speakers learning English (cf. Stockwell, Bowen, and Martin 1965).

article in the phrase *Picture is very dark* (Schumann 1978) is not attributable to Spanish since a Spanish translation of the sentence would require an article (see Section 3.2).

While error analysis research has done much to show the complexity of acquisition behaviors, it is not without its own problems (Schachter and Celce-Murcia 1977; Long and Sato 1984). One of the major challenges for error analysts is deciding what category to assign a particular error to. For example, omitting an article in English may quite arguably be a case of simplification with a Spanish speaker but a case of transfer with a Korean speaker (see Section 3.2). Moreover, there is reason to believe that processes such as transfer and simplification *interact* (see Section 3.3). Aside from such problems, the error analyses of the 1960s and 1970s often found some evidence of native language influence, even while opinions varied about the importance of such influence.

Despite the evidence of cross-linguistic influence in some error analyses, the credibility of contrastive analysis had been seriously damaged by the 1970s. Some scholars (e.g., Lee 1968; Wardhaugh 1970) suggested that contrastive analysis had no predictive power and that contrastive studies could only be useful after the fact. In other words, a comparison of the native and target languages would be useful for explaining why certain errors arise, but in the absence of actual data about learners' errors little if anything could be reliably predicted. Other researchers (e.g., Schachter 1974) nevertheless offered empirical arguments for the predictive ability of certain kinds of contrastive analysis (Section 6.2). How much a contrastive analysis can or should predict has remained a controversial question up to the present (Section 3.3).

Universal processes in acquisition?

Aside from casting doubt on the value of contrastive analysis, the empirical studies of the 1960s and 1970s contributed to skepticism about transfer in other important ways. The research showed not only the similarity of some errors made by learners of many different language backgrounds, but also the similarity of some errors in both first and second language acquisition, which led many to wonder how different the two processes really were.

The error analyses of the 1960s and 1970s showed that some types of errors are common in the emerging second language of speakers of virtually any native language. For example, the omission of *is* in cases such as *That very simple* is an error made not only by Spanish speakers but also by speakers of Chinese, Japanese, and other languages (Huang and Hatch 1978; Itoh and Hatch 1978). In some cases the omission of *is* would be predicted from a contrastive analysis, as in the case of the stereotypical Russian's monologue given in Chapter 1. Likewise, the omission of the verb in *That very simple* by a Chinese speaker might be predicted from structural facts about the use of copula forms in Chinese. Nevertheless, the success of this contrastive prediction seems unimpressive in light of the omission of English copula forms by speakers of Spanish, Japanese, and other languages that do have present-tense copulas. Moreover, the transfer explanation for such errors seems questionable in light of the fact that the omission of *is* and other copula forms also occurs in the speech of children learning English as their native language: for example, *That a kitchen* (Brown 1973).

For many researchers, such errors are nothing more or less than indicators of developmental processes found in both first and second language acquisition, and accordingly such errors are often termed **developmental errors**. The stages of development, many have argued, are evident in the relative accuracy that learners show in using particular structures. For example, Dulay and Burt (1974) observed similar accuracy orders for several English structures in the speech of two groups of bilingual children, one group speaking Spanish as their native language and the other group speaking Chinese. Part of the accuracy order is given below:

Most accurate	contractible copula (*'s*)[12]
	regular past tense (*-ed*)
Least accurate	possessive (*'s*)

Thus, errors such as *That very simple* were less frequent than tense errors such as *I play a new game last night*, which in turn were less frequent than omissions of the possessive marker, as in *John book*.

The methodology of studies of accuracy order rests largely on two assumptions: (1) that learners have reached a particular developmental stage if they make very few or no errors with particular types of structures; and (2) that the more frequent particular errors are, the further learners are from attaining a particular stage. If one accepts these assumptions, the succession of structures that are mastered constitutes a **developmental sequence**, that is, a succession of phases of learning to master new structures. The most important evidence for any particular sequence comes from **longitudinal** studies, in which learners' progress with various structures is charted over some interval of time (e.g., Hakuta 1976). Though not as persuasive, evidence for a sequence can also come

---

12 In spoken English the copula may be contracted most of the time. In some cases, however, the full form of the copula is required. For example, when the copula follows a word that ends with a strident sound such as /S/ (as in *The glass is fragile*), one cannot omit the vowel of the copula. In order to separate difficulties due to grammar problems from difficulties due to pronunciation problems, researchers have generally distinguished contractible and uncontractible copulas.

from **cross-sectional** studies, in which individuals' relative performances are measured at a single interval.[13]

In the debate on language transfer, the notion of developmental sequences has been a key concept, especially since the appearance of the first studies of accuracy orders by Dulay and Burt (e.g., Dulay and Burt 1973; Dulay and Burt 1974). Their cross-sectional studies have often been viewed as strong evidence for the existence of developmental sequences in second language acquisition, since rather similar results have been evident in studies of other groups of learners, including adults and speakers of other languages besides Spanish and Chinese (e.g., Bailey, Madden, and Krashen 1974; Fathman 1975). Moreover, there are some similarities in these results with those in child language research (cf. Brown 1973; de Villiers and de Villiers 1973; Van Patten 1984). Although the accuracy orders shown by children are not the same as those shown by second language learners, many researchers have seen enough similarities to begin paying serious attention to the idea that all language acquisition, first and second, proceeds largely in terms of a set of fixed developmental sequences.[14] Aside from the particular structures studied by Dulay and Burt, developmental similarities between child language and second language acquisition have been documented in other areas, such as the evolution of negation patterns (Section 6.3). Moreover, research on the relative clause patterns of adult second language learners indicates developmental similarities regardless of the native language of the learners (Section 6.2).

Largely from the evidence for developmental sequences, Dulay, Burt, Krashen, and others have argued that transfer plays only a minimal role in the acquisition of grammar. The study of Chinese and Spanish speakers by Dulay and Burt (1974) illustrates the basic thrust of such arguments. Despite the fact that the copula is often absent in Chinese, speakers of that language were nearly as successful in using the contractible copula *is* as Spanish speakers were. And despite the fact that Chinese and Spanish are very different languages, the accuracy orders for all structures studied were comparable for both groups. In other words, the native language appears to have little influence on whether one target language structure will be easier than another.

13 From a methodological point of view, longitudinal studies are superior to cross-sectional studies. From a practical point of view, however, cross-sectional studies are usually much more feasible. In studying most kinds of human behavior over long stretches of time, researchers often find it difficult to keep track of the individuals under study.

14 It is not entirely clear how good the evidence is for developmental sequences in the cross-sectional studies of Dulay, Burt, and others. While problems with the methods and data interpretation of Dulay and Burt are beyond the scope of the present discussion, such problems have been discussed by many researchers (e.g., Rosansky 1976; Andersen 1977; Hatch 1983; Huebner 1983).

If native language influence does not determine the accuracy orders or the developmental sequences presumably represented by those orders, some other influence (or influences) must account for the relative ease or difficulty of a target language structure. Dulay and Burt saw in the results of their Spanish and Chinese study evidence

that universal cognitive mechanisms are the basis for the child's organization of a target language and that it is the L2 system [the target language] rather than the L1 system [the native language] that guides the acquisition process. (1974:52)

Krashen (1981) and others have argued that this position is just as applicable to adult second language acquisition, at least in those cases in which formal instruction plays little, if any, role. Dulay, Burt, Krashen, and others claim that second language acquisition is essentially no different from child language acquisition. While they acknowledge that there frequently are differences in the success achieved in second language acquisition in comparison with first language acquisition, they see such differences as related to motivation, anxiety about making errors, the learner's environment, and other factors. The claim made about the fundamental identity of first and second language acquisition is thus exactly the opposite of the one made by Fries in the 1950s.

The skepticism about transfer did not result simply from the growth of empirical research. For many scholars, transfer was a behaviorist concept that had been appropriated by structural linguists such as Fries, and in the 1960s and 1970s both behaviorism and structuralism were becoming unattractive, as major theoretical shifts occurred in linguistics and psychology (cf. Section 3.1). Where structuralist analyses of grammar had prevailed during much of the twentieth century, transformational syntax now became the dominant form of grammatical analysis (cf. Fries 1952; Chomsky 1957; Robins 1979). Where the vast differences between some languages had made many linguists hesitant to see any common patterns, the similarities of languages now became clearer to scholars more and more interested in the notion of language universals (cf. Section 3.4). Where an earlier generation of scholars thought little about biological predispositions to learn language, a new generation looked back to the old philosophical problem of innate ideas. Where the behaviorist doctrine of habit formation had once dominated psycholinguistic investigations (including investigations of language acquisition), cognitive psychology stressed the creative capacities of human thought and language. For many scholars, transfer was too much the theoretical creature of dubious psychology and dubious linguistics.

Some doubts about the case against transfer

The empirical failures of contrastive analysis and the important similarities between first and second language acquisition did much to bring the notion of transfer into disrepute. Nevertheless, the most skeptical positions taken on transfer and contrastive analysis are highly questionable on both theoretical and empirical grounds. Since much of this book presents evidence that rebuts the most skeptical positions, the shortcomings of those positions will be discussed only briefly in this section.

There are many theoretical difficulties with the arguments that minimize the importance of transfer. One problem with many of these arguments is their focus on errors (e.g., Whitman and Jackson 1972). While errors no doubt provide important evidence for the strength or weakness of particular native language influences, they are far from being the only evidence (cf. Section 3.3). Another problem lies in an assumption frequently made in the consideration of language universals: namely, that if universal developmental sequences play a major role in acquisition, transfer cannot play much of a role. In fact, however, there are reasons to believe that cross-linguistic influences work in tandem with the psychological factors governing developmental sequences (Sections 6.2, 6.3). Still another difficulty is the assumption sometimes still made that theories of transfer are inextricably linked to theories of habit formation. Yet by no means is there any necessary connection between such theories (Section 3.1).

One further theoretical shortcoming found in many of the most skeptical positions on transfer also warrants mention: their overemphasis on morphology and syntax. Even though the motivations have been somewhat different, there is a clear similarity between the positions on language mixing taken by Müller, Whitney, and others in the nineteenth century and the positions on transfer taken by Dulay, Burt, and others in the twentieth. As in the nineteenth century, grammar often continues to be seen as the "blood and soul" of language (cf. Section 2.1). In contrast to grammatical transfer, transfer affecting second language pronunciation has been less controversial – even though empirical studies have identified many of the same problems in contrastive analyses of phonetics and phonology that have been evident in analyses of morphology and syntax (e.g., Johansson 1973). Too often in polemics on transfer the evidence from research not only on pronunciation but also on discourse and vocabulary is either taken for granted or simply ignored. Obviously the question of grammatical transfer is important and warrants much of the research that has been undertaken. Nevertheless, the studies surveyed in Chapters 4 through 7 indicate that: (1) transfer can occur in *all* linguistic subsystems, including morphology and syntax; and (2) other influences besides transfer affect all subsystems.

The theoretical shortcomings evident in the more skeptical positions on transfer are more than matched by empirical shortcomings. In virtually none of the most extreme polemics on transfer has there been a careful look at some of the most relevant language contact evidence.

Dulay and Burt (1974/1983), for example, equate the bilingual situations in Weinreich's study with those in Haugen's research (which concerned borrowing transfer), and claim that Weinreich's research has little to do with contrastive analysis (cf. Section 2.1). Haugen's study, it is true, focuses on borrowing transfer and thus is only indirectly relevant to transfer in second language acquisition. However, Weinreich's study cites a great deal of research not only on borrowing but also on substratum transfer (e.g., Schuchardt 1884/1971; Marckwardt 1946; Harris 1948). While Weinreich's use of the term *interference* to refer to both kinds of transfer (and also to code-switching) was no doubt confusing, many of the cases discussed in his book involve native language influence on the second language of bilinguals having varying degrees of linguistic proficiency.

Along with the relatively early studies cited by Weinreich, much of the empirical research in the 1970s and 1980s has led to new and ever more persuasive evidence for the importance of transfer in all subsystems. A rather large number of studies comparing the grammar, vocabulary, and so forth of learners with different native languages indicate acquisition differences attributable to cross-linguistic influence (e.g., Ringbom and Palmberg 1976; Schachter and Rutherford 1979; Jansen, Lalleman, and Muysken 1981; Ard and Homburg 1983; Andrews 1984; Appel 1984; White 1985; Schumann 1986; Singler 1988). Furthermore, there are studies indicating the influence of a second language on the acquisition of a third (Sections 3.3, 8.3). And with the growth of transfer research, there have appeared more studies that give some idea of how transfer interacts with many other factors in acquisition (cf. Chapter 8). From the nineteenth century on, the standards of evidence for transfer have been rising, and the empirical support for the importance of cross-linguistic influences on grammar, vocabulary, pronunciation, etc., is now quite strong. Before a detailed look is taken at empirical work on specific subsystems, however, it is worthwhile to consider some basic problems in doing research on transfer. Chapter 3 addresses several of those problems.

Further reading

The role of language contact in language change is discussed at some length by Bynon (1977) in a very readable introduction to historical linguistics. Surveys by Appel and Muysken (1987) and by Mühlhäusler (1986) offer more detailed discussions of many of the same issues. Though somewhat dated, an article by Sridhar (1981) is a very thoughtful survey of problems related to error analysis and transfer. Hakuta (1986) offers useful insights not only on transfer but also on many other issues important in the study of bilingualism.

3 Some fundamental problems in the study of transfer

There are many theoretical and practical problems that attend the study of transfer. It is beyond the scope of this chapter to review them all, but problems in four areas have an especially important bearing on the discussion in subsequent chapters: definition, comparison, prediction, and generalization.

3.1 Problems of definition

The terminology used to study language reflects – and sometimes creates – vexing problems, and in the terminology of second language research, the term *transfer* is as problematic as any. The issue of cross-linguistic influence is controversial with or without the term, but the long-standing use of *transfer* has itself led to differences of opinion. Some scholars have advocated abandoning the term or using it only in highly restricted ways (e.g., Corder 1983; Kellerman and Sharwood Smith 1986), yet many others continue to use it without restriction. In this section, a definition of the term *transfer* will be presented, along with a critique of that definition. However, before any observations are made about what transfer is (or at least seems to be), some observations about what transfer is *not* are appropriate.

Transfer is not simply a consequence of habit formation. A discussion of contrastive analysis and behaviorism by Carroll (1968) makes clear that the behaviorist notion of transfer is quite different from the notion of native language influence (cf. Section 2.2). For one thing, the behaviorist notion of transfer often implies the extinction of earlier habits, whereas the acquisition of a second language need not (and normally does not) lead to any replacement of the learner's primary language.[1] This and other considerations suggest that behaviorism may never have been relevant to the study of transfer (cf. Hakuta 1986). Even though behaviorism has

1 The acquisition of a second language *can* lead to borrowing transfer and attrition, and to that extent the behaviorist conception might apply to second language behavior (cf. Section 2.1). However, in many acquisition contexts the effects of such attrition are extremely negligible.

contributed extremely little to the study of transfer since the 1970s, much of the dislike of the term *transfer* comes from its traditional association with behaviorism. Yet as Kellerman (1984) has observed, there is less and less danger of people associating transfer with habit formation, which has in many ways been superseded by concepts from cognitive psychology (cf. Section 2.2). In fact, behaviorism is now so widely discredited in the field of psycholinguistics that some leading textbooks in that field give virtually no attention to behaviorist analyses (e.g., Clark and Clark 1977; Foss and Hakes 1978). It is worth noting that over a hundred years ago Whitney (1881) used the term *transfer* to refer to cross-linguistic influences – long before any linguists thought of linking it to the notion of habit formation. In all likelihood, no amount of scholarly protestation will keep that term from being used far into the future.

Transfer is not simply interference. With or without any behaviorist connotations, the notion of interference does seem applicable in the description of some aspects of second language performance, such as phonetic inaccuracies that resemble sounds in the learner's native language (Section 7.2). Not surprisingly, then, the term *interference* continues to be widely used. Nevertheless, much of the influence of the native language (or of some other previously learned language) can be very helpful, especially when the differences between two languages are relatively few. For example, the number of Spanish-English cognates (e.g., *público* and *public*) is far greater than the number of Arabic-English cognates.[2] Accordingly, native speakers of Spanish have a tremendous advantage over native speakers of Arabic in the acquisition of English vocabulary (Section 5.2). The term *interference* implies no more than what another term, **negative transfer**, does, but there is an advantage in using the latter term since it can be contrasted with **positive transfer**, which is the facilitating influence of cognate vocabulary or any other similarities between the native and target languages.

Transfer is not simply a falling back on the native language. In an elaboration of an analysis originally proposed in the 1960s, Krashen (1983:148) claims that:

Transfer ... can still be regarded as padding, or the result of falling back on old knowledge, the L1 rule, when new knowledge ... is lacking. Its cause may simply be having to talk before "ready," before the necessary rule has been acquired.

In addition to this claim, which might seem plausible, is another: "Use of an L1 rule ... is not 'real' progress. It may be merely a production strategy that cannot help acquisition" (Krashen 1983:148). There are

2 From a historical point of view, the similarity of *public* and *público* is not a cognate relation in the same sense that *mother* and *madre* are cognates. From the learner's point of view, however, *any* lexical similarities may be considered cognates.

several problems with analyzing transfer as merely a falling back. First, it ignores the head start that speakers of some languages have in coming to a new language (cf. Singleton 1987). For example, the similarities in vocabulary, writing systems, and other aspects of English and Spanish reduce the amount that may be utterly new in English for Spanish speakers in comparison with, say, Arabic speakers (cf. Sections 3.3, 5.2, 7.4). Second, Krashen's statements imply that native language influence is always manifested in some transparent "L1 rule." In fact, however, native language influences can *interact* with other influences so that sometimes there is no neat correspondence between learners' native language patterns and their attempts to use the target language (cf. Section 3.3). Third, Krashen's claim that transfer may be a mere "production strategy" fails to recognize that cross-linguistic influences can be beneficial in listening or reading comprehension. Fourth, Krashen's analysis cannot account for the long-term results of language contact in some settings. In the case of Ireland, for example, learners of English seem to have fallen back frequently on knowledge of Irish, but such falling back was never entirely eradicated nor did it halt the wide-scale adoption of English. While the Hiberno-English that bilinguals – and later, monolinguals – spoke was often a nonstandard variety, the bilinguals of Ireland had indeed acquired English (Section 8.3).

Transfer is not always native language influence. Throughout this book, the phrase *native language influence* is used as a synonym for *transfer*. Such usage, however, is only a convenient fiction. When individuals know two languages, knowledge of both may affect their acquisition of a third (Section 3.3). Most probably, knowledge of three or more languages can lead to three or more different kinds of source language influence, although pinning down the exact influences in multilingual situations is often hard (Section 8.3). Since knowledge of a single native language is the most typical basis for substratum transfer, such cases will have priority in this book.

Although the four conceptions of transfer just discussed do not adequately characterize the phenomenon, a working definition of transfer is nevertheless feasible. The following definition of substratum transfer applies to all subsequent discussions in this book:

Transfer is the influence resulting from similarities and differences between the target language and any other language that has been previously (and perhaps imperfectly) acquired.

This, it should be stressed, is only a working definition, since there are problematic terms within the definition. While the word *influence* seems appropriate, it is somewhat vague. Just how does the influence work? Without question, the influence arises from a learner's conscious or unconscious judgment that something in the native language (most typically) and something in the target language are similar, if not actually the same. However, the conditions that trigger judgments of similarity or identity remain incompletely understood. The term *acquired* also remains only partially understood. Various models of second language acquisition have been proposed, but the time seems distant when scholars will agree on a definitive model (cf. Ellis 1985).

A fully adequate definition of transfer seems unattainable without adequate definitions of many other terms, such as *strategy, process,* and *simplification.* Such definitions may presuppose an account of bilingualism that accurately characterizes relations between transfer, overgeneralization, simplification, and other second language behaviors. An adequate account of bilingualism would in turn have to include an accurate neurological model of language since, presumably, the influence of one language on another has something to do with the storage of two knowledge systems within the same brain (Albert and Obler 1979). Thus, one might plausibly argue that a fully adequate definition of transfer presupposes a fully adequate definition of language.

3.2   Problems of comparison

The study of transfer depends greatly on the systematic comparisons of languages provided by contrastive analyses. While it may seem obvious that any investigation of transfer presupposes such comparisons, Thomason and Kaufman (1988) cite instances of historical linguists attempting to study language contact situations without knowing much about the languages involved. The essential criteria for sound contrastive analyses are easy enough to state, but the development of comparisons based on those criteria has proved to be difficult. As a result, there is considerable variation in the quality of cross-linguistic comparisons. Yet no matter how good a contrastive analysis is, more than just *structural* comparisons are necessary for a thorough understanding of transfer, since native language influence interacts with *nonstructural* factors. And aside from native–target language comparisons, a second type of comparison is useful, and often necessary, to establish the occurrence of transfer: a comparison of the performance of two or more groups of learners with different native languages.

Descriptive and theoretical adequacy

An ideal contrastive analysis would provide much of the same information that ideal grammars of the native and target language would.[3]

---

3 The use of the term *grammar* here is in the more general sense – it describes not just the morphology and syntax of a language but also its phonology, lexicon, etc.

By the criteria discussed by Chomsky (1965), an ideal grammar would be both descriptively and theoretically adequate, and the same criteria apply to a contrastive analysis. Accurate and thorough descriptions are obviously important. Yet just as important are descriptions that embody sound theoretical principles which enable contrastive analysts to predict better what will be easy or difficult to learn.

While many contrastive analyses provide useful and sometimes highly perceptive information about languages they compare, none comes close to meeting in full the criteria of descriptive and theoretical adequacy. The descriptive shortcomings of contrastive accounts are quite evident; even much-studied languages such as English have not been thoroughly described, and many languages have yet to be studied in any detail. Consequently, no theoretically adequate grammar exists, since descriptive adequacy is, as Chomsky has observed, a precondition for theoretical adequacy. Moreover, the range of unsolved theoretical problems is immense and has led to very different opinions about the foundations of grammatical analysis (e.g., Givón 1979; Chomsky 1981; Comrie 1981; Gazdar et al. 1985; Lakoff 1987).

Despite this lack of consensus, certain theoretical approaches have found much favor among contrastive analysts and students of second language acquisition. Chomskyan approaches have long been especially popular (e.g., Stockwell, Bowen, and Martin 1965; Di Pietro 1971; James 1980; Sharwood Smith 1986). Scholars have often called both for rigorous analyses and for a set of analytical principles relevant to a general understanding of human language, and in the opinion of many scholars the generative analyses of Chomsky and others speak to such concerns. Yet whatever a contrastive analysis gains through the use of Chomskyan formalisms, it also inherits their theoretical and empirical liabilities. Aside from the analyses by Lakoff, Givón, and the others cited above, there have been numerous other discussions of linguistic theory that challenge the assumptions and methods of Chomskyan approaches (e.g., Labov 1972; Bolinger 1975; Coulmas 1981a). In this book there will not be a great deal said about Chomskyan analyses, as most of the research described in it provides important insights about transfer with little or no reliance on Chomskyan theories and formalisms.[4]

4 Some researchers (e.g., Flynn 1984) do formulate their analysis within a Chomskyan framework, but rarely does that framework seem to be the only way to explain the results the researchers obtained. It might be mentioned that other varieties of formal linguistics, such as Generalized Phrase Structure Grammar, have received little or no attention from second language researchers. Whatever advantages any particular formalist approach may have, the methods of investigation employed often show many of the same limitations of Chomskyan approaches, including an overreliance on introspection (cf. Labov 1975; Chaudron 1983; Trudgill 1984).

Some problems in contrastive descriptions

Whether contrastive analysts use a Chomskyan or some other approach, they encounter formidable problems in trying to formulate sound descriptions. One of the most fundamental problems is *idealization*, which is the characterization of the most important aspects of a language with the elimination of unneeded details. Idealization of linguistic data is unavoidable since there are many minute variations in the speech of individuals who consider themselves to be speakers of the same language. The more idiosyncratic variations in a speech community clearly have no place in a contrastive description. However, too much idealization amounts to distortion. For example, contrastive descriptions of Arabic and English do not always specify the *regional* varieties in question, and while such generalized comparisons are often appropriate, there do exist important differences in, for instance, the pronunciation of Arabic speakers in Iraq and Egypt. As Broselow (1983) has pointed out, differences such as those between Iraqi and Egyptian Arabic can result in differences in learners' pronunciation of English. Social variation can matter as much as regional variation in contrastive descriptions (Wolfram 1978; Gonzo and Saltarelli 1983). For example, Classical Arabic enjoys greater social prestige than does Egyptian or any of the other regional varieties of Arabic, and this sociolinguistic fact seems to influence formal and informal speech not only in the Arabic but also in the English of Egyptians (Section 8.3).

As noted earlier, criticisms of contrastive analysis have frequently attacked the Lado-Fries assumption that linguistic *difference* is equivalent to linguistic *difficulty* (Section 2.2). More refined approaches to contrastive analysis have attempted to deal with this problem by identifying the types of differences that will lead to difficulties and the types that will not (e.g., Stockwell, Bowen, and Martin 1965). For example, one difference that frequently, if not always, leads to difficulty is that in which a structure in one language has not one but two (or more) counterparts in another language. As mentioned previously (Section 2.2), Spanish, for instance, has two verbs, *conocer* and *saber*, that correspond to different senses of the English verb *know*, and this lexical discrepancy constitutes a real area of difficulty that English speakers encounter with Spanish vocabulary, even though this lexical difference does not seem to be problematic for Spanish speakers learning English. A fully developed contrastive analysis would include an accurate hierarchy of difficulty, that is, a definitive statement about which contrasts are most and least likely to cause problems. That hierarchy would have to account for, among other things, those cases in which similarities between languages prove to be more troublesome than some differences.[5] For ex-

5 A claim is frequently made that similarities between languages are a greater source

ample, the formal resemblance between English *embarrassed* and Spanish *embarazado* (which means "pregnant") can lead an embarrassed Englishman to make the embarrassing statement *Estoy muy embarazado* ("I am very pregnant") (Section 5.2).

Another challenge for any contrastive description is the *interaction* of linguistic subsystems. Psycholinguistic research has demonstrated a strong interdependence among discourse, syntax, phonology, and other subsystems in the comprehension and production of language (e.g., Sanford and Garrod 1981; Bock 1982). For example, the production of discourse has important effects on the pitch contours, pauses, and other **suprasegmental** aspects of phonological structure (Section 7.2). Similarly, the treatment of **topics** in discourse often has important effects on word order and other syntactic structures (Section 6.1). Some systematic analyses of language have taken these interactions into account, but relatively few contrastive analyses have explored in much detail the interdependence of various subsystems (e.g., Schachter and Rutherford 1979).

Structural and nonstructural factors

In this book, the term *structure* is roughly synonymous with the term *tagmeme*, a unity of form and function (Pike 1954). In other words, nothing is a structure unless it has both a *form* (some definite pattern) and a *function* (some definite use). Such a notion of structure has been implicit in much contrastive research, but with the increased interest in discourse from the 1970s onward the boundaries of contrastive analysis no longer seem as clear-cut as they once did.[6] There do exist units of discourse structure, such as paragraphs and narratives, that clearly involve form-function relations analogous to those in phonology, syntax, and other subsystems (Section 4.2). Nevertheless, discourse involves much more than what a purely structural analysis covers. For example, politeness is an aspect of discourse that is very important for any cross-linguistic comparison, but it is also one that involves many nonlinguistic factors. Differences between, say, apologies in English and apologies in Japanese may reflect differences in cultural beliefs and values (Section 4.1). In such areas, the boundaries between anthropology, philosophy,

---

of difficulty than differences (e.g., Pica 1984). While some similarities doubtless can occasion great difficulty, it is an oversimplification to deem similarities to be the greater problem. Such claims generally rely on data from error analyses (Section 2.2), but do not account for other relevant evidence. If the claim that similarities cause more difficulties were fully true, some very improbable events would be normal; for example, students literate in Chinese would have a big advantage over students literate in Spanish in learning the English alphabet (cf. Section 7.4).

6 The notion of *structure* here includes categories (e.g., past tense), rules (e.g., number agreement), relations (e.g., word order), and vocabulary items.

and linguistics become very hazy. In attempting to deal with the question of just what a contrastive analysis of discourse should contrast, some researchers have proposed intricate systems encompassing a myriad of variables (e.g., Hartmann 1980). However, practical tests of the merit of one system over another would be extremely complicated.

Another problematic relation between structural and nonstructural factors is **language distance**, or the degree of similarity between two languages. As discussed in Chapter 1, intuition suggests that some languages are more closely related than others. For example, English seems more closely related to French than to Eskimo, and Spanish seems more closely related to French than to English. While resemblances such as those just cited often arise from various historical relationships (Section 2.1), there are clear resemblances between languages whose historical relationships are not certain (e.g., Korean and Japanese), and even between languages having no known historical relationship (e.g., Japanese and Quechua). Objective measures of the distance between languages can be established through careful comparisons of structural similarities, which would show, for example, that the patterns of noun phrases in Spanish are more like those of French than like those of English. While the cumulative similarities between languages might be quantified in an objective manner, the *subjective* judgments of language distance by learners can matter considerably. For example, although English and Dutch have many cognates, Dutch students of English appear to be frequently skeptical about the possible use of certain cognate forms (Section 8.3). Other nonstructural factors, which are discussed in Chapters 4 and 8, also suggest that there is more to transfer than what a good contrastive analysis will indicate.

Comparison of performances

While a contrastive analysis is a necessary condition to establish the likelihood of transfer, it is not always a sufficient condition. By comparing the performances of speakers of at least two different native languages, researchers can better determine any effects of negative transfer. Such comparisons are frequently necessary since transfer interacts with other factors, and explanations based only on contrastive analyses are sometimes misleading. For example, there are problems in attributing only to Persian language influence the errors that Persian speakers make by using **resumptive pronouns**, as seen in the last word in the sentence *I know the man that John gave the book to him*. A contrastive analysis of relative clauses in Persian and English does suggest that the use of resumptive pronouns would be a Persian speaker's error; Persian relative clauses often have resumptive pronouns. Simply relying on a contrastive description would be misleading, however, since such errors are also made by speakers of languages not having resumptive pronouns in equivalent relative clauses (e.g., most Romance languages). Nevertheless, comparisons of speakers of languages such as Persian, on the one hand, and speakers of languages such as French, on the other, indicate differing propensities to use such pronouns in the target language; in other words, the presence of resumptive pronouns in the native language can lead to a greater use of them in the target language (Section 6.2).

In some cases the need for a formal comparison of performances is not very great. Certain spelling errors made by ESL students reflect characteristic pronunciation problems of speakers of particular native languages. For example, the spelling of *playing* as *blaying* is more likely to be the spelling error of an Arabic speaker than of a Spanish speaker (cf. Sections 3.3, 7.4). Moreover, while grammatical errors such as resumptive pronouns and the omission of the copula occur in the English of speakers of many different languages, other errors are characteristic of speakers of very few languages. For example, the anomalous verb form found in Hiberno-English sentences such as *He's after telling a lie* ("He's told a lie") is rarely if ever cited in error analyses of the English of speakers of other languages. While formal comparisons of such spelling and verb errors are possible, the distinctiveness of the errors amounts to an implicit comparison. In cases where an error is rather common among speakers of several different native languages, explicit comparisons are preferable.

While explicit comparisons are often desirable in determining negative transfer, they are indispensable in determining positive transfer. Research on articles clearly illustrates this need. Like the omission of the copula, the omission of articles is common even among speakers of languages having articles. For example, the following error comes from a native speaker of Spanish: *Picture is very dark* (Schumann 1978). A contrastive analysis of Spanish and English would not predict this error since there is a word-for-word grammatical correspondence between Spanish and English:

El   cuadro es muy oscuro.
The picture is very dark.[7]

Because of examples such as *Picture is very dark*, many linguists believe that the native language helps learners very little in their acqui-

---

7 The context of this statement is not given, so it is not clear that *cuadro* is the best translation of *picture*. However, this uncertainty does not affect the grammatical analysis of article use in the two languages. It should be noted that another (and highly probable) Spanish translation involves a different word order in which the subject appears in sentence-final position: *Es muy oscuro el cuadro* (cf. Section 6.1).

sition of English articles. Spanish-speaking learners, it might be argued, learn correct use of articles (e.g., *The picture is very dark*) not as a result of any positive transfer from Spanish but simply as the result of sufficient exposure to the definite article in English. Several comparative studies, however, suggest that this argument is dubious. Three studies of student performances on written tests of ESL indicate that speakers of languages having articles tend to use them more accurately than do speakers of languages not having articles (Oller and Redding 1971; Kempf 1975; Ringbom 1976). Moreover, speaking tests of learners' abilities to use articles produced results similar to those of the written tests (e.g., Dulay and Burt 1974; Fathman 1977), as did comparisons of learners' speech in naturalistic contexts (Zobl 1982; Gilbert 1983). The similarity of results in several studies thus suggests that some positive transfer occurs even when the contrastive prediction is stated in a very crude way (e.g., "Having articles in the native languages will make articles in the target language easier to acquire"). It is likely that more refined comparisons of learner performances would show even better evidence of positive transfer. Errors of article omission in the English of Spanish speakers appear to correspond closely – though not entirely – to areas of contrast between English and Spanish: for example, where indefinite articles are used in English but not in Spanish (Andersen 1977).

The existence of differences in acquisition patterns seen in comparative studies may not in all cases be due to cross-linguistic influence alone. It is conceivable, for example, that some of the differences reflect transfer of training, such as schooling that encourages learners to translate from their native language (cf. Krashen 1983). Such an explanation, however, cannot explain a number of findings in the comparative studies. For one thing, some of the studies are of children who probably have not had formal training in translation (e.g., Zobl 1982), and some other studies are of adults having little or no schooling (e.g., Schumann 1986). Moreover, other research suggests that schooling may decrease – not increase – the likelihood of negative transfer (Section 8.3). Even if schooling did invariably encourage all forms of cross-linguistic influence, transfer-of-training explanations could not account for results such as those seen in work on the perception of tones (Section 7.2) and on alterations of structures to forms that do not closely resemble structures in either the native or target language (Section 3.3).

Regardless of how much or how little any training in translation or other second language behaviors may encourage substratum transfer, there is strong evidence that different acquisition patterns are associated with different native language backgrounds. Not only articles but several other areas of second language performance have been the focus of comparative research – over three dozen empirical studies which provide explicit comparisons of learners' behaviors and which show effects of transfer are cited in this book.[8]

3.3 Problems of prediction

Forecasts and explanations

The literature on contrastive analysis frequently refers to predictions that are determined by cross-linguistic comparisons. In reality, however, the "predictions" of learners' behavior are often derived after the fact: What counts as a prediction is frequently based on data about learner performances already known to a linguist who has interpreted the data record with the help of cross-linguistic comparisons (cf. Wardhaugh 1970). Such a record does have the predictive value that other kinds of knowledge of past events have. A record of temperatures in the month of July in Texas for several years is likely to be a good predictor of average temperatures in Texas next July. Similarly, a record of errors in French made by English-speaking students in previous years can serve as a predictor of errors that English-speaking students will make in a French course next year. However, such predictions are clearly different from the kind made before the actual performance of learners is investigated.

One could argue, as Wardhaugh and others have, that the ultimate test of a contrastive analysis is one in which the predictions are based only on comparisons of the linguistic systems. Successful contrastive analyses developed in such a way could make it easier to discover general principles for making sound predictions about transfer in any language contact situation that might arise in the future. Yet while such predictions may constitute the ultimate test, the *explanatory* power of any cross-linguistic comparison is another important test. In other words, a good contrastive analysis should make it easier to explain *why* transfer will or will not occur in any given instance. Without a clear understanding of the conditions that occasion transfer, there is little hope of developing highly sophisticated contrastive analyses that make predictions of the kind discussed by Wardhaugh. Thus, while good predictions may be the ultimate goal, good explanations are a crucial part of achieving that goal. In view of the descriptive and theoretical problems of comparison already discussed (Section 3.2), it is not surprising that contrastive anal-

8 Other problems involving comparison, such as the notion of translation equivalence, are discussed in Section 3.4. Sridhar (1981) discusses in some detail still other problems of comparison.

yses have yet to succeed completely as either explanations or forecasts. Part of the challenge in developing better explanations and predictions is to understand better the many possible outcomes of cross-linguistic similarities and differences.

A classification of outcomes

The following classification offers some idea of the varied effects that cross-linguistic similarities and differences can produce:

   I. Positive transfer
  II. Negative transfer
     A. Underproduction
     B. Overproduction
     C. Production errors
     D. Misinterpretation
 III. Differing lengths of acquisition

POSITIVE TRANSFER

The effects of positive transfer are only determinable through comparisons of the success of groups with different native languages (Section 3.2). Such comparisons often show that cross-linguistic similarities can produce positive transfer in several ways. Similarities between native language and target language vocabulary can reduce the time needed to develop good reading comprehension, as discussed later. Similarities between vowel systems can make the identification of vowel sounds easier (Section 7.2). Similarities between writing systems can give learners a head start in reading and writing in the target language (Section 7.4). And similarities in syntactic structures can facilitate the acquisition of grammar: Learners speaking a language with a syntax similar to that of the target language tend to have less difficulty with articles, word order, and relative clauses (Sections 3.2, 6.1, 6.2). Future research is likely to show that cross-linguistic similarities in other areas will also promote acquisition.

NEGATIVE TRANSFER

Since negative transfer involves divergences from norms in the target language, it is often relatively easy to identify. Although negative transfer tends to be equated with production errors, there are other ways in which an individual's second language performance may differ from the behavior of native speakers.

Underproduction.   Learners may produce very few or no examples of a target language structure. Often the examples learners produce result in comparatively few errors, but if the structure is more infrequent than it is in the language of native speakers, the infrequency constitutes a divergence from target language norms. There is good evidence for one form of underproduction related to language distance: *avoidance*. If learners sense that particular structures in the target language are very different from counterparts in the native language, they may try to avoid using those structures. Schachter (1974) found that Chinese and Japanese students of ESL tended to use fewer relative clauses than did students whose languages have relative clause structures more like those of English (Section 6.2). Similarly, Kleinmann (1977) found evidence of avoidance involving other structures (Section 8.1).

Overproduction.   Overproduction is sometimes simply a consequence of underproduction. For example, in an effort to avoid relative clauses, Japanese students may violate norms of written prose in English by writing too many simple sentences. Overproduction can also arise for other reasons, however. For example, the use of apologies appears to be more frequent in American English than in Hebrew, and English speakers learning Hebrew appear to follow the norms of their native language in making apologies (Section 4.1).

Production errors.   In speech and writing there are three types of errors especially likely to arise from similarities and differences in the native and target languages: (1) **substitutions,** (2) **calques,** and (3) alterations of structures. Substitutions involve a use of native language forms in the target language. For example, Ringbom (1986) noted the following use of the Swedish word *bort* ("away") in an English sentence written by a native speaker of Swedish: *Now I live home with my parents. But sometimes I must go bort.*

Calques are errors that reflect very closely a native language structure. For example, Fantini (1985) notes the following sentence spoken by a Spanish-English bilingual child:

Vamos rápido   a poner   el   fuego   afuera.
Let's   quickly put   the   fire   out.

The child made a literal translation of the English expression *put the fire out,* which normally translates into Spanish as *extinguir el fuego.* Aside from such idiomatic expressions, certain word-order errors can also be evidence of calques. For example, an error made by a Spanish-speaking ESL student shows the same word order as the translation equivalent in Spanish: *the porch of Carmen,* as opposed to the more natural English phrase, *Carmen's porch* (Section 6.1).

Substitutions and calques are frequently the types of errors to which writers on bilingualism refer when they discuss transfer errors, and these types might suggest that transfer always involves an obvious correspondence between the native and target languages. Krashen (1983), for example, characterizes transfer as a falling back on some "L1 rule" (Section 3.1). While this assumption holds in the case of errors due to calques and substitutions, it cannot explain some of the most important cases of cross-linguistic influences which involve alterations of structures, as seen, for instance, in **hypercorrections**. Sometimes hypercorrections are overreactions to a particular influence from the native language. For example, Arabic speakers occasionally make ESL spelling errors that involve substitutions of the letter *b* for the letter *p*, as in *blaying* (Section 7.4); however, Arabic speakers also use *p* inappropriately (e.g., in *hapit*) in mistaken attempts to avoid *b/p* substitutions (Ibrahim 1978). Other alterations resemble hypercorrections insofar as they do not reflect any direct influence from the native language. For example, Schachter and Rutherford (1979) discuss cases of Chinese and Japanese students inappropriately using English syntactic structures involving forms such as *There is* and *It is*, as in: *There were many new patriots in my country gathered together and established a new country.* Schachter and Rutherford argue that although Chinese and Japanese do not have syntactic structures comparable to *There is* and *It is*, sentences such as the one just cited reflect discourse influences from those languages. Still other cases of alterations may lead to phonological errors. For example, Thomason (1981) discusses errors observed in the Serbo-Croatian stress patterns of Hungarians; the stress rule reflects influence from Hungarian, but the stress rule applied by Hungarian learners does not exist either in Serbo-Croatian or in Hungarian.[9]

Misinterpretation.   Native language structures can influence the interpretation of target language messages, and sometimes that influence leads to learners inferring something very different from what speakers of the target language would infer. Variant interpretations can arise from misperceptions of target language sounds that become categorized in terms of native language phonology (Section 7.2). Misinterpretations may also occur when native and target language word-order patterns differ (Section 6.1) and when cultural assumptions differ (Section 4.2).

DIFFERING LENGTHS OF ACQUISITION

The distinction between positive and negative transfer is useful, but the study of these types of transfer tends to focus on specific details and not on the *cumulative effects* of cross-linguistic similarities and differences on the acquisition process. One way of assessing such effects is to look at the length of time needed to achieve a high degree of mastery of a language. As noted in Chapter 1, native speakers of one language often

9 Calques are the only type of error invariably reflecting native language influence; substitutions and alterations may arise from sources besides the native language.

believe that they will find certain other languages especially hard to learn. While little research has been carried out to demonstrate the validity of that belief, some relevant evidence does exist, such as the lengths of language courses offered to members of the U.S. diplomatic corps. The following list shows the maximum lengths of intensive language courses at the Foreign Service Institute (1985) of the U.S. State Department:

Language	Number of Weeks
Afrikaans	24
Amharic	44
Arabic	44
Bengali	44
Bulgarian	44
Burmese	44
Chinese	44
Czech	44
Danish	24
Dari	44
Dutch	24
Finnish	44
French	20
German	20
Greek	44
Hebrew	44
Hindi	44
Hungarian	44
Indonesian	32
Italian	20
Japanese	44
Korean	44
Lao	44
Malay	32
Norwegian	24
Pilipino	44
Polish	44
Portuguese	24
Rumanian	24
Russian	44
Serbo-Croatian	44
Spanish	20
Swahili	24
Swedish	24
Thai	44
Turkish	44
Urdu	44

In all of the FSI language courses listed, the aim is to develop students' linguistic skills to a high level of proficiency that is comparable in each of the languages. For example, students who spend twenty-four weeks studying Swedish are expected to be as proficient as students who spend forty-four weeks studying Finnish. In each course, students spend the same amount of time in class each week (thirty hours), and there are no significant differences in the language-learning aptitudes of the groups studying any particular language.[10] Accordingly, the most straightforward explanation for the varying FSI course lengths is that the languages themselves are of varying difficulty for students who (usually) are native speakers of English. The notion of language distance is clearly relevant to differences seen in the list (cf. Section 3.2). The least difficult languages, as determined by course lengths, are mainly Germanic and Romance languages, which are similar to English in many respects.[11] The most difficult languages are diverse, but in general they share fewer structural similarities with English.

Such differences in course lengths have occasionally been noted, but in only a few discussions of transfer (e.g., James 1971; Ringbom 1987) has there been much attention given to the issue of time. This issue is, however, quite important, since it indicates that there may be a fundamental difference between first and second language acquisition. Linguists by and large agree that children acquire their native languages in approximately equal periods of time. That is, both Turkish-speaking children and Italian-speaking children, for example, master the essentials of linguistic structure in about the first five years of childhood, even though not all the particulars of each language prove to be equally easy (Slobin 1982). On the other hand, the FSI figures suggest that it will take an English-speaking adult over twice as long to become highly skilled in Turkish as to become highly skilled in Italian.[12]

There is, however, a counterargument to claims about the importance-

10 The lengths of shorter FSI courses are not cited since they often reflect administrative and not pedagogical considerations. In the case of Arabic and some other languages, certain regional varieties are taught in separate courses but these show no divergences in the overall pattern of course length. I would like to express my gratitude to Willow Shlanta and Hedy St. Denis of the FSI for this information and for help in interpreting it.

11 Actually, the course-length data give only a conservative estimate of the difference in difficulty of various languages. Oxford and Rhodes (1988) discuss estimates that suggest that it will take *ninety-two*, not forty-four weeks, to reach a rather high level of proficiency in Arabic, Chinese, and Japanese comparable to what learners studying French, Spanish, or Swedish can achieve in twenty-four weeks (cf. Ringbom 1987).

12 The greater amount of time needed by English speakers to learn Turkish may well be due in part to greater cultural differences (cf. Sections 4.1, 4.2). However, it is highly instructive that FSI course lengths differ between languages spoken in areas where the cultures are very similar (e.g., Hungarian versus Rumanian, and Finnish versus Swedish). Thus, linguistic structure seems to play more of a role in course length than culture does.

of transfer that are based on course-length data. As Littlewood (1973) has noted, one might argue that "correct" methods of teaching could eliminate the differences in course lengths that seem to be necessary. Yet, while the correct-methods argument is taken seriously by some researchers (e.g., McLaughlin 1978), the logic of the argument leads to predictions that are, to say the least, implausible. As noted earlier, the difference between Spanish and Portuguese is close enough to be considered a dialect difference (Section 2.1). Nevertheless, the correct-methods argument would lead one to predict, for example, that some teaching method would enable Spanish-speaking students to learn Japanese as quickly as they can Portuguese. Such a method would be truly miraculous.

Aside from course-length data, another kind of evidence that suggests a strong relation between language distance and length of acquisition comes from a study of reading comprehension of Dutch by English-speaking university students (Singleton and Little 1984). In that study, *none* of the students had had any instruction in Dutch, but one subgroup had already had some instruction in German, and that subgroup showed a better understanding of the Dutch text that they were given to read. The other subgroup in the study did succeed in understanding some of the text (largely because of a modest number of Dutch-English cognates), but they did not have the advantage of the subgroup that had studied German, a language highly similar to Dutch.[13] These results clearly support the belief that several years of study of one foreign language can greatly reduce the time needed to acquire a similar language.

Transfer and simplification

The taxonomy of transfer effects in the previous section is not comprehensive, largely because the relation between transfer and other processes in second language acquisition remains only partially understood. Distinguishing between transfer and simplification is often quite difficult. There are cases in which cross-linguistic influence is not a very compelling explanation – for example, the omission of the English copula by Spanish speakers (Section 2.2). On the other hand, the omission of pronouns seen in the following statements of a Spanish speaker may or may not reflect transfer:

In Saturday no like, no time. watch TV...
On Saturday I don't like [to go to the movies], I don't have any time. I watch TV... (Givón 1984b:124)

---

13 Some of those in the non-German subgroup had studied other foreign languages, but such language study helped them little.

Spanish frequently allows pronoun omission, and a study of learners' grammaticality judgments by White (1985) indicates that Spanish speakers are more tolerant of pronoun omissions than are speakers of French, which, like English, does not usually allow pronoun omission. Yet pronoun omissions can result from other influences, such as interactions between discourse and syntax (Section 6.1). It remains unclear how much of a role native language influence has in the omission of pronouns, prepositions, articles, and other structures in particular acquisition contexts. Such uncertainty is reflected in the conflicting estimates of native language influence seen in error analyses (Section 2.2); as Ellis (1985) has suggested, such estimates often seem to reflect theoretical biases on the part of the researchers. However, comparative studies such as those of article usage offer hope of further understanding. When cross-linguistic differences have some real influence, there should be evidence in the form of different performances on the part of groups of learners speaking different languages. Comparative research in fact indicates that transfer and simplification may sometimes converge in some errors, such as the omission of articles (Section 3.2).

Individual outcomes

Up to this point, the discussion of predictions has not distinguished between the performance of *groups* and the performance of *individuals*. Since contrastive analyses compare linguistic *systems*, they are more relevant to collective than to individual behavior. Contrastive analysts have a hard enough time in predicting, for example, the range of possible ESL errors of Spanish speakers as a group. The difficulty of predicting the specific errors that any particular Spanish speaker will make is obviously far greater (cf. Lee 1968). Individuals vary in many ways, including in their experience and aptitude for learning languages, and such variation can definitely affect transfer (Section 8.1).

The effects of individual variation make any contrastive prediction subject to probabilities. Contrastive analysts have often been criticized for hedging their predictions with words such as *probably* and *tend to* (cf. Dickerson 1974). However, such hedges reflect a strong sense of realism about human behavior. The physical sciences have yet to develop to the point where meteorologists can flawlessly predict tomorrow's weather or where geologists can long foresee any occurrence of an earthquake. It should thus come as no surprise that in the study of complex individuals who speak complex languages, predictions are statements of probabilities. Progress, such as it may come, will result from refining contrastive predictions so that they more frequently tally with actual outcomes.

3.4   Problems of generalization

The discovery of valid generalizations about transfer depends very much on the discovery of valid generalizations about the nature of language, that is, about language universals. Along with structures found in all languages or in most languages, structures that distinguish certain types of languages from others are the focus of many universalist investigations and are often important for the understanding of cross-linguistic influences.

Language universals

Two of the most distinctive approaches to the study of universals are associated with the linguists Noam Chomsky and Joseph Greenberg. As Comrie (1981) observes, the Chomskyan approach favors the intensive analysis of one language as part of an effort to identify abstract principles of a Universal Grammar, whereas the Greenbergian approach favors cross-linguistic comparisons. Much, though by no means all, of the work in the Chomskyan approach has focused on various characteristics of the syntax of standard written English. In contrast, Greenbergian analyses have generally focused on the cross-linguistic variations seen in particular structures such as word order. Some researchers (e.g., Hawkins 1983) have attempted to combine both approaches, but many investigators of universals have favored one approach over the other.

In some respects, the Chomskyan approach is the more ambitious of the two since it advances many more claims about language structure, language acquisition, and linguistic theory. One key hypothesis is that Universal Grammar is a biological inheritance which simply requires activation in child language acquisition. Just as there seems to be a biological "program" that guides infants in their efforts to walk, there seems to exist, according to Chomskyan views, a program that guides them in their efforts to talk. With its basis in Universal Grammar, the language program is generally successful: Under normal conditions children will inevitably learn to talk, just as under normal conditions they will inevitably learn to walk.[14] The interest of some Chomskyan linguists in child language acquisition has intensified in recent years, and many linguists who differ in their adherence to Chomskyan views have nevertheless agreed about the importance of Universal Grammar in language acquisition (cf. Wexler and Culicover 1980; Bickerton 1981). Still more

---

14 Examples of abnormal conditions include such cases as where children are severely retarded or deprived of opportunities to speak with others. Even in cases where their speech organs are hopelessly damaged, children can acquire a sign language as highly structured as any spoken language (de Villiers and de Villiers 1978).

recently, Chomskyan analyses have led to empirical investigations in second language acquisition that aim to determine the extent to which Universal Grammar is still "available" to guide the progress of adults learning a second language (e.g., Flynn 1984; Eubank 1986).

The Greenbergian approach involves relatively few theoretical assumptions, but the cross-linguistic regularities identified in that approach have provided the basis for much research on grammatical theory and language acquisition. Greenberg's own work on word order exemplifies the usefulness of cross-linguistic surveys (Greenberg 1966). The basic word order of English is one in which grammatical subjects precede verbs (or verb phrases), which in turn precede objects, and thus the abbreviation SVO characterizes the canonical order of constituents in an English clause (e.g., *John bought the car*). While the SVO order is quite common in the world's languages, Greenberg found two other orders also to be common:

Order	Examples	Cross-linguistic frequency
VSO	Irish, Classical Arabic	Somewhat common
SVO	English, Russian	Very common
SOV	Persian, Japanese	Very common
VOS	Malagasy	Rare
OVS	Hixkaryana	Very rare
OSV	Apurinã	Very rare[15]

At first glance there would seem to be little "universal" in such findings. However, the fact that the first three word-order types (VSO, SVO, SOV) account for the vast majority of languages in Greenberg's survey is itself highly significant. It appears that subjects tend to precede objects in most languages. That tendency does not constitute a universal in the strictest sense of the word, but it is too consistent a regularity to be the result of chance; there seems to be a strong preference for having subjects appear early in sentences (Keenan 1978). Greenberg found, moreover, that other word-order patterns were often predictable from basic word order. For example, one can predict with considerable accuracy that an SOV language will use postpositions instead of prepositions, as in Japanese (e.g., *tookyoo ni* – "Tokyo to"), and one can predict with even more accuracy that a VSO language will use prepositions (e.g., in Irish *sa bhaile* – "at home"). Linguists frequently put such predictions in the form of **implicational** statements. Thus one would state, for example, that if a language is VSO it will also have prepositions (cf. Hawkins 1983).

---

15 Scholars have often been skeptical about the existence of OSV languages, but there is growing evidence that some languages in the Amazon region rely primarily on OSV (Derbyshire 1986). A discussion of the notion of basic word order appears in Section 6.1.

The great interest in universals during the last thirty years or so has undoubtedly led to a greater appreciation of both the complexity and the unity of human languages. Nevertheless, that interest has not resulted in the discovery of many facts about linguistic structure that are universal in the strictest sense of the term, that is, facts which hold for *all* human languages. Linguists usually do concede the truth of some universalist statements, such as the claim that all languages have vowels. However, the number of uncontroversial claims is small, and what agreement there is in the study of universals has generally been about implicational universals, which provide useful information for the study of language types.

Linguistic typologies

Languages may be classified in many different ways. **Typology**, the study of such classifications, benefits work in many fields, including historical linguistics, grammatical theory, and contrastive analysis. A very rudimentary example of a typological comparison of English, Classical Arabic, and Thai is given below:

Language	Inflectional morphology	Basic word order	Resumptive pronouns?	Lexical tones?
English	Simple	SVO	No	No
Arabic	Complex	VSO	Yes	No
Thai	Negligible	SVO	No	Yes

The comparison indicates various structural similarities and differences. Among the ways that Arabic, for example, differs from English and Thai is in its intricate system of inflections to express gender, number, and other categories. On the other hand, Thai is different from both English and Arabic in that it uses tones to distinguish meanings of words (Section 7.2).

Typological analyses contribute to the study of transfer in three ways. First, they provide a basis for estimating *language distance*. While the example given cites only four structural characteristics, it does suggest that the language distance between Thai and English may be smaller than the distance between Thai and Arabic. Second, typological analyses encourage the study of transfer in terms of *systemic* influences. For example, research indicates that speakers of Japanese sometimes have difficulty both with word order and relative clause structure in English (Sections 6.1, 6.2). Since there is a fairly strong implicational relation between word order and relativization, the difficulties that Japanese learners have in these two areas may be related. Finally, typological analyses allow for a clearer understanding of relations between transfer and *developmental sequences*. For example, Greenbergian research on negation suggests that certain patterns of negation occur much more often than others. These typologically common patterns are also frequent in first language acquisition both as errors and as correct forms, and in second language acquisition these negation patterns may sometimes reflect native language influences, sometimes developmental factors, and sometimes perhaps both transfer and developmental factors (Section 6.3).

Typologically common features give clues to universal preferences in linguistic structure. For example, the five-vowel system of Spanish is extremely common, whereas the eleven-vowel system of Vietnamese is rare (Maddieson 1984). The reasons for widespread preference for the "Spanish" system probably reflect both physical and psychological factors. The five vowels in Spanish (/i/, /e/, /u/, /o/, /a/) are among the easier ones that the human vocal tract can produce, and their acoustic distinctiveness makes perceptual confusions between them unlikely. A wide range of physical and psychological factors must be involved in typologically common (or universal) characteristics of linguistic structure (cf. Gass and Ard 1984). Accordingly, the hierarchy of difficulty in a refined contrastive analysis would have to take into account the significance of such factors (Section 3.2).

Universalist assumptions

Even though their focus is often on particular kinds of human languages, typological analyses and contrastive analyses often involve universalist assumptions. One of the most important is the assumption that there are *categories* applicable to the analysis of all languages. For example, Greenberg's classification of languages in terms of basic word order assumes that categories such as *Subject* are universal. Many researchers accept that assumption, but there is no consensus about a set of necessary and sufficient conditions to define the category Subject. Some have argued against viewing linguistic categories as sets of necessary and sufficient conditions, and attempt to define categories such as Subject and Object as highly correlated bundles of syntactic, semantic, and discourse properties (e.g., Lakoff 1972; Keenan 1976; Comrie 1981; Bates and MacWhinney 1982). Whatever the merits of such proposals, it is clear that until the general nature of linguistic categories is well understood, all analyses assuming the universality of particular categories are highly tentative (cf. Lakoff 1987).

Another crucial universalist assumption in typological and contrastive analyses is that there are certain *meanings* that are equivalent in the discourse and semantic systems of all human languages. Without some notion of translation equivalence, there can be no useful cross-linguistic comparison of structures. In constructing a typology of syntactic negation, for example, linguists assume that negation is a logical construct found in all languages (cf. Sections 5.1, 6.3). Yet how much translation equivalence exists between the discourse and semantic systems of two languages is problematic. Areas in discourse such as politeness expressions show considerable variation, and not all areas of semantic structure are necessarily uniform (Sections 4.1, 5.1, 5.2). The most extreme forms of linguistic **relativism** have ascribed highly distinct worldviews to members of different cultures and have minimized similarities not only in meanings in different languages but also in speakers' perceptions of the world (Section 4.1). Yet despite many important differences in beliefs and attitudes in different cultures, such differences probably affect language less than what extreme relativist claims suggest. In areas such as color vocabulary, a long-cherished topic in relativist analyses, there are reasons to believe that semantic universals exist (Berlin and Kay 1969; Rosch 1973; Mervis and Roth 1981).

There is one assumption of universalist analyses that is found in many other kinds of research – that a reasonably good sample of behavior allows for reasonable inferences about *all* such behavior. However, "large" samples in Greenbergian analyses usually cover only a small fraction of the known languages of the present and past, and they obviously cannot say much about undiscovered languages or about the many languages that once existed but that were never written down. Similarly, studies in second language acquisition sample only a small number of the language contact situations in the world, and caution is certainly advisable in claims about how universal the results of such studies are. As the discussion of discourse in the next chapter indicates, there is good reason to be cautious in assessing the importance of either universals or transfer.

Further reading

Texts by Clark and Clark (1977) and Foss and Hakes (1978) are somewhat dated introductions to the psychology of language, but are still worth consulting. While these texts offer almost no discussion of second language research, a survey by Hatch (1983) provides a useful look at the implications of psycholinguistic studies for second language acquisition. James (1980) raises a number of important issues related to the development of contrastive analyses. One of the best discussions of typologies and universals is a text by Comrie (1981).

4 *Discourse*

Of all the areas of contrastive analysis, cross-linguistic comparisons of discourse are probably the most challenging. As noted in Chapter 3, discourse analysis involves a wide array of nonstructural as well as structural characteristics, and the boundaries between contrastive discourse and other disciplines such as cultural anthropology are not clear-cut.[1] Moreover, models of discourse are necessarily complex and are thus quite difficult to test (Section 3.2). Yet despite the lack of comprehensive cross-linguistic descriptions, there has been progress in the study of contrastive discourse. Researchers now have detailed information about specific cross-linguistic contrasts in requests, apologies, monologues, and other forms of discourse. Such information points to some probable cases of discourse transfer.

While there are many difficulties attending the study of discourse transfer, such study is undeniably important. As Richards (1980) has noted, when learners violate norms of conversation in the target language, the violations are potentially much more serious than syntactic or pronunciation errors since such violations can affect what is often termed "the presentation of self." Two areas of discourse in which effects on the presentation of self can be especially dangerous are *politeness* and *coherence*. While politeness is probably a universal notion, the expression of politeness in different societies varies considerably. Similarly, the notion of coherence is applicable to conversations and monologues in every society, but the relations between sentences, phrases, and other units can vary a great deal in the discourse patterns of different languages. If native language patterns influence learners in inappropriate ways, the language that a learner uses may seem impolite or incoherent. Cross-linguistic differences in discourse may affect comprehension as well as production. A learner may interpret conversations and monologues in the target language in terms of

1 Many of the topics discussed in this chapter are sometimes considered to fall within the realm of *pragmatics*, which some scholars (e.g., Levinson 1983) see as a field distinct from discourse analysis. However, there is no consensus about terminology in such matters, and in the interests of terminological simplicity, only the term *discourse* will be used.

native language norms, and may mistakenly believe that native speakers are being rude in situations where they are actually behaving appropriately according to the norms of their speech community. A learner may also have difficulty in seeing the coherence of target language discourse and fail to grasp the points a speaker or writer is trying to make. Since much of the research on contrastive discourse has dealt either with politeness or coherence, this chapter focuses on research in those areas.

4.1 Politeness

Types of politeness

One of the basic challenges in the study of politeness is understanding the differences of *interpretation* that different cultures make of certain kinds of behavior. What counts as an apology in one culture may be seen as an expression of thanks in another, and what constitutes a proper request in one culture may seem very rude in another. Brown and Levinson (1978) have provided a useful framework for understanding how politeness may be interpreted by different cultures in different ways.[2] According to their analysis, all people have a strong interest in preserving *face*, which has two aspects: (1) **positive face**, the self-image and self-respect that a person has; and (2) **negative face**, the claim to privacy, freedom of action, and other elements of personal autonomy. Since individual and social needs often lead to actions that threaten the positive or negative face of other people, it is important for individuals performing such actions to minimize the sense of threat created by an action. Brown and Levinson describe a large number of options individuals can use to minimize the impact of a face-threatening action, but most options are instances of either **positive** or **negative politeness**, which are strategies that minimize threats to positive or negative face.

Which politeness strategy may be chosen in any given discourse context depends on many situational and cultural factors. Brown and Levinson assert that in some societies speakers will generally opt for strategies aimed at positive politeness, whereas in other societies they will opt for ones aimed at negative politeness. Comparisons of the norms of politeness in two communities are therefore possible in terms of how

2 Brown and Levinson (1978) criticize the characterization of behaviors described in speech-act theory as "norms" or "rules," and suggest that an approach emphasizing "strategies" can better characterize the dynamism of speech acts. Yet, while their objections to the static characterization of discourse in some analyses are warranted, the "strategies" they propose resemble rules.

much the members of those communities use positive or negative politeness in their **speech acts**, which are the requests, apologies, and other purposive uses of language (cf. Levinson 1983). Such comparisons suggest that there can be important divergences in the speech acts of two communities even when the sociolinguistic norms of both communities are generally similar. For example, the norms of linguistic politeness in France and the United States are the same in many situations, but there is at least one context in which the norms differ considerably – using the telephone. According to Godard (1977), telephone calls in France are seen as impositions more often than they are in the United States, and thus the etiquette of making calls in France more frequently requires callers to make an apologetic statement (which is a form of negative politeness) at the beginning of the call. Consequently, phone calls between French and American individuals who are bilingual but unfamiliar with the differences in telephone etiquette may give rise, as Godard notes, to perceptions of bizarre or rude behavior. A somewhat similar problem resulting from differing norms is described by Gumperz (1982) in an analysis of the communicative difficulties between a speaker of British English and a Pakistani who had nativelike control of English syntax and vocabulary but whose conversational strategies differed from the norms of British English.

Whether the norms of polite speech in two languages vary a great deal or only a little, there do seem to be norms that are shared and that are related to the universals of politeness suggested by Brown and Levinson. In their analysis, negative politeness is most likely to be used to redress actions that are serious threats to face, whereas positive politeness is more likely to be used in less threatening situations. Grammatical mood is one area of linguistic structure where the positive-negative distinction appears very useful: the evidence presented by Brown and Levinson shows that questions are correlated with negative politeness and statements with positive politeness. In one sense, then, grammatical moods can be viewed in terms of a politeness scale: interrogative mood is somewhat "more polite" than indicative mood, since the former can do more to diminish threats to face; by the same token, imperative mood is the "least polite," since imperative forms often seem to be face-threatening acts. This politeness scale has empirical support from both first and second language acquisition research indicating that learners are sensitive to the correlation between politeness and grammatical mood (Bates 1976; Rintell 1979; Walters 1979a, b; Carrell and Konneker 1981; Obilade 1984). For example, Carrell and Konneker found that ESL students who were native speakers of Spanish, Arabic, Persian, Japanese, or other languages consistently ranked sentences such as *Could you give me a pack of Marlboros?*, *I want a pack of Marlboros*, and *Give me a pack of Marlboros* on a scale of politeness: the first sentence was consistently deemed the most polite and the third the least polite.[3] Such similarities in judgments among students of very different backgrounds indicate that learners can sometimes successfully use their intuitions about what is "naturally polite" as an aid in distinguishing between target language expressions which have the same referential meanings but different social meanings. Yet such intuitions can be perilous. Much of what seems "naturally polite" in one society will not necessarily be so in another, as research on requests and apologies indicates.

Requests

Some contrastive studies indicate that speakers of different languages prefer different levels of directness in their requests. In a detailed empirical study, Kasper (1981) showed that native speaker norms in German and English differ; German usage allows for more directness in requests than does British English usage. For example, German speakers show a strong preference for modal forms suggesting a sense of obligation, as in *Du solltest das Fenster zumachen* ("You should close the window"), whereas English speakers prefer modal forms with a weaker force, as in *Can you close the window?*. Moreover, it appears that German speakers more often prefer declarative statements in contrast to English speakers, who more often prefer interrogative statements to make requests, as in the preceding example. In terms of the relation between grammatical mood and politeness described previously, the preferred request strategies in English seem "politer."

Nevertheless, it would be mistaken to use any scale, no matter how carefully constructed, as a means of determining how polite speakers of one language are in comparison with speakers of another language. Using an approach common in tagmemic analyses of language and culture (Pike 1954), House and Kasper (1981) contend that a universal scale of politeness must always be interpreted in language-specific terms. In other words, even though a universal scale will determine the range of points on the politeness scale in every language, individual speech communities determine the specific points on the scale that mark deference, neutrality,

---

3 Thomas (1983) claims that because correlations between mood and politeness are only "probabilistic," they contribute little to the understanding of problems in the acquisition of discourse. She also notes that there are many counterexamples involving polite statements in the imperative form and impolite ones in the interrogative. Such objections, however, cannot account either for cross-linguistic correlations between mood and politeness, or for a similar correlation between utterance length and politeness, or for the heuristic value that such correlations may have in acquisition.

imposition, and so forth. Thus, while the sentences *Du solltest das Fenster zumachen* and *Kannst du das Fenster zumachen?* have formally equivalent counterparts in English, *You should close the window* and *Can you close the window?*, they are not, in social terms, translation equivalents. On a German politeness scale, the two German sentences do not have such different politeness values as do the two English sentences on an English politeness scale.

The notion of language-specific politeness scales is not altogether novel – good translators intuitively make use of the notion, as do good language teachers. The notion does, however, warrant greater attention in classrooms. The speech act study of Kasper (1981) indicates that speakers of German often produce requests in ESL that are too direct, and that finding has obvious implications for the teaching of English in German-speaking countries. In other acquisition contexts, however, the problems of directness can be just the opposite of those described by Kasper. Blum-Kulka (1982) found that native speakers of English often make requests in Hebrew that are, by the standards of native speakers of Hebrew, not direct enough; apparently the English politeness scale induces learners of Hebrew to use structural correlates of modals such as *can* in requests, whereas politeness in Hebrew does not require such forms.

The distinction between positive and negative politeness proposed by Brown and Levinson suggests a possible generalization about the differences in politeness scales. English speakers more often seem to prefer negative politeness in their requests: Respect for the autonomy of people who have the power, but not necessarily the desire, to grant favors seems to explain the frequent use of modals such as *could, would,* and *can*. In contrast to English speakers, German and Hebrew speakers appear to make more use of positive request strategies, in which social bonds between the speaker and hearer are assumed to be strong. Thomas (1983) gives an interesting example of such an assumption among speakers of Russian, who may use extremely direct requests even with strangers in cases where the imposition is considered slight: for example, *Daite sigaretu!* ("Give [me] a cigarette!"). This example suggests that speakers of a language such as English might have difficulty in learning to make requests that seem rude in their native language. Moreover, the example points to a clear danger that speakers of Russian might have in making requests in English. The problem for Russian speakers is especially great since some of the polite equivalents of *Daite sigaretu* in English are syntactically more complex (e.g., *Excuse me, you wouldn't happen to have a cigarette, would you?*). Research in both first and second language acquisition suggests that learning the full range of polite formulas often poses grammatical problems that less capable learners avoid through the use – and often misuse – of simpler forms, such as *Please* (Bates 1976; Scarcella 1979).

Apologies

Apologies also show considerable cross-linguistic variation and pose problems for second language learners. Research indicates that the problems may arise from two kinds of cross-linguistic differences: differences in the frequency of use of apologetic formulas, and differences in the relations between apologies and other speech acts. Important differences in the frequency of apologies are evident in comparisons of the verbal behavior of speakers of Hebrew, Russian, and English (Cohen and Olshtain 1981; Olshtain 1983). The comparisons, which involved various role-playing tasks, showed the following tendency:

English > Russian > Hebrew

That is, English speakers used apologetic formulas the most, and Hebrew speakers used them the least. The evidence furthermore suggests that native speakers of English generally use apologies when using Hebrew more often than native speakers of Hebrew do, and that native speakers of Hebrew generally use apologies when using English less often than native speakers of English do. These tendencies are not necessarily seen in all contexts, however. Native speakers of Hebrew, for example, may be more likely to make apologies that imply personal responsibility in auto accidents.[4]

Differences in the relations between apologies and other speech acts can lead to inappropriate uses of apologetic formulas. Borkin and Reinhart (1978) claim that *Excuse me* and *I'm sorry* are often used inappropriately by Thai and Japanese ESL students because of imperfect matches between those forms and analogous forms in the students' native languages. Borkin and Reinhart cite as an example a Japanese student responding "I'm sorry" to an American saying, "I have so much homework to do!" The relations between apologies and expressions of gratitude seem to occasion particular difficulty. The underlying similarities between these speech acts are analyzed by Coulmas (1981b), who shows, for example, that in English, French, and German, expressions of both thanks and apology from speaker A can elicit identical responses to both types of speech act from speaker B:

4 The lesser willingness of English speakers to take responsibility for auto accidents may have a legal explanation. If the English speakers in the role-playing situations were of American or British origin, they may have been thinking of the legalistic advice that American and British insurance companies routinely give to clients to not admit any fault at the scene of an accident.

A: Thank you so much.   A: Excuse me, please.
B: That's all right.   B: That's all right.

A: Merci Monsieur.   A: Excusez-moi.
B: De rien.   B: De rien.

A: Danke schön.   A: Verzeihung.
B: Bitte.   B: Bitte.

In Japan, the relations between thanks and apologies are more overt, and expressions of gratitude are often formulated with terms that in other languages only express apologies. Westerners may find strange the double function of phrases expressing either thanks or apologies, such as O-*jama itashimashita* ("I have intruded on you"), but in the analysis of Coulmas it has a straightforward explanation:

> In Japan, the smallest favor makes the receiver a debtor. Social relations can be regarded, to a large extent, as forming a reticulum of mutual responsibilities and debts. Not every favor can be repaid, and if circumstances do not allow proper repayment, Japanese tend to apologize. They acknowledge the burden of the debt and their own internal discomfort about it. (1981b:88)

Other speech acts besides thanks and apologies probably also show underlying similarities, similarities that might have a great deal to say about the relation between discourse universals and language-specific forms in speech acts. Since cross-linguistic research on speech acts is, as Levinson (1983) has noted, still in its infancy, it would be premature to speculate on such relations. However, there is sufficient evidence to indicate that the differences between speech acts in a target language will create problems for speakers of a language in which the differences between the same speech acts are less evident. It does seem to be true that Japanese speakers have transfer-based difficulties in predicting the use of *I have intruded on you*, *Thank you*, and *I'm sorry* (Coulmas 1981b; Loveday 1982a). An important implication of the work on Japanese speakers is that future research on discourse transfer should contrast not only individual speech acts in two languages but entire speech act *systems*.

Other speech acts

Requests and apologies are not the only types of speech acts that can cause difficulties in learning to be polite in a foreign language. While *greetings* are a likely language universal (Ferguson 1981), the rules governing the use of them can vary considerably. In parts of the West Indies, for example, greetings are expected in almost every social encounter, whereas in the United States they are used less often (Reisman 1974). Moreover, some languages (e.g., English) show variable patterns of greeting, while others (e.g., Arabic) show fixed patterns (Applegate 1975). *Proverbs* are another likely discourse universal (Taylor 1962), but their role in polite speech varies considerably in different cultures. In many countries, including much of the Middle East and Africa, proverbs and other formulaic utterances are frequently employed as aids in arguing, in complimenting, in expressing condolences, and so forth (Tannen and Öztek 1981; Wolfson 1981). While proverbs (as well as related phenomena, such as commercial and political slogans) are common in English-speaking countries, there are stylistic constraints on their use both in speech and in writing (as seen, for example, in advice offered by Hornby 1974).

Formulaic statements in one language do not always have close translation equivalents in other languages. Some of these expressions are quite simple, as the formula *bon appétit* said by French speakers at the beginning of a meal, but others are quite complex, such as the chanting ceremonies of Cuna Indians (Sherzer 1974). These language-specific speech acts pose additional challenges for second language learners. Unlike requests and apologies, which may in some sense be already "known" to learners even when details of the patterning are not clear, language-specific speech acts require learners to become familiar with very new patterns of culture. It is safe to say that the more dissimilar two cultures are, the more learners will need to make use of speech acts that appear in one speech community but not in the other.

Along with speech acts, the rules governing turn-taking and other procedural aspects of conversation show considerable cross-linguistic variation. Sacks, Schegloff, and Jefferson (1974) and other analysts of social interaction have noted complex rules related to who can take a turn at what point, who can "hold the floor," and so forth. While there may be a universal element in some of the rules they have identified, much about turn-taking involves culture-specific rules that can cause problems for learners. For example, German sociolinguists have observed that Turkish workers in Germany often have difficulty in participating in conversations where turns are exchanged rapidly. According to Barkowski, Harnisch, and Krumm (1976), the norm in rural Turkey is for individuals to take extended turns without having to deal with questions, comments, or other interruptions. Similarly, Applegate (1975) has noted different levels of tolerance of interruptions between Scandinavians, Americans, and people from the Middle East.

Conversational style

Many linguists (e.g., Tannen 1981) consider the totality of discourse devices that signal the imprint of a specific culture on an individual's speech to be the domain of *style*.[5] From one language to the next, conversational style can vary along many dimensions, some of which are not related to politeness. However, one of the most important stylistic dimensions is very much related to politeness: formality. Structural distinctions signaling formal and informal speech are found in many, and perhaps in all, societies. However, there are considerable differences in *when* formal speech is necessary and *what* aspects of language are used to convey formality. For example, most dialects of English do not make use of pronoun distinctions for purposes of formality, but such distinctions are common in many languages.[6] For instance, the distinction in French between *tu* ("you" singular) and *vous* ("you" plural) can signal a difference in number, but often it only signals a difference in formality: *Vous* is the expected form to use when addressing one individual in formal situations. The acquisition of pronouns in languages such as French is thus a special challenge for speakers of a language such as English. Successful acquisition requires coming to grips early with sociolinguistic norms in the target language. In French, as in other languages, pronouns constitute basic vocabulary; moreover, French sociolinguistic norms are often coded not only in the pronoun system but also in the verb inflection system, as in the different verb endings for *tu penses* ("you think," singular) and *vous pensez* ("you think," plural). In the latter case, again, the phrase can be used in formal situations to refer to one individual. With other target languages (e.g., Persian, Thai, and Japanese) the challenges are even greater because formality distinctions extend to first- or third-person pronouns. Moreover, in such languages there is often a complex system of honorifics involving other types besides pronouns (Brown and Gilman 1960; Hinds 1975; Beeman 1976; Richards and Sukwiwat 1983).

Along with purely linguistic elements such as pronouns, many paralinguistic elements can also serve to mark a conversational style: intonation and related characteristics such as loudness and speech rate, gestures, facial expressions, physical posture, and the like. The importance of these elements is as great as the complications they cause for contrastive analysis. The problem of style would be far simpler if para-

---

5 The question of style is far more complex than the discussion in this chapter may indicate. Some discourse analyses distinguish *registers* (e.g., the baby talk that adults use with children) from styles. Moreover, the role of norms is a basic issue that would be covered in a more detailed analysis of style. Some scholars have viewed style largely in terms of norms, whereas others have seen it as the systematic departure from norms. This and a host of other questions would have to be considered in order to arrive at a fully adequate theory of style. For further discussion, see Sebeok (1960), Crystal and Davy (1969), Kinneavy (1971), and Corbett (1971).

6 Some British dialects still use *thou* forms to signal familiarity, and the use of *ya'll* serves a somewhat similar function in parts of the United States.

linguistic elements were always language-specific; however, there are probably some universals of paralanguage. A cross-cultural experiment by Ekman (1972) suggests, for example, that some facial expressions (e.g., smiles) can serve as signals of the same emotional state in any society. Thus, Ekman found that Americans could accurately infer the emotional states of Japanese photographed with various facial expressions, New Guineans could infer the same from pictures of Americans, and so forth. However, there also are culturally specific uses of facial expressions. For example, Loveday (1982b) has observed that in northern Germany adults talking in the "baby talk" register with infants pucker and protrude their lips. The mix of universal and specific elements is also found in voice quality. Shouting, for instance, has a natural advantage everywhere in that it can attract the attention of a distant individual. However, what people consider to be an acceptable level of volume in conversation is culturally variable. Thus, Americans speaking at "normal" volume by American standards might be considered rather quiet in some parts of Africa and rather loud in some parts of the Far East (cf. Applegate 1975).

Similar problems involving universal and culture-specific norms are seen in the uses of silence. For example, Japanese and English speakers appear to have very different interpretations, as Loveday observes:

Japanese performing in English often do not realize how much distress is caused by remaining silent for long periods. A hesitancy to speak out and verbalize one's thoughts and feelings may be interpreted in the L2 setting as coldness, hostility, unconcern and even wiliness. Of course, well-meaning attempts to make the Japanese partner "speak up" often tend to cause silent frustration and resentment, since, from the Japanese viewpoint, the Westerner is the culprit who should rather be taught how to shut up. (1982a:8)

Differing community standards on the role of talk and silence are also known to affect other language contact situations, such as those involving speakers of English and speakers of some American Indian languages (Scollon and Scollon 1981).

In second language acquisition, much of the difficulty in becoming a competent speaker (and listener) is likely to come from the simultaneous existence of universal and specific elements in spoken interactions. The difficulty may be compounded by beliefs on the part of learners that their requests, their greetings, their facial expressions, their volume, and so on, are not arbitrary in the way that words in their native language are. That is, learners may suspect – not altogether mistakenly – that the rules guiding their interactions are natural and therefore universal. Information that sorts out the seemingly natural from the truly natural in paralanguage thus has an important place in foreign language instruction in oral skills.

4.2   Coherence

Differences in norms of politeness are only one of the ways in which cross-linguistic variation can lead to misunderstandings. Differences related to expectations about *coherence* in discourse may create special problems for learners in their reading or listening comprehension efforts. Alternatively, those differences may lead members of a speech community to consider the speech or writing of non-native speakers incoherent. It is not yet clear just how often such differences actually result in negative transfer (Section 4.3). What is clear is the potential that cross-linguistic variations in discourse have for creating misunderstandings.

The notion of coherence is closely related to the notions of logicality and relevance, with an absence of either one seriously jeopardizing the coherence of a discourse. Sometimes only an *apparent* absence of either can create an impression of incoherence. That is, conversations or monologues may seem incoherent if they appear to lack sufficiently logical relations between ideas, or more technically, **propositions** (Section 5.1). Conversations or monologues may also seem incoherent if there appears to be too little relation between a focus of information in a discourse (i.e., a **topic**) and other information, in other words, if too much appears to be "off-topic" (cf. Section 6.1).

Incoherence is sometimes very real. For example, the speech of disturbed people can be quite illogical or full of irrelevancies. On the other hand, the incoherence that readers or listeners may perceive sometimes has little to do with logicality or relevance. In some cases a particular audience may simply lack sufficient knowledge of the topic to make sense out of a discourse. The language in technical reports in various fields may seem incoherent to those unfamiliar with the subject matter, whether or not the discourse is really incoherent. Similarly, discourse that presupposes some familiarity with another culture may seem incoherent when listeners or readers lack sufficient knowledge of the culture. In other cases, audiences may not have problems with the content of the discourse but with the presentation of information. For audiences unfamiliar with certain patterns of organization, the information presented through those patterns may prove difficult or even impossible to understand.

Narratives

Like linguistic expressions of politeness, narratives probably constitute a discourse universal. Appearing in most, and perhaps all, societies, narratives allow for many cross-linguistic comparisons of discourse form. Some types of narratives recur in an extremely wide variety of cultures. Myths and folktales have long been a focus of study by anthropologists and literary theorists on account of pervasive characteristics both in content and form. Stories about the creation of the world, a flood, a return of a god or hero, and so forth have appeared in a remarkable number of communities. Moreover, traditional narratives are known to have formulaic characteristics that recur in the oral literature of many communities (Lévi-Strauss 1955; Dundes 1964; Propp 1968). On the basis of some of these formulaic characteristics, scholars have developed *story grammars* and other methods of analysis to understand narratives and related forms of discourse (e.g., Thorndyke 1977; Mandler et al. 1980). In story grammars, relations between settings, themes, plots, episodes, and characters are made explicit through a series of rules similar to those in generative descriptions of syntax. While such rules do not entirely account for the coherence seen in narratives, they do suggest the role that linguistic organization plays in signaling coherence.[7]

The range of possible stories is far greater than what is found in the narratives analyzed in terms of story grammars, and it seems unlikely that that or any other analytic system will ever account for the entire range. However, many of the narratives characterized in story grammars are quite common in storytelling traditions and have a number of recurrent properties. Among such properties are chronological and causal order, as well as a sense of narrative tension. That is, the events in such stories show a succession of events in time, with many of the events being causally related to each other, and a problem introduced early in the story is often not resolved until the end of the story, with the audience being kept in suspense during most of the narrative. In many cultures children are introduced to such stories at an early age, and adult listeners (or readers) are quite able to recognize and *expect* patterns of chronology, causality, and narrative tension.

These patterns certainly recur in storytelling in many lands. However, it is not clear that such recurrences are universal. Kintsch and Greene (1978) have claimed that there are culturally specific patterns of narratives and that cultural differences in narrative form have consequences for language comprehension. This claim has some experimental support, including the results of studies showing that English-speaking undergraduates had more success in remembering European than Amerindian folktales (Kintsch and Greene 1978). Others, however, have criticized the conclusions that Kintsch and Greene drew from such evidence and

---

7 Carrell (1982) and others have observed that coherence in discourse (including narratives) comes not from the formal structure of discourse but from the coherence of content – that is, from the thought processes underlying any discourse form.

have argued that cultural differences in narrative are far less than what they seem to be (Mandler et al. 1980).

However culturally specific or universal certain patterns of narrative may be, it is undeniable that stories from other cultures can seem rather strange. The following story from the Kathlamet of the Pacific Northwest is a classic example of just how different stories can appear:

One night two young men from Egulac went down to the river to hunt seals, and while they were there it became foggy and calm. Then they heard war-cries, and they thought: "Maybe this is a war-party." They escaped to the shore, and hid behind a log. Now canoes came up, and they heard the noise of paddles, and saw one canoe coming up to them. There were five men in the canoe, and they said:

"What do you think? We wish to take you along. We are going up the river to make war on the people." One of the young men said: "I have no arrows."

"Arrows are in the canoe," they said.

"I will not go along. I might be killed. My relatives do not know where I have gone. But you," he said, turning to the other, "may go with them."

So one of the young men went, but the other returned home.

And the warriors went on up the river to a town on the other side of Kalama. The people came down to the water, and they began to fight, and many were killed. But presently the young man heard one of the warriors say: "Quick, let us go home: that Indian has been hit." Now he thought: "Oh, they are ghosts." He did not feel sick, but they said he had been shot.

So the canoes went back to Egulac, and the young man went ashore to his house, and made a fire. And he told everybody and said: "Behold I accompanied the ghosts, and we went to fight. Many of our fellows were killed, and many of those who attacked us were killed. They said I was hit, and I did not feel sick."

He told it all, and then he became quiet. When the sun rose he fell down. Something black came out of his mouth. His face became contorted. The people jumped up and cried.

He was dead.

(Bartlett 1954:65)

While the story is coherent, the supernatural events in it cause compre-hension problems for readers who do not note some important details. In a famous psychological experiment, Bartlett (1954) showed that Brit-ish students had considerable difficulty in remembering much of the story, while students had considerably less difficulty in recalling details of an African story with a pattern rather similar to that of many English stories. Although the Kathlamet ghost story does show formulaic char-acteristics, the formula of the story was apparently hard for English speakers to recognize (Dundes 1964).

Lack of familiarity with a discourse pattern is not the only possible source of comprehension difficulties. When listeners or readers are not familiar with another culture, they may not succeed in correctly inter-preting the content of a discourse. In a study of reading comprehension,

Steffensen, Joag-Dev, and Anderson (1979) prepared two passages in English, one describing a wedding in the United States and the other a wedding in India. In both cases the passages were constructed to resemble a narrative letter written by someone who had attended one of the weddings and who was a member of the same culture: for example, the Indian wedding was described by an Indian writer for an Indian reader. Test results indicated that subjects needed less time to read the narrative describing the type of wedding more familiar to them and that they were able to recall the gist of the familiar type of wedding better than the gist of the unfamiliar type. An especially significant finding is that subjects' recollections showed fewer distortions of facts in the text of the familiar wedding. For example, Indians readily understood such statements as "After two days of marriage she was taken to Nagpur. Her father-in-law accompanied her." The Indian readers understood this to mean that the bride was going to Nagpur to live with her in-laws, as they knew that the norm for marriages in India is for the bride to live with the groom's family. In contrast, a number of the American readers interpreted that statement to mean that the bride was going to Nagpur for a honeymoon.

Culturally specific knowledge can affect not only the *comprehension* but also the *production* of discourse, as shown in a study by Winfield and Barnes-Felfeli (1982). Two groups of ESL students, Spanish-speaking and non-Spanish-speaking, were asked to read paragraphs of about two hundred words and then write summaries of the paragraphs. One of the two paragraphs was about the Spanish classic *Don Quixote*, while the other was about the Japanese Noh theater. The Spanish-speaking students were able to write significantly longer descriptions of the Quixote paragraph than were their non-Spanish-speaking counterparts, although in some other respects there were no clear-cut differences between the two groups. Since most of the Spanish-speaking students were already familiar with the Quixote story but not with Noh theater, cultural knowledge apparently contributed to their relative fluency. Aside from fluency, more subtle effects of cultural knowledge appear in discourse production. For example, Greek and American students produced rather different narrations about a short film that they had seen (Tannen 1984). The Greek students tended to provide more details about possible social or psychological characteristics of the individuals seen in the film, whereas the Americans tended to provide more details about actions performed by the individuals and about the film-making technique.

Indirection in discourse

Research on narratives provides some evidence of cross-linguistic differences in discourse, but there is even stronger evidence from recent studies of Japanese and Korean. These studies suggest that cross-linguistic differences can affect not only comprehension and memory but also value judgments of writing. The evidence comes from prose that shows a great deal of *indirection*.

In an effort to categorize the ESL writing of students from various countries, Kaplan (1966) compared the writing done in various countries in terms of different types of lines (cf. Section 2.2). In Kaplan's analysis, writing in English resembles a straight line since it supposedly is direct and "to the point." In contrast, writing in Russian, for example, resembles, according to Kaplan, a zigzag, and writing in Oriental languages "a widening gyre."[8] Kaplan provided examples in support of his impressionistic linear characterizations, although there is still much uncertainty about the nature of cross-linguistic variation in discourse (Section 4.3). Despite that uncertainty, however, Kaplan's analysis has had much intuitive appeal among scholars who have encountered paragraphs such as the following translation from Korean:

Foreigners who reside in Korea as well as those who study the Korean language in foreign countries are, despite their deep interest, ignorant of the basis on which the Korean alphabet, Hangul, was formulated. The Korean alphabet, composed of combinations of lines and curves, at first seems more difficult than Japanese kana for those who use the Roman alphabet, and as the combination of vowels and consonants multiplies, it appears more difficult to memorize all the combinations. This seemingly complicated combination of vowels and consonants can, on the contrary, be mastered with no more effort than is needed to learn the Roman alphabet or Japanese kana, for one must merely memorize two dozen vowels (Eggington 1987:154).

The first sentence seems to set the stage for a discussion of the history of the Korean alphabet. However, the focus of information in the paragraph then shifts without any warning to a description of the seeming difficulty of Hangul. Such a sudden change in topic is not unusual in Korean prose, according to Eggington (1987), who sees abrupt shifts as a normal feature of Korean style. Similarly, Hinds (1983, 1984) has cited several examples of Japanese news stories written in a form known as *ki-shoo-ten-ketsu*. According to Hinds, the *ki-shoo-ten-ketsu* form has its origins in Chinese poetry and constitutes a norm of Japanese style.

---

8 The "straight line" pattern may not be characteristic of all English discourse, as the following remarks by a Scandinavian linguist (Dahl 1979a:199) on John Lyons's (1977) *Semantics* suggest. Dahl criticizes Lyons's "tendency to write in the rambling essay style not uncommon among British scholars...he may get off the main line of discussion to elaborate on some minor point at length, after which the reader will have lost the thread." Moreover, correspondence in other languages sometimes shows a "linear" pattern even in cases where influence from English may be minimal. The Vai people of West Africa, for example, are known to use a very direct type of paragraph structure in their letters (Scribner and Cole 1981).

Texts in this form have a four-part pattern of development, as seen in the following translation of an article in a Japanese newspaper:

(ki) This columnist first learned to drive and obtained a driving license in New York City. At the time, what the driving instructor most naggingly stressed was "harmony." He said that the knack of driving lay first in harmony, second in harmony, no third and fourth and fifth in harmony.

(shoo) Ignoring the question of how to shift gears, he lectured, while on the road, on the importance of maintaining the minimum necessary distance between cars. There were times when this writer became sick and tired because he kept harping on the matter so much. It may be questionable whether American drivers actually place importance on "harmony," but at least that aged instructor kept insisting on it all the time.

(ten) The most frightening thing in the accident in the Nihonzaka Tunnel of the Tomai Expressway on July 11 was that there were about 170 vehicles within the tunnel and most of them burned. Why were there so many as 170 vehicles inside the tunnel?

In order to run at a speed of 80 kilometers per hour within the tunnel, vehicles must keep a distance of 80 meters between each other. If the vehicles had been running at 80-meter intervals, the total of vehicles on the two lanes from the entrance to the site of the accident about 1.6 kilometers away should have been 40 at the most. Since the expressway was crowded that day, the speed may have been less than 80 kilometers per hour. Still, 170 vehicles are just too many.

First, there was disregard of the proper distance between vehicles. On expressways, there are cases of vehicles running at 100 kilometers an hour with only 10 or 20 meters between them. Even if a driver tries to maintain the proper distance between vehicles, other vehicles cut into the space in front of that driver, immediately destroying harmony. Drivers are aware of the danger of a collision and pile-up but keep on driving, comforting themselves with the thought, "It will be all right." The piling up of such disharmony is dangerous.

There was also the fact that warnings were ignored. Immediately after the accident occurred, the panel at the tunnel entrance lit up with the warning, "Fire Outbreak, Entry Banned." But it appears that a considerable number of cars entered the tunnel after the warning had been posted. Did they speed into hell, unable to apply brakes suddenly because the distance between vehicles was too small?

(ketsu) The preventive measures taken by the Japan Highway Public Corporation were grossly inadequate. Experts should be well aware of what a lack of water for firefighting means in emergencies. They knew but closed their eyes to the fact. The psychology of "It will be all right" on the part of the drivers and of the corporation caused this major accident.

(Hinds 1983:188–89)

While the first two parts of this rhetorical format will not likely seem strange to an English-speaking audience, the third part (the *ten*) seems to be an abrupt shift away from the topic originally introduced. In fact, the rhetorical norm is for the *ten* to introduce a subtopic that is only indirectly related to the *ki* and the *shoo*. Hinds's research indicates that

Japanese readers are quite accustomed to reading such articles. In comparison with an American group that read translated passages such as this one, a group of Japanese readers more accurately recalled information in news articles in the *ki-shoo-ten-ketsu* form.

Taking a somewhat different experimental approach, Eggington found that Korean readers were often able to recall more information when it was presented in "nonlinear" forms like the *ki-shoo-ten-ketsu* than when it was presented in the "linear" form that Kaplan deemed to be characteristic of writing in English. The indirection seen in some Japanese and Korean prose thus seems to produce no adverse effects on comprehension among readers used to such forms. There is, furthermore, evidence that readers in the Far East consider indirection to be quite acceptable: results of a survey by Hinds (1983) indicate that Japanese readers are more likely than American readers to consider articles in *ki-shoo-ten-ketsu* form as well written. The results of such investigations thus suggest that a passage may be more readable or less readable depending on readers' expectations, which are partially shaped by language and culture.[9]

4.3   Discourse transfer and other factors

Most of the research discussed up to this point has shown considerable evidence of cross-linguistic *differences* in discourse, but less evidence of cross-linguistic *influences*. There is strong evidence of discourse transfer in a small number of studies. However, just as other factors besides transfer can affect the acquisition of syntactic competence in a second language, other factors can affect the acquisition of discourse competence.

Cross-linguistic differences and influences

The earlier discussion of the cross-linguistic dimensions of politeness and coherence cited many discourse contrasts evident in human languages. While there is still only fragmentary information available about

---

9 Some other interesting evidence for cross-linguistic differences in discourse comes from the literature being written in several former colonies of Western powers. Several authors have perceived language-specific discourse differences and have attempted to convey them in poems, short stories, and novels. For example, in Raja Rao's novel *Kanthapura* (1963), which was written in English, there are several stylistic devices used to convey a sense not only of the oral tradition in a village in south India but also of the syntax of the language spoken there (cf. Kachru 1969; Richards 1979; Platt, Weber, and Ho Mian Lian 1984).

such contrasts, the available evidence suggests that English and Japanese, for example, show a number of differences, such as the following:

English	*Japanese*
Less overlap in expressions of gratitude and apology	More overlap
Simple pronoun system	Complex honorific system
More avoidance of silences	Less avoidance
Less use of "nonlinear" patterns of organization	More use

Observations by Loveday (1982b) and others suggest that a fully developed contrastive analysis of discourse in Japanese and English would show even more differences than these, but the full range of differences will probably remain unknown for a long time to come. For languages less investigated than English and Japanese, even preliminary contrastive studies of discourse are often lacking.

Along with the differences, however, there probably are typological similarities in discourse between languages just as there are typological similarities in phonology and syntax (Section 3.4). While such resemblances are not well understood, typological research is certainly feasible for some aspects of discourse, such as indirection. Yamuna Kachru (1983) has argued that indirection is highly characteristic of discourse in Hindi and other Indian languages (cf. Pandharipande 1983). It is natural to wonder if the kinds of indirection found in Hindi closely resemble the kinds found in Korean and Japanese.[10]

While the differences and similarities of discourse warrant further study, their effects on second language acquisition remain only partially understood. There is some evidence that negative transfer occurs in certain situations. Some of the best evidence comes from an investigation by Bartelt (1983) of repetition in the ESL writing of American Indian students. In Amerindian languages such as Navajo and Apache, repetition is frequently used for emphasis, and Bartelt's study indicates that Navajo and Apache students writing in English use repetition so much that their papers often seem verbose in the eyes of teachers conscious of the norms of English style. The students are most likely to use repetition when they have strong feelings toward a topic, as seen in the following excerpt from an English composition written by a student describing a raid the Navajos suffered at the hands of a marauder:

Carson invaded the Canyon De Chelley to destroyed Navajo crops and livestocks and capture or kill all the Navajos, so they burned all their crops

---

10 Hinds (1987) has proposed still another typology, one involving the variations in "responsibility" that writers and readers may have in different societies. The Japanese, he claims, more frequently put the burden of responsibility for understanding a text on the reader rather than on the writer.

and bring all their livestock, all their livestock. Finally when the Navajos found they have destroyed all their crops and livestock they shoot down all their livestock ... (Bartelt 1983:299)

Since livestock and crops were the heart of the Navajo economy, the repetitions doubtlessly serve to emphasize the scale of the calamity. Such reiteration is not characteristic of all ESL writers, although some evidence suggests that Arabic discourse may encourage Arab students to repeat words and phrases in English (Koch 1983). Since the use of repetition seems to be characteristic of only some groups and since there is evidence of the use of repetition in the students' native languages, the case for discourse transfer in Bartelt's study is quite strong.

Some of the evidence for discourse transfer also involves syntactic transfer – such an overlap of evidence is not surprising in view of the important influence of discourse on syntactic structure (Section 6.1). English makes considerable use of cleft sentences for purposes of emphasis, as in the following examples: *It's the transmission that isn't working* and *It was the copilot who saw the oncoming plane*. In cleft sentences there is often a contrast between an entity referred to in the sentence and one known from the discourse context; thus, the first sentence could serve to contrast a broken-down automobile transmission with a smoothly running carburetor, and the second sentence could serve to contrast an attentive copilot with an inattentive pilot. In certain other languages the use of cleft sentences is more pervasive. Irish, for example, makes use of a wide range of cleft patterns, and the language contact situation in Ireland has led to a use of cleft sentences unlike those found in other English-speaking regions: *It's flat it was* ("It was flat") and *It must be working for her he was* ("He must have been working for her") (Henry 1957). As Henry and others have observed, such Hiberno-English sentences reflect cleft patterns in Irish (cf. Stenson 1981; Bliss 1984). The case for transfer is also supported by the fact that cleft sentences seem to be especially common in counties of Ireland where Irish is still spoken (Filppula 1986).

The use of repetition by American Indians writing in English and the use of cleft sentences by speakers of Hiberno-English are cases of transfer in which the comparisons of performance of different native language groups are *implicit*. That is, since only certain groups of non-native speakers of English produce certain patterns, the divergences from target language norms are not seen in all language acquisition and they therefore suggest the influence of particular native languages (Section 3.2). In studies that make *explicit* comparisons of target language speech or writing by speakers of different languages, there is also some credible evidence for discourse transfer. For example, the study of apologies in Hebrew by Olshtain (1983) compared native speakers of Hebrew with immigrants from the United States and the Soviet Union (Section 4.1).

The English and Russian groups differed in their use of apologies not only from the native speaker group but also from each other.

Despite such evidence for cross-linguistic influences in discourse, the extent of discourse transfer is not clear. Some studies of contrastive discourse have found little or no evidence for transfer (e.g., Connor and McCagg 1983, 1987; Scarcella 1984; Mohan and Lo 1985). The dearth of evidence in such studies suggests that the discourse influences from the native language may be weaker than, for example, phonological influences, although the relative likelihood of transfer in phonology and other subsystems is still very much an open question. In any case, the enormous complexity of linguistic factors related to politeness, coherence, and so forth suggests that a learner's native language may well be only one of a host of influences on second language discourse.

Other possible influences

In second language discourse (and also in syntax, phonology, etc.), the relative importance of factors besides transfer is not clear. Nevertheless, there is evidence that other factors can be quite important.

OVERGENERALIZATION

Just as morphological errors may result from false generalizations (e.g., *We sleeped a long time*), inappropriate discourse may result from generalizations carried too far. In her detailed study of speech acts of German ESL students, Kasper (1981) noted many instances such as the following:

Y: Could you show me the drawings?
X: Yeah.[11]

In a role-playing task, a student (X) made the response *Yeah* to a request from an older woman (Y) whom he had never met before. While *Yeah* might be polite enough as a response to a request from a friend of the same age, it could be seen by an older person as extremely curt. Since the norms of politeness in German and English are not very different in this regard, transfer is not as good an explanation for X's response as overgeneralization is.

A subclass of false generalizations probably results from transfer of training, specifically from foreign language instruction. Kasper cites a case that seems to reflect an inappropriate use of a polite formula: *Would you like to drink a glass of wine with me?*, which was used in a context in which *Can I get you another glass of wine?* would have been more

---

11 The capitalization and punctuation of this example differ in minor ways from the system used by Kasper.

appropriate. The overuse of formulas such as *Would you like* ... probably results from ESL instruction that does not make clear the limits on the use of polite formulas.

DEVELOPMENTAL INFLUENCES

In some respects the mastery of writing in a second language resembles the development of writing in one's native language. For example, children writing in their native language and adults writing in a second language often show a preference for discourse constructed with very simple syntactic structures (Homburg 1984; Hillocks 1986). This fact complicates the study of transfer, since some discourse characteristics that appear to be due to native language influence may instead reflect little more than a normal development of writing abilities. For example, writing in Persian shows considerably more use of coordinating conjunctions than English writing does (Dehghanpisheh 1978). It therefore is tempting to attribute to transfer any overuse of *and* or other coordinating conjunctions by Persian-speaking ESL students. However, the frequent use of simple and coordinate sentences is a common developmental characteristic among both native and non-native speakers of English (cf. Shaughnessy 1977; Larsen-Freeman 1978). Accordingly, transfer is not necessarily the best explanation for this aspect of Persian speakers' writing, just as transfer is not always the best explanation for certain syntactic errors.[12]

LITERACY

Many of the problems that second language writers face may be due primarily to inexperience in reading or writing in *any* language. For example, the problems that Japanese ESL students have in writing classes may more reflect a lack of skill in composing in Japanese than an influence of the *ki-shoo-ten-ketsu* form (Section 4.2). In fact there is evidence that native-language literacy skills affect a number of aspects of second language performance, including writing (Section 8.1).

---

12 The use of coordinate clauses might seem to be an issue primarily related to syntax and not to discourse. However, the developmental preference for coordinate clauses over subordinate clauses may result from a need of inexperienced writers to concentrate on the global demands of discourse construction instead of on syntactic elaboration. There is empirical support for the idea that differences in discourse tasks can affect linguistic performance. Working with English-speaking children, Levin, Silverman, and Ford (1967) found that when children were asked to explain simple physical processes (in English), they paused more often and spoke more slowly than they did when asked to describe objects. That finding is consonant with some ESL writing teachers' intuitions that it is more difficult for students to write accounts of processes than descriptions of objects.

A *word about positive transfer*

Up to this point, most of the discussion of cross-linguistic influences in discourse has focused on negative transfer. While the likelihood of positive transfer also being important is high, most research on contrastive discourse has not addressed this issue. Such transfer is virtually impossible to document in the absence of studies comparing the performance of speakers of different language backgrounds (Section 3.2), and so far there have been few comparative studies in the area of discourse.

One hindrance to doing comparative research is the dearth of information about discourse similarities (or differences) in various languages. There is a clear need for several kinds of information, including: (1) discourse universals such as those hypothesized by Brown and Levinson about politeness (Section 4.1); (2) stylistic variation in different languages; (3) the teaching of rhetoric for written communication; (4) the teaching of rhetoric for spoken communication (e.g., Albert 1964); and (5) the influence of English and other Western languages on spoken and written discourse in Asia, Africa, and elsewhere. On that last point, it seems likely that the impact of Western science, education, and journalism on many cultures can explain some of the similarities seen in the non-narrative prose of many speech communities. For example, Yamuna Kachru (1983) has shown that some scientific writing in Hindi follows the (supposedly) "linear" pattern of English prose. Such influences constitute a kind of borrowing transfer, and in some languages the effects of such transfer are evident in the wide range of styles used in writing (e.g., in Persian). As more information is becoming available about the teaching of writing in various countries (e.g., Purves 1986), future studies of contrastive discourse should be better able to take into account such factors as borrowing transfer and stylistic variation.

4.4   Summary and conclusion

Although the evidence is still fragmentary, enough exists to indicate that transfer involving discourse can often occur in second language acquisition. The probability of future research showing more instances of such transfer seems high since much research has already identified considerable cross-linguistic differences in discourse. Some of those differences can cause misunderstandings and may also lead to second language speech or writing that differs greatly from the discourse norms of the target language. Misunderstandings related to politeness and coherence are especially dangerous, and thus discourse transfer should be a matter of special concern for teachers. As with phonology, syntax, and other

subsystems, however, transfer is not the only source of divergences between native speakers' and learners' use of target language discourse.
At present, it would be hard to quantify the importance of cross-linguistic
influences on discourse. Nevertheless, it appears that discourse transfer
has considerable potential to interact with other subsystems, including
syntax, as seen in the case of Hiberno-English sentences such as *It must
be working for her he was*. Other interactions involving transfer also
seem likely; as research described in the next chapter indicates, semantic
transfer often requires the study of several kinds of interaction.

Further reading

Two highly useful surveys of problems related to discourse are texts by
Levinson (1983) and Brown and Yule (1983). Many of the problems
especially important to second language discourse are discussed by Loveday
(1982b). Although their views on discourse transfer are rather different,
articles by Hinds (1983) and by Mohan and Lo (1985) provide much-needed
critical assessments of some of the work on contrastive rhetoric.

5 *Semantics*

The study of discourse transfer and the study of semantic transfer overlap a great deal. Since discourse normally consists of sequences of statements, discourse analysis is closely related to **propositional** semantics, or the study of meaning in statements (cf. Section 4.2). Moreover, since statements normally consist of sequences of words, discourse analysis is also related to lexical semantics, which is the study of meaning in words.[1] Accordingly, if discourse transfer occurs, as evidence discussed in Chapter 4 suggests, semantic transfer is also probable. The discussion of semantic transfer in this chapter is divided into two sections: first, a look at cross-linguistic differences evident in propositional semantics, and then a look at lexical transfer.

5.1 Propositional semantics

Semantic universals and linguistic relativism

A fundamental issue in the study of semantic transfer is the relation between language and thought. Expressions such as "learning to think in French" reflect a common belief that learning a particular language requires adopting a worldview which, to some extent, is unique to that language. One implication of this belief is that if learners do not "think in French," for example, they must still be using their native language as a reference point for cognitive activities. It is still very much an open question just how closely language and thought are related (cf. Whorf

---

1 Scholars frequently point out that discourse is more than the sum of its structural parts. That is, while words are components of statements, and statements are components of discourse, discourse also involves aspects of meaning not truly amenable to a componential analysis. Another caution seems advisable here: The term *statement* should not be construed in the narrow sense of an assertion or a description, but in a broader sense to include speakers' communications about their attitudes and feelings. Sentences are the most typical statements, but words and phrases can also be statements, as in the case of the response *Yes* to the question *Is Paris the capital of France?*.

1956; Foss and Hakes 1978; Lakoff 1987). Accordingly, it is also an open question just how much native-language semantic structure can influence performance in a second language. Some research, however, does suggest that cross-linguistic differences in structure sometimes reflect differences in thinking, and a look at such differences is therefore appropriate.

Whatever differences there may be in the thought patterns of people in different speech communities, there are indications of universals in cognition. Propositional reasoning is a case in point. Although not all cultures have developed an explicit study of logic and although cultures in which logic is studied have not all developed exactly the same type of logical analysis, human reasoning processes show considerable similarities in empirical cross-cultural research. For example, an investigation by Hamill (1978) of reasoning in conversations in Mende (a West African language) and in English showed there was little cross-cultural variation in either successes or failures in reasoning. In conversations in both languages, speakers showed an awareness of such basic logical rules as contradiction: that is, if a proposition "X" is true, a negation of the same proposition (i.e., "not X") must be false. Thus, the statements *Paris is the capital of France* and *Paris is not the capital of France* cannot both be true. In Hamill's study, English speakers and Mende speakers seemed to make use of the same basic rules in both valid and fallacious interpretations of chains of statements (cf. Hutchins 1981).

Despite such evidence for the universality of basic reasoning processes, cross-cultural differences in cognition do seem to exist. One important source of differences is probably the form of education that children receive (Scribner and Cole 1981). Another probable source of differences – and one more directly relevant to the problem of contrastive analysis – is linguistic variation. Many scholars have claimed that differences in thought processes are somehow reflected in differences in language. A passage from an essay by Whorf (1956:212–13) states some of the strongest claims:

the background linguistic system (in other words, the grammar) of each language is not merely a reproducing instrument for voicing ideas but rather is itself the shaper of ideas, the program and guide for the individual's mental activity, for his analysis of impressions, for his synthesis of his mental stock in trade. Formulation of ideas is not an independent process, strictly rational in the old sense, but is part of a particular grammar, and differs, from slightly to greatly, between different grammars. We dissect nature along lines laid down by our native language. The categories and types that we isolate from the world of phenomena we do not find there because they stare every observer in the face; on the contrary, the world is presented in a kaleidoscopic flux of impressions which has to be organized by our minds – and this means largely by the linguistic system in our minds.

Several of the statements in this passage are consonant with the so-called strong **relativist** position, which claims that language can determine cognitive processing, as exemplified in the statement "We dissect nature along lines laid down by our native language." Yet, as many scholars have observed, this determinist position is beset with insurmountable problems (cf. Section 3.4). For example, if individual languages (and thought patterns) were as radically different as the determinist position claims, the acquisition of a second language might sometimes be impossible. That is, there might be some language whose speakers were utterly incapable of learning even a rudimentary amount of English because of radically different structures in their native language; or by the same token, there might be some language that speakers of English would find utterly impossible to learn. While the results of second language acquisition often fall short of what is desired, there are no known cases of an absolute "acquisition barrier" between speakers of different languages. This and many other considerations suggest that the differences seen between languages and cognitive processes are far less vast than what determinist arguments claim (cf. Penn 1972; Rosch 1974; Foss and Hakes 1978; Bloom 1981).

Although the "strong" position is discredited, the "weak" relativist position is plausible; as the last sentence in the passage of Whorf quoted earlier suggests, language may have an important – but not absolute – influence on cognition.[2] One structural characteristic found in many languages that might influence cognition is grammatical gender, as in the case of French, which classifies every noun as either masculine or feminine. For example, *mot* ("word") is masculine and *langue* ("language") is feminine. Gender classification may encourage mental associations that differ according to the languages that individuals speak (cf. Guiora and Acton 1979; Clarke et al. 1981). In certain cases, cultural traditions may encourage or discourage certain types of thinking, and those cultural patterns may be reinforced by the structural characteristics of a particular language. A contrastive study of English and Chinese (Bloom 1981) illustrates one possible instance of interaction between language and culture, but also illustrates exceedingly well the difficulties of achieving conclusive evidence that supports the relativist position. Like speakers of other languages, Chinese speakers are perfectly capable of talking about unreal states of affairs. However, the syntactic structure of Chinese does not explicitly encode some semantic differences asso-

---

2 Much of the controversy surrounding linguistic relativism has arisen from ambiguities in statements by Whorf and others, with the result that discussions of language and cognition do not always distinguish the "strong" and the "weak" relativist positions (cf. Penn 1972).

ciated with unreality; in contrast, the English verb system explicitly codes differences, such as those seen in the sentences *If you burned your finger, it would hurt* and *If you had burned your finger, it would have hurt.* The syntax of Mandarin allows for one type of sentence construction to apply to both types of conditions described in the two English sentences. Thus, there is no special syntactic device in Chinese to signal the difference between a hypothetical state of affairs (in the first sentence) and a counterfactual state of affairs (in the second) in which an event that did not take place (e.g., a finger burned) is talked about as an imaginary event in the past. The absence of such an overt distinction is, according to Bloom, consonant with certain Chinese intellectual traditions.

However plausible relativist analyses, such as that of the Chinese case, may appear, they can be difficult to validate. Bloom has provided interesting but controversial evidence in support of his Whorfian interpretation of counterfactuals in Chinese. Some of his strongest evidence comes from the results of a reading test given to Chinese monolinguals, English monolinguals, and Chinese-English bilinguals. The passage used on the reading test contained many counterfactual statements and the state of affairs described in the passage was explicitly unreal: the effect that a certain philosopher might have had – but actually did not have – upon the development of science. In answers to questions designed to establish how well readers understood that the philosopher had actually had no effect on the development of science, the English monolinguals proved the most successful and the Chinese monolinguals the least successful.

Bloom argues that the performance of the bilingual group constitutes further evidence for his Whorfian analysis since the performance of that group fell in between those of the monolingual groups; by virtue of having studied English, this group had become more sensitive to counterfactual states of affairs in abstract discourse. In effect, such study may have resulted in a form of borrowing transfer. Bloom's research has met with vigorously argued rebuttals from other researchers who have claimed, among other things, that Bloom's reading test was poorly translated into Chinese, and who have provided counterevidence from other reading tests (cf. Au 1983; Bloom 1984; Liu 1985). Bloom's claims are likely to be controversial for a long time to come, but some other evidence besides the reading test argues for a limited Whorfian position and also suggests a more straightforward methodology for investigating some issues in linguistic relativism.[3] Bloom searched for examples of coun-

---

3 Birdsong and Odlin (1983) present a detailed discussion of several aspects of
   Bloom's analysis. In that article and in this chapter, the use of *counterfactual* differs
   somewhat from Bloom's terminology.

terfactual arguments in a Chinese newspaper and found only one, which happened to be in a translation of a speech of an American statesman. While Bloom described this survey as "informal," a controlled textual analysis comparing, for example, hundreds of editorials in English with hundreds of editorials in Chinese might establish – or disconfirm – that counterfactual arguments are indeed rarer in Chinese discourse. Such comparative studies might conceivably also work for other aspects of the Whorfian question.

While the results of Bloom's investigation are not conclusive, they do suggest intriguing implications for the study of transfer. Celce-Murcia and Larsen-Freeman (1983) note that the syntax of English hypothetical and counterfactual statements is an area of exceptional difficulty for learners. Some of the difficulty is no doubt related to the intrinsic complexity of the English system, but some of the difficulty may be related to differences between languages such as English and Chinese. If borrowing transfer can occur, as suggested earlier, substratum transfer is also conceivable.

Semantic case

One of the most important concepts in propositional semantics is the notion of **semantic case**, or semantic roles. Many relationships between syntactically different sentences can be specified with a small number of cases, as in the correspondence between active and passive voice in the following sentences: *Bob stole the tomatoes* and *The tomatoes were stolen by Bob*. While the syntactic structures of the two sentences are obviously different, the sentences share an identical proposition.[4] Semantic case analysis allows the semantic relation between the two sentences to be specified in some detail. In both sentences the noun *Bob* has the same semantic case of *agent* and the noun *tomatoes* has the same case of *patient* (i.e., an entity that is affected through an action). The analysis of propositions in terms of semantic case is useful not only for an understanding of the semantic system of a language but also for crosslinguistic comparisons of morphology and syntax (cf. Fillmore 1968; Chafe 1970; Lyons 1977). For example, the possessive constructions of English and Spanish differ somewhat in their morphosyntactic characteristics. Thus, the Spanish phrase *los héroes de la nación* can translate into English either as *the heroes of the nation* or *the nation's heroes*. A contrastive description of Spanish and English grammar in this area would posit a morphosyntactic but not a semantic difference; that is,

4 The traditional criterion determining that identity is that the two sentences must share the same truth conditions; in other words, one sentence must be true if the other is also true, or false if the other is also false.

while **genitive** (i.e., possessive) constructions are common to both languages, the morphosyntactic manifestations are only partially the same – English makes use of both a possessive inflection (as in *nation's*) and a prepositional construction (as in *of the nation*), whereas Spanish only allows a prepositional construction (e.g., *de la nación*). This contrast is significant for the analysis of some of the difficulties that Spanish speakers encounter with possessive constructions in English (Section 6.1).[5]

Since there is a fairly high degree of similarity in the Spanish and English structures just described, the notion of semantic case might not seem especially original or useful. However, case analyses are just as applicable in comparisons of two languages that are typologically very different. For example, Russian differs from Spanish and English in that it relies greatly on **morphological case**, which (in Russian) is primarily a system of noun endings that signal semantic case.[6] The fact that Russian relies so much on word endings to signal semantic case is relevant to the considerable flexibility seen in Russian word order (cf. 6.1). A propositional analysis employing the notion of semantic case allows for a clear and consistent comparison of very different uses of morphology and word order in Russian and English. In general, the notion of semantic, as opposed to morphological, case is essential to any contrastive analysis since, as was stated earlier, only when sentences in two languages have comparable meanings can aspects of their morphological and syntactic structure be compared (Section 3.4). By referring to a (presumably) universal inventory of semantic cases as well as to other characteristics of propositional structure, contrastive analysts can be explicit about how sentences in two languages have comparable meanings.

The notion of case is also useful in the study of interactions between propositional and lexical semantics. For example, in Irish there is no word closely corresponding to the English verb *have*. The closest translation of *I have money* is as follows:

Tá airgead agam.
Is   money   at-me.

Airgead is the syntactic subject of the sentence and *agam* is an example of the "prepositional pronouns" that are common in Irish. While the semantic case relations of *Tá airgead agam* and *I have money* are iden-

5 In many theoretical analyses of semantic case, the genitive construction is not treated as a basic case but instead as a derivative of some other case (cf. Fillmore 1968; Lyons 1977). Aside from a further consideration of basic case relations, a more detailed look at Spanish and English possessive constructions would have to include a description of the restrictions on the use of prepositional constructions: for example, the constraint that makes *Tom's book* more often acceptable than *the book of Tom*.

6 Often the relation between semantic case and morphological case is rather weak (cf. Jespersen 1929; Fillmore 1968).

tical, the syntactic forms of the two sentences are very different due to Irish lacking a verb like *have*. This lexical difference between Irish and English has had grammatical consequences. Hiberno-English often employs prepositional constructions where other varieties of English do not, and it therefore makes more extensive use of the objective morphological case found in the pronoun forms *me, him, her, us,* and *them.* Thus, the standard English sentence *He had a bad heart* has a unique counterpart in Hiberno-English: *The heart was bad on him* (Henry 1957). Such uses of prepositions in Hiberno-English are highly systematic.[7] As in other varieties of English, the most common antonym of *on* in Hiberno-English is *off*, which can sometimes be used to express the idea of *not having* something. Thus, a counterpart of the standard English *You won't have money worries* is *The money will be off you* (Henry 1957).

5.2 Lexical semantics

Transfer and cognate vocabulary

Many language teachers and linguists have believed that similarities and dissimilarities in word forms, along with similarities and dissimilarities in word meanings, play a major role in how quickly a particular foreign language may be learned by speakers of another language; intuition suggests that the similarity between, say, French *justifier* and English *justify* will give English speakers studying French (and French speakers studying English) a head start in the acquisition of vocabulary. Commenting on the comparative difficulties that speakers of European languages encounter in learning to read European and Oriental languages, Sweet observed:

Mastering the vocabulary of most European languages means simply learning to recognize a number of old friends under slight disguises, and making a certain effort to learn a residue of irrecognizable words, which, however, offer less difficulty than they otherwise would through being imbedded in a context of familiar words. The higher vocabulary of science, art, and abstract thought hardly requires to be learnt at all; for it so consists either of Latin

---

7 Lass (1986) has noted some dubious claims about Irish-language influence in Hiberno-English, including claims about prepositional constructions. Despite the skepticism shown by Lass, there is strong evidence pointing to Irish influence in certain prepositional constructions. First, some sentences involving such constructions do appear to be unique to dialects in Ireland (e.g., *The heart was bad on him*). Second, the wide range of uses of certain Hiberno-English phrases, such as *in it*, suggests Irish influence even though such phrases are found in other English dialects. Third, some prepositional constructions, such as *with a while*, occur as part of phrases that are calques of Irish idioms (Section 8.3).

and Greek terms common to most European languages or of translations of
them.

It is very different with a remote disconnected language such as Arabic or
Chinese. The abstract vocabulary of Arabic shows Greek influence, although
this affords very little practical help; but the terminology of Chinese
philosophy and science is independent of Western influence, so that every
extension of the vocabulary requires a special effort of memory and
reasoning. The task of mastering such languages is literally an endless one.
Enough Arabic grammar for reading purposes is soon acquired, the
construction being always perfectly simple – at least in ordinary prose, but
the student may read one class of texts for years, and then, when he proceeds
to another branch of the literature, he may find that he can hardly
understand a word, this being almost entirely the result of the unfamiliarity
of the new vocabulary required. (Sweet 1899/1972:64–65)

Sweet's observation has been expressed in somewhat different ways by
many other scholars, but only recently has there been much intensive
study of the effects of lexical similarity. In a comparison of the success
of Finnish- and Swedish-speaking students on an ESL test, Sjöholm
(1976) found that the former group did not do as well as the latter on
vocabulary questions, probably because Finnish does not share nearly
as much cognate vocabulary with English as Swedish does.[8] In a somewhat similar study in the United States, Ard and Homburg (1983) compared the performances of ESL students speaking two different native
languages, Arabic and Spanish. Here again, the speakers of the language
having more lexical similarities with English (in this case, Spanish) were
considerably more successful on vocabulary questions. While both the
Finnish and American studies controlled for such factors as the linguistic
proficiency of the test takers, the American study went a step further.
In looking closely at the performance of Spanish speakers, Ard and
Homburg determined that those students did especially well with the
words on test items that had spelling identical or at least similar to that
found in Spanish forms (e.g., *exiled* and *exilado*). The benefits of recognizing cognates may not be the only advantage that Spanish speakers
have in learning English; as Ard and Homburg observe, another likely
advantage is that Spanish speakers will have more time to concentrate
on unfamiliar vocabulary.

Despite the advantages of a large lexicon common to two languages,
there are nevertheless pitfalls in the form of "faux amis," the "false
friends" notorious to many language teachers. For example, the forms
of French *prévenir* and English *prevent* seem to be as reliable signals of
a cognate relation as the forms of *justifier* and *justify*. Yet while the
latter pair is a true instance of a cognate relation, the former is not:

8 As suggested in Chapter 3, the use of the term *cognate* in second language
   acquisition research is broader than the use of the term by historical linguists.

Prévenir means "to warn," and thus the pair *prévenir* and *prevent* is a pitfall for English learners of French and French learners of English (Holmes 1977).

False friends come in other guises as well. One of the most common problems in second language acquisition is when there is only a partial semantic identity of cognates. Thus, the translation of English *succeed* into Spanish as *suceder* will be acceptable in some contexts but not in others: For example, while *Truman sucedió a Roosevelt* ("Truman succeeded Roosevelt") is acceptable Spanish, *Sucedió en su trabajo* ("He succeeded in his work") is not (Anthony 1952–3). Lexical transfer can also occur when there is no morphological similarity between words that appear to be semantically equivalent, as is seen in the following error made by a Finnish student: *He bit himself in the language.* In Finnish, a single form, *kieli*, is used for both "tongue" and "language" (Ringbom 1986).

While a pair of cognates may be semantically similar, there are often grammatical restrictions found in one language but not in another, and such restrictions can occasion difficulty. For example, Adjemian (1983) notes a cognate problem in the English of a French-speaking student: *At sixty-five years old they must retire themselves because this is a rule of society.* While the form *retire* reflects a true French-English cognate, the French lexical item has a grammatical restriction that the ESL student applied erroneously to the English form – the use of the reflexive pronoun is necessary in French (the infinitive verb form is *se retirer*), whereas the use of the English reflexive *themselves* is not grammatical in the context of the sentence. Transfer can also occur when the word forms are not similar but the meanings are. For instance, the Swahili auxiliary *weza* is roughly equivalent to English *can*. However, the Swahili auxiliary often suggests the moral capacity for doing something. Hocking (1973) claims a likely transfer error for a Swahili speaker trying to suggest a person's capacity for cruelty would be to say *He's a very cruel man – he can beat his children with a hoe.* It is an open question whether this type of transfer is as likely as in cases where there is an overt formal similarity of lexical forms in two languages. Whatever the relative advantages or disadvantages that cognate forms occasion, more and more research on contrastive lexical semantics shows that *recognition* of cognates is often a problem. Learners may not always note the formal similarities that mark a cognate relation, and they may not always believe that there is a real cognate relationship (cf. Sections 8.1, 8.3).

Yet, even with the problems attendant in lexical similarities, there can be little doubt that learners will find one language far easier to learn than another if the one language shows many lexical similarities with their native language and the other does not. Much of the advantage in lexical similarity is likely to be evident in reading comprehension. The

Ard and Homburg study suggests, for example, that Spanish-speaking students can be exposed to written texts with great lexical variety much earlier than Arabic speakers can.

Lexical universals and acquisition

Even while transfer can play a major role in the acquisition of vocabulary, other factors are also at work. Although relatively little systematic investigation has been undertaken, there appear to be important similarities between first and second language learners in their patterns of lexical acquisition. For example, Strick (1980) compared judgments made by native speakers of Persian about the lexical similarity of words in their own language and their judgments about words in English. He found that the judgments Persian speakers made about the similarity of English words differed from their intuitions about Persian words. To a considerable extent, their judgments about English words resembled semantic intuitions of English-speaking children (Clark 1973). For example, the Persian speakers tended to classify the four terms *Mr., Mrs., John,* and *Mary* more frequently on the basis of a perceptible attribute (i.e., male or female sex) than on the basis of social affiliation (i.e., formal terms of address in contrast with personal names). Such results suggest that there may be a universal core of semantic information accessible to all learners and which may aid in the acquisition of new vocabulary. Determining the exact nature of that core is difficult, however. Even while there seems to be a strong similarity between the semantic classifications of first and second language learners, there are limits to the similarity.[9] In children the evolution of lexical competence is accompanied by major steps in cognitive development (Nelson 1974). Although the notion of continuing cognitive development in adults is plausible, there is little reason to believe that the acquisition of lexical semantics in a second language is a close recapitulation of all earlier developmental processes.

Whether they are communicative errors or simply innovations, the uses of words in a second language often show influences besides those from the native language, and some influences probably have a universal basis. Although no classification has proven wholly satisfactory, there seems to be a rather wide range of semantic innovations. Overextension of word meanings is as likely as any other kind of overgeneralization. Bamgbose (1982) notes that while many lexical innovations in Nigerian

---

9 Even in Strick's study there is evidence of nonuniversal influences in the form of transfer in some similarity judgments made by the Persian speakers. And in a study using methods similar to those of Strick, Ijaz (1986) found that cross-linguistic influences affected learner judgments of similarities between pairs of English prepositions.

English have resulted from transfer from West African languages, some have not. For example, in Nigerian English *My father has traveled* is equivalent to *My father is away*. The Nigerian use of *travel* reflects a new semantic range that has not resulted from transfer, according to Bamgbose, but from a natural process of semantic extension, a process found just as commonly among monolinguals (cf. Clark and Clark 1979; Clark 1982; Lakoff 1987).[10] When learners are not familiar with the customary uses of a word, they may have recourse to approximation, which is similar to overextension in that it is not a direct reflection of either the native or target languages. For instance, Blum and Levenston (1978) note that English speakers learning Hebrew may consider the phrase *asaf kesef* (literally, "gather money") an acceptable construction to express the idea of saving money, even though the phrase does not correspond directly to any phrasing either in Hebrew or in English. Some approximations clearly result from metaphoric coinages that function in lieu of the normally accepted target language form. For example, Bartelt (1982) notes the description by an Apache ESL student of rotting food as *dead food*, and Varadi (1983) notes instances of Hungarian ESL students describing a balloon as an *air ball* or *gas ball*. Overextensions and approximations as well as other types of semantic innovations are also found in first language acquisition (Clark 1973; Clark and Clark 1977; de Villiers and de Villiers 1978). Accordingly, some of the errors seen in lexical semantics are among the best evidence of the universality of processes at work in all language acquisition contexts.

Such universality, however, coexists with language-specific nuances in the lexicon. For example, while many languages have a word roughly equivalent to the English word *family*, the kinship concept signaled by the form can vary from complex extended families to nuclear families. Indeed, the form *family* signals different meanings in different varieties of English, such as Nigerian and American English (Platt, Weber, and Ho 1984). One cross-linguistic study of universals and language-specific nuances in the lexicon (Osgood, May, and Miron 1975) supports a limited form of linguistic relativism. While Osgood, May, and Miron found quite similar connotations associated with certain words (e.g., *girl* and its translation equivalents) in various languages, the emotional significance of some words can vary considerably (e.g., *policeman* and its translation equivalents). Such variation appears to have important

---

10 The use of the term *overextension* is not meant to suggest that lexical innovations such as that seen in the case of *travel* are "errors" in the Nigerian context. However, it is clear that in varieties of English found in Nigeria, Ireland, India, and elsewhere, lexical innovations and other types of innovations have resulted from such natural processes in second language acquisition as transfer and overgeneralization.

effects on synonymy judgments of second language learners (e.g., Blum and Levenston 1980).

Lexicon and morphology

As the "dictionary" component in the structural description of a language, the lexicon contains not only information about the meaning of words but also morphological and syntactic information. In the case of cognate forms, occurrences of lexical transfer are generally cases of both *morphological* and *semantic* transfer. The studies of Sjöholm (1976) and Ard and Homburg (1983) cited earlier suggest that morphological transfer involving independent words is as likely as any other kind of transfer. However, in speech and writing there may be very strong constraints working against the transfer of **bound morphemes**, which are prefixes, suffixes, and any other forms that are meaningful yet incapable of standing alone. For example, it may be the case that Spanish speakers do not have any special advantage in using the English plural suffix seen in *tops, kites,* and *cakes* even though the form is almost identical with the Spanish form (cf. Dulay, Burt, and Krashen 1982). Yet while there is skepticism about such transfer, some studies show instances of pluralization rules in one language being used in another, as in the phrase of a Spanish-English bilingual child *too manys cars*, which reflects a number agreement rule in Spanish whereby adjectives must agree in number with the nouns they modify (Fantini 1985).

A number of scholars have claimed that the transfer of bound grammatical morphemes is rare or nonexistent (e.g., Whitney 1881; Krashen 1978). Nevertheless, Weinreich (1953/1968) found a number of cases where such transfer seems to have occurred. While noting the apparent rarity of these cases, he suggested a formal criterion regarding the use of native-language bound morphemes in another language:

> it stands very much to reason that the transfer of morphemes is facilitated between highly congruent structures; for a highly bound morpheme is so dependent on its grammatical function . . . that it is useless in an alien system unless there is a ready function for it. (Weinreich 1953/1968:33)

Thus, for example, it seems unlikely that an Arabic speaker trying to learn Thai would attempt using the complex rules of Arabic word formation in Thai, which has virtually no inflectional morphology (cf. Section 3.4). Weinreich's notion of "highly congruent structures," as well as a related notion of "crucial similarity," may well be essential to any adequate account of language transfer in syntax as well as in morphology (cf. Section 6.3). However, just how much congruence there has to be remains problematic (cf. Andersen 1983b).

The existence of general lexical similarities is probably a major influence on how much transfer of bound morphemes will take place. In the case of two languages with many lexical similarities, such as Spanish and Italian, the transfer of bound morphemes in speech appears to be quite possible, as indicated in research by Meo Zilio (1959, 1964) on both borrowing and substratum transfer. For example, in the Spanish of Uruguay, where many Italian immigrants settled, the adjective *nubladeli* ("rather cloudy") reflects a fusion of Spanish *nublado* ("cloudy") and an Italian suffix -*eli*. Even in very dissimilar languages, however, there do appear instances of morphological transfer. The Greek spoken in some parts of Turkey earlier in this century frequently showed borrowing transfer in the form of Turkish suffixes on Greek nouns and verbs (Dawkins 1916). And morphology in a variety of the Chinese language Hui has apparently been affected by substratum transfer; in the dialect studied by Li (1984) there are morphological case suffixes unlike those found in other varieties of Chinese but very much like those of some Mongolian and Turkic languages spoken in the same region of western China.

Whatever the constraints may be on the transfer of bound morphemes in *production*, there are probably fewer constraints on transfer in *comprehension* processes. In other words, the similarity of bound morphemes in two languages may facilitate reading and listening in the same way the similarity of free morphemes does. For example, the similarity of suffixes in English and Spanish, such as -*ous* and -*oso* in *scandalous* and *escandaloso*, is likely to help readers identify words as cognates.

5.3 Summary and conclusion

There is little question that lexical similarities in two languages can greatly influence comprehension and production in a second language. Cognates can provide not only semantic but also morphological and syntactic information, and while some of the information may be misleading, some can facilitate acquisition. What is less clear is the importance of linguistic relativism. In all probability, anything that can be said in one language can also be said in any other, although it might be easier to express a particular thought in one language (cf. Hockett 1954). A moderate Whorfian position has some empirical support (e.g., some of the findings of Osgood, May, and Miron 1975), but there remains considerable uncertainty about how much influence semantic structures in one language can have on production and comprehension in another language. Whatever the importance of relativism, the need for the study of universals is evident in some cross-linguistic research on cognition and in studies of the development of word meaning in first and second language acquisition. It seems clear that second language research on universals and relativism cannot make great progress without a clearer understanding of the problem of meaning not only in discourse and semantics but also in interactions between syntax and other subsystems. In the next chapter, there is considerable attention given to interactions between syntax, discourse, and semantics.

Further reading

Lyons (1977) provides a very detailed discussion of the vast literature on propositional and lexical semantics. Good historical reviews of the problem of linguistic relativism are found in studies by Penn (1972) and Bloom (1981). Ard and Homburg (1983) discuss not only lexical transfer but also some methodological problems in determining such transfer.

6 *Syntax*

The notion of syntactic transfer has long been controversial, and empirical studies of second language syntax have fueled much of the debate (Sections 2.1, 2.2). Despite the apparent absence of cross-linguistic influence in some studies, however, there is considerable evidence for positive transfer involving articles and other syntactic structures (Section 3.2). There is also evidence for negative transfer in cases such as the Hiberno-English verb phrase seen in *He's after telling a lie* (Sections 2.1, 3.2). And a great deal of evidence has also been found for syntactic transfer (both positive and negative) in studies of *word order, relative clauses,* and *negation.* An extended look at research in those three areas is appropriate for several reasons. First, the number of studies in those areas is rather large. Second, several studies have involved target languages other than English. Third, such work is related in important ways to work in other areas of linguistics, such as discourse analysis and syntactic typology. Finally, many of the studies indicate that transfer interacts with other factors in acquisition.

6.1 Word order

Word order has been one of the most intensively studied syntactic properties in linguistics, and in second language acquisition research there are now numerous studies of learners' word-order patterns. The study of second language word order has been useful not only for a better understanding of transfer but also for an understanding of discourse, syntactic typology, and other factors affecting second language acquisition.

Word-order rigidity

As discussed earlier, the vast majority of human languages have either VSO, SVO, or SOV as their basic word order (Section 3.4). Yet while most languages can be compared in terms of these three patterns, a contrastive analysis based only on such comparisons could be misleading. In the case of Russian and English, for example, both languages have SVO as their basic order but they vary considerably in terms of *rigidity*. For instance, each of the following Russian sentences cited by Thompson (1978) has a different word order, whereas most of the English translations have SVO order:

Kolja	kupil	mašinu	Kolya bought the car (neutral)
Kolya	bought	car	
S	V	O	

| Kolja | mašinu | kupil | Kolya BOUGHT the car |
| S | O | V | |

| Kupil | Kolja | mašinu | Kolya did buy the car |
| V | S | O | |

| Kupil | mašinu | Kolja | KOLYA bought the car |
| V | O | S | |

| Mašinu | Kolja | kupil | The car, Kolya BOUGHT it |
| O | S | V | |

| Mašinu | kupil | Kolja | The car, it was Kolya who |
| O | V | S | bought it |

The flexibility of Russian word order is readily explained. The form *mašinu* signals the syntactic role of direct object in contrast with other forms such as *mašina*, which can signal the role of subject.[1] Such a reliance on **bound morphology** (as in the use of the morphological case suffix *-u*) is often seen in languages having flexible word orders.

The relative rigidity of word orders is, according to Thompson (1978) and others, just as important a typological property as basic word order. VSO, SVO, and SOV languages can thus be subcategorized according to the rigidity of their word order, as illustrated below:

Language	*Word order*	*Rigidity*
Irish	VSO	Rigid
Biblical Hebrew	VSO	Flexible
English	SVO	Rigid
Russian	SVO	Flexible
Persian	SOV	Rigid
Turkish	SOV	Flexible

1 The flexibility of word order in languages such as Russian raises the question whether all languages have a "basic" order such as SVO or SOV. Some linguists are more skeptical than others on this question (cf. Hawkins 1983; Givón 1984a). Certain analyses suggest that it may be possible to develop criteria for "basicness" even when word order is quite flexible (e.g., Keenan 1976, 1978). Even if a consensus ever develops on such criteria, there are still other reasons to be cautious in using the concept of basic word order in a contrastive analysis. For example, a

Languages designated as rigid can vary; Irish may be more rigid than English (Filppula 1986). Similarly, languages designated as flexible can vary; Russian is probably more flexible than Spanish (Thompson 1978). Nevertheless, the classification of languages as either rigid or flexible allows for a more detailed characterization of syntactic contrasts between languages.

Rigidity appears to be a transferable property. Speakers of a flexible language, for example, may use several word orders in English even though English word order is quite rigid. Evidence of such transfer appears in a study by Granfors and Palmberg (1976), which lists numerous errors in English word order in a guided composition task performed by native speakers of Finnish, a flexible SVO language. One example of negative transfer that resulted is *This weekend got F. any fish* ("This weekend F. caught no fish"). Granfors and Palmberg attribute such errors to the flexibility of Finnish word order; in the same study, native speakers of Swedish, a more rigid SVO language, made far fewer errors. Similarly, Trévise (1986) notes cases that reflect the relatively flexible word order of French: for example, *I think it's very good the analysis between the behavior of animals and the person.*

Aside from studies of production, studies of comprehension also point to the importance of rigidity (Bates and MacWhinney 1981; Gilsan 1985; Gass 1986). For example, the results of Gilsan's study indicate that English speakers learning Spanish experience comprehension difficulties related to the relatively flexible word order of Spanish. Sometimes, however, rigid word order may be quite helpful in the comprehension and production of a second language by younger learners. There is evidence that some children in the early stages of acquisition are likely to prefer rigid word order regardless of whether word order is rigid in either the native or target language. For example, a study by Pienemann (1981) of Italian children learning German shows a frequent use of a rigid SVO order, and many of the children's sentences do not seem to be based on word-order patterns of either German or Italian (cf. Section 8.2).[2]

single language can employ word-order patterns that seem diametrically opposed. German, for instance, often has SVO in main clauses but SOV in subordinate clauses, and thus scholars have often debated whether the basic order in German is SVO or SOV (cf. Comrie 1981; Zobl 1986).

2 While reliance on rigid word order appears to be a common developmental characteristic, it is not found universally in first language acquisition. Slobin (1982) has shown that the morphological typology of the language being acquired can affect children's reliance on word order. Such typological factors might also affect second language acquisition (cf. Zobl 1983).

Discourse factors in word order

With the exception of Pienemann's study, most of the results discussed in the preceding section are compatible with the predictions of a contrastive analysis that takes word-order rigidity into account. However, some of the production and comprehension difficulties that learners experience with word order in a second language have little to do with native language influence. Pienemann's study and others indicate that a rigid word order is advantageous because it simplifies (or at least seems to simplify) language processing routines (cf. Clahsen 1984). On the other hand, flexible word order also has advantages, since variations in word order can signal special discourse conditions. Flexible word order in learners' use of a second language may at times reflect discourse constraints in the native language, but at other times it may reflect discourse signals found in all languages.

The expression "free word order" is sometimes used to characterize languages having a flexible order, but discourse considerations suggest that that expression is misleading. Surveys of Ute, Turkish, and Serbo-Croatian, all languages with a very flexible order, show that some of the six possible permutations (i.e., SVO, SOV, VSO, VOS, OSV, OVS) are much more frequent than others (Slobin 1982; Givón 1984a). Far from being "free" or random, word order in flexible languages seems to reflect constraints imposed by the discourse needs of speakers and listeners. The constraints are complex and some seem to be language-specific, but some of the most important constraints are evident in the limited number of patterns used to signal information about **topics** in discourse (Section 4.2). Definitions of the term *topic* are problematic, partly because topics and grammatical subjects are often distinct, as the discussion later indicates (cf. Li and Thompson 1976; Brown and Yule 1983). Nevertheless, a necessary condition for something to qualify as a topic in conversation or writing is that it be a *focus* of information. Once a focus has been established, speakers (or writers) typically elaborate on the information already presented, with any elaboration functioning as a **comment**.

A conventional way to present information is through the use of a topic-comment sequential order. In English syntax, this order frequently – though not always – coincides with a subject-predicate order. Such ordering seems to play an important role in first and second language acquisition. Establishing the topic in a stretch of discourse can be difficult for learners, and the use of a topic-comment order is one way of minimizing the difficulty. As Givón (1984b:128) observes:

If one has difficulty establishing a new topic, or if one suspects that the hearer is likely to experience such difficulty, the most sensible strategy is first to make sure that the topic is *firmly established* [emphasis in the original] and only then to come up with the new information.

There is detailed evidence for the heavy reliance of some learners on topic-comment patterning in the early stages of acquisition. In a highly detailed study of the speech of a Hmong refugee in Hawaii named Ge, Huebner (1983) presents evidence that topic and comment are basic categories in Ge's early speech and that topic-comment order is likely when both categories are overtly signaled, as in the following sentences:

mii wok
As for me, I walked

hos, ai reis
As for horses, I raced (them)[3]

In both sentences, the first word can be identified as the topic and all subsequent words as the comment. It is possible that Ge was influenced by word-order patterns in Hmong, but other research suggests that a learner's use of topic-comment order need not result from native language influence. The following example from a Spanish immigrant in Germany (Klein 1986) shows a patterning just as rigid as Ge's:

Heute – vier Schule neu meine Dorf; ich klein Kind – eine Schule vielleicht hundert Kind; heute vielleicht ein Chef o Meister – zwanzig oder fünfundzwanzig Kind; ich Kind – vielleicht hundert Kind

Today – four school new my village; I little child – one school perhaps hundred child; today perhaps one boss or master – twenty or twenty-five child; I child – perhaps hundred child

The comparison that this speaker attempted to make is that: (1) there are now four schools in his village whereas when he was a young child, there was only one school with about one hundred children; (2) while the student–teacher ratio today is twenty or twenty-five to one, when the speaker was a child the ratio was about a hundred to one. This comparison is analyzable in terms of a topic-comment analysis:

Topic	Comment
today	four schools
in the past	one school
today	twenty children
in the past	one hundred children

3 Huebner notes that such clear cases of overtly expressed topics and comments are somewhat rare because Ge seemed to know that some topics were easily identifiable and therefore did not need to be expressed.

The word order of Spanish does not require that information be presented in such a rigid sequence, and Givón's explanation quoted earlier may best account for the speaker's performance (cf. Schumann 1984).[4]

Although Huebner's study and others have shown the importance of the topic-comment pattern, an explicit indication of the topic is not as frequent in the speech of learners as one might expect. Once topics have been clearly established, they are predictable for listeners and therefore are not incessantly signaled, even by speakers with very little proficiency. Technically known as **zero anaphora**, the omission of a form signaling a predictable topic (here, the speaker) is seen in the following example from a Spanish speaker responding to a question about going to the movies:

In Saturday no like, no time. Watch TV...
On Saturday I don't like [to go to the movies], I don't have any time. I watch TV... (Givón 1984b)

Instead of being omitted, topics may *follow* comments, as seen in another example from the same speaker:

...(me come-back Mexico in 1974), is come my family...
...(I came back from Mexico in 1974), they came too, my family did...
(Givón 1984b)

The appearance of *family* after *come* instead of before it is known technically as **right dislocation**, as opposed to **left dislocation**, which is seen in the following example from a Korean speaker:

...diploma my son high school get...
...diploma, my son got a high school diploma... (Givón 1984b)

Learners probably do not use these different word-order patterns randomly. In a study of the discourse of second language learners with three different native language backgrounds, Givón (1984b) has argued that the striking similarities in learners' word-order patterns reflect universal principles of signaling topic continuity. The basic principle is summarized thus by Givón (1984b:126):

Of topics that are fully expressed as an independent word or pronoun, those that are most continuous/predictable will display COMMENT-TOPIC (VS, VO) word order; while those that are less continuous/predictable will display TOPIC-COMMENT (SV, OV) word order.

---

4 Klein uses a different set of terms, which may in fact be preferable to *topic* and *comment*. However, his evidence is very similar to that of Huebner, who does employ *topic* and *comment*. In the interest of terminological consistency, only Huebner's classification is used in this chapter.

The signaling system thus reflects speakers' judgments about how continuous and predictable a topic is.[5] Aside from word order, other syntactic devices play a role in the system, part of which is given in the following scale:

Most continuous topic
   Zero anaphora
   Unstressed pronoun
   Right dislocation
   Neutral order
   Left dislocation[6]
Least continuous topic

This analysis has been consistently applied not only to some aspects of learners' syntax but also to syntactic characteristics of a wide variety of languages, including Japanese, Ute, Amharic, Spanish, and English (Givón 1983a). In light of such cross-linguistic regularities, the word-order errors of speakers of Finnish and French noted earlier might not reflect transfer so much as universal principles of topic continuity. Several researchers have in fact argued that what appears to be word-order transfer is often a reflex of discourse constraints (e.g., Muysken 1984). There are, however, problems with such arguments as an explanation for *all* cases of anomalous word order. First, many of the errors are remarkably like flexible patterns in the native languages of some learners (cf. Andersen 1984). Second, comparative evidence cited by Granfors and Palmberg (1976) suggests that native speakers of a language with rigid word order (Swedish) make fewer errors than do speakers of a language with flexible word order (Finnish). Finally, negative transfer accounts better for many errors made in cases where the basic word orders of two languages differ, as evidence in the next section suggests.

Transfer in basic word-order patterns

Among the most controversial topics concerning the acquisition of second language syntax is the extent of word-order transfer, especially regarding the two basic word orders, SVO and SOV. Despite reported

5 The Spanish speaker's clause cited earlier, *is come my family*, might seem to contradict Givón's generalization about more predictable topics having a VS order; such a clause could well be the first time that speaker has mentioned his family. The generalization about VS word order is still tenable, however, if such a clause appears early in a discourse "paragraph" (Givón 1983b). It should be noted that the word order in *is come my family* does not rule out the possibility of transfer interacting with discourse universals, since the VS order here has a close translation equivalent in Spanish.
6 In the interest of brevity, some details (e.g., the role of definiteness in noun phrases) have been omitted from the discussion of Givón's analysis.

instances of basic word-order transfer, a number of skeptics have contended that such transfer does not take place, and others have argued that if it does take place, it is a negligible phenomenon. Arguments against word-order transfer have generally rested on universalist interpretations (cf. Section 3.4). One is that what appears to be transfer may be an artifact of discourse manipulations related to topic continuity and the like (e.g., Muysken 1984). Another universalist argument is that some constraint of Universal Grammar blocks the use of basic word-order transfer (e.g., Zobl 1986). While both arguments are universalist, there is a crucial difference between them: The discourse-based argument suggests that in the early stages of acquisition, learners' word-order patterns are "asyntactic" and reflect universal principles of discourse organization. On the other hand, the Universal Grammar argument suggests that some innate principle of syntactic organization is available in second as well as in first language acquisition. Clearly, whatever the facts are with regard to word-order transfer, they are relevant to fundamental questions in the study of second language acquisition.

The universalist arguments are relatively easy to test when they involve predictions directly the opposite of those of a contrastive analysis. Rutherford, for example, has claimed that "Japanese learners of English do not at any time produce writing in which the verb is wrongly placed sentence-finally" (1983:367). Since the basic order of Japanese is SOV and the basic order of English SVO, transfer might take place. Yet in a word-order study by Rutherford, virtually no evidence of such transfer emerged, a finding supported by other studies (cf. Zobl 1986). Nevertheless, universalist arguments cannot be true in any absolute sense for the simple reason that some studies do show clear evidence of basic word-order transfer. For instance, a highly detailed study of Japanese speakers of Pidgin English in Hawaii contains examples of full-fledged SOV patterns, as, for example, *mi: cu: stoa gécc* (me two store get = "I got/acquired two stores") as well as several examples of clauses in which objects appear before verbs (i.e., OV), as in *hawai kam* ("I came to Hawaii") (Nagara 1972).

With regard to OV patterns, the claim has sometimes been made that they do not reflect native language influence but instead discourse strategies. For example, native speakers of English sometimes use OSV order for purposes of contrast. The clause *The soup we ordered*, for instance, can be used contrastively in sentences such as *The soup we ordered, the salad we did not*. If the subject were omitted, this pattern would be *The soup ordered*. Evidence in the preceding section suggests that zero anaphora is common in the early stages of second language acquisition. Thus, it is possible to argue that even when a Japanese speaker uses OV patterns, a discourse strategy instead of transfer is at work. Such arguments have not, however, been substantiated with studies of second language discourse like those described in the previous section. More important, such claims do not square with comparative data on Hawaiian Pidgin English. Bickerton and Givón (1976) found that speakers of Philippine languages such as Ilocano and Tagalog, which are VSO, produced a large number of VSX sentences, and they found that speakers of Japanese produced a large number of SXV sentences.[7] Two additional facts strongly suggest that word-order transfer is the best explanation of these findings. First, the immigrants from the Philippines produced almost no SXV sentences, and the immigrants from Japan produced almost no VSX sentences. Second, the least proficient speakers in both groups tended to produce the largest number of variant patterns (whether SXV or VSX). Still other comparative evidence is seen in Givón's (1984b) study of topic continuity in second language acquisition. The Korean-English text in that study shows more instances of OV than VO phrases, whereas the Philippine-English text shows many VO but almost no OV phrases. Since Korean is, like Japanese, an SOV language, the data in Givón's study parallel those of the Bickerton and Givón study comparing Japanese and Filipinos.

Studies of Andean Spanish also provide evidence of word-order transfer. Many of the Indians of Peru and Ecuador speak both Spanish, an SVO language, and Quechua, an SOV language, and studies of both child and adult bilinguals indicate that Quechua word order influences the local varieties of Spanish.[8] A study of the Spanish spoken by Peruvian children shows that five-year-olds used as many OV patterns as they did VO ones, and while seven- and nine-year-olds used more VO patterns, OV patterns were still quite common (Luján, Minaya, and Sankoff 1984). The decrease in OV patterns appears to continue as speakers grow older and speak a less distinctly regional variety of Spanish. Other research indicates that adults who use Quechua more also tend to use OV patterns more (Muysken 1984). As in the case of Hiberno-English, the speech of bilinguals (past or present) has probably influenced the speech of monolinguals; Ecuadorean Spanish speakers who do not know any Quechua also frequently use OV patterns (cf. Section 8.3).[9]

7 As with some other scholars whose work is discussed in this section, Bickerton and Givón contrast the patterns of the pidgin speakers in terms of a difference between SVX, VSX, and SXV instead of SVO, VSO, and SOV. The use of X allows grammarians to account for other patterns besides ones involving a direct object. For example, the indirect question seen in *I asked what she was doing* can be described as X in an SVX pattern.
8 Non-Andean varieties of Spanish do use SOV patterns with pronoun objects, but there is little doubt that the basic word order of Spanish is SVO.
9 Muysken (1984) attempts to show that word-order transfer is only indirectly involved in the basic SOV patterns of Andean Spanish. Space does not permit a fully detailed analysis of Muysken's claims, but the most important one he makes should be noted (cf. Odlin 1987). Muysken claims that the reason that objects

Studies of Dutch and German offer particularly intriguing examples of where word-order transfer can lead to different acquisition patterns.[10] Both languages employ SOV in subordinate clauses and SVO in main clauses, although other main-clause word orders are possible under special circumstances. Examples of Dutch word orders cited by Jansen, Lalleman, and Muysken (1981) appear below:

ik zag gisteren een beer I saw yesterday a bear	Independent clause, SVO
gisteren zag ik een beer yesterday saw I a bear	Independent clause, VSO[11]
omdat ik gisteren een beer zag because I yesterday a bear saw	Subordinate clause, SOV

A study of the speech of immigrant workers by Jansen, Lalleman, and Muysken indicates that speakers of Moroccan Arabic, a language that mainly uses SVO, tend to identify the basic word order of Dutch as SVO, whereas speakers of Turkish, an SOV language, tend to identify the basic order as SOV. Consistent with such identifications, the Dutch word-order patterns of the Arabic speakers showed a strong preference for SVO and those of the Turkish speakers for SOV (cf. Appel 1984). The transfer-based preferences of the workers for SVO or SOV were especially evident among the less proficient speakers of Dutch; as in the study of Bickerton and Givón, there seemed to be an inverse relation between transfer and proficiency (cf. Section 8.1).

Research on Italian and Spanish workers in Germany also provides strong evidence of transfer of basic word-order patterns (Meisel, Clahsen, and Pienemann 1981). The SVO order of Italian and Spanish appears to have influenced some workers' use of SVO instead of SOV order in German subordinate clauses (cf. LoCoco 1975). These findings are especially significant in light of research on the acquisition of German (Clahsen 1982). Children acquiring German as their native language

occur before verbs so often in Andean Spanish is not a result of transfer but a result of "stylistic" (i.e., discourse) strategies. His claims are not, however, supported by any actual analysis of discourse. Moreover, if one accepts Muysken's discourse-based explanation, one has to account for why Peruvian five-year-old bilinguals use OV patterns so much more than do seven-year-olds, who in turn use them much more than do nine-year-olds (cf. Luján, Minaya, and Sankoff 1984). In fact, Zobl (1983) provides evidence suggesting that four- and five-year-old children seldom use word orders influenced by discourse factors (Section 8.2).

10 Zobl (1986) has seen the German and Dutch cases as examples of word-order transfer. Nevertheless, his analysis cannot account for – and indeed it is contradicted by – the cases of Hawaiian Pidgin English and Andean Spanish. Moreover, there are other cases that contradict the analyses of Zobl and Rutherford (cf. Odlin 1987).

11 The presence of a sentence-initial adverb is one condition under which VSO order is employed in Dutch and German.

rarely seem to use SVO in subordinate clauses, and thus the evidence suggests that the development of basic word order can and sometimes does proceed differently in first and second language acquisition.

Evidence from the acquisition of English, Spanish, Dutch, and German thus strongly suggests that basic word order is one kind of syntactic pattern susceptible to native language influence. Accordingly, universalist arguments cannot fully account for the acquisition of basic word order. Yet a contrastive analysis may sometimes overpredict word-order problems. The transfer of basic word order does not always occur in situations where, for example, the native language is SOV and the target language is SVO. Although there has yet to appear any satisfactory explanation for cases in which transfer does not occur, several factors are probably involved. Target language patterns can lead to overgeneralizations (Section 2.2). For instance, a study by Snow (1981) shows that English speakers may overgeneralize the SOV order of Dutch subordinate clauses and thus produce them in main clauses. Aside from tendencies of learners to overgeneralize target language patterns, there seem to be other cases in which cross-linguistic influences are highly improbable, such as when a native language pattern is not really "basic." For example, French and Spanish, which are clearly SVO languages, nevertheless have a rigid SOV order when pronouns instead of nouns signal objects; however, Zobl (1980) has noted that virtually no cases of transfer into English of such SOV patterns (e.g., *I them see*) have appeared in the second language acquisition literature.[12] In addition to such structural factors, there are probably other factors that inhibit transfer, such as the linguistic awareness of the individual (Odlin 1987). Accordingly, even while a contrastive analyst may justifiably predict basic word-order transfer in some acquisition contexts, an array of structural and nonstructural factors may affect the prediction – in some cases basic word-order transfer may not take place, and in other cases such transfer may be seen in only the earliest stages of acquisition.

Word order within the clause

Other constituents besides S, V, and O are also subject to word-order rules. In noun phrases (NPs) in English, for example, articles normally precede adjectives and nouns in the noun phrase (e.g., *the fierce lion*), and languages generally have rules specifying the occurrence of elements within noun phrases, verb phrases, and other constituents. Even languages with a somewhat flexible order can show considerable rigidity

---

12 Transfer may, however, take place in the opposite direction, as when an English speaker learning French uses SVO instead of SOV patterns regardless of whether the object is a noun or a pronoun (cf. Zobl 1980; Andersen 1983b).

in some areas of their syntax (Hawkins 1983). Since the rules governing the position of adjectives, adverbs, and other word classes vary considerably from one language to the next, it is natural to expect to find cases of word-order transfer in constituents within clauses, and indeed such cases exist. Yet, as with basic word order, learners may encounter difficulty for reasons besides native language influence.

Some of the clearest evidence of within-clause transfer comes from a study by Selinker (1969) of Hebrew speakers learning ESL. Using data obtained from interviews with Israeli students, Selinker found a strong tendency for speakers to follow Hebrew instead of English norms for the placement of adverbial elements, as seen in the following error: *I like very much movies.* Selinker did not attribute all adverbial errors to transfer, but native language influence did account well for the vast majority of the errors. Other research on the English of non-native speakers also shows strong evidence of transfer. In a study of possessive constructions in ESL papers written by Spanish-speaking students, Andersen (1979) found frequent examples of NPs that were word-for-word translations from Spanish, as in *the porch of Carmen* from *el balcón de Carmen*. Nevertheless, Andersen also found many NPs that could not be explained in terms of native language influence but that could be explained in terms of overgeneralization: for example, *the United State President*, which does not conform to Spanish word order. In addition to these types of errors, another type described in Andersen's study suggests that some errors may result from an interaction of transfer and syntactic overgeneralization. For example, *the flute's lessons* reflects not only the English word order (i.e., *flute lessons*) but also the Spanish use of an overt signal of a genitive construction (cf. Section 5.1). That is, the use of the inflection *'s* seems to serve as a semantic counterpart of the Spanish preposition *de* in the translation equivalent *lecciones de flauta*.

In studies of the acquisition of other languages besides English, there is also considerable evidence for the importance of cross-linguistic as well as other types of influences on the production of within-clause word order (e.g., Snow 1981; Veronique 1984; Luján, Minaya, and Sankoff 1984). One area of special interest is the implicational statements formulated by Greenberg (1966), Hawkins (1983), and others (Section 3.4). Some researchers have tried to determine, for example, if there is a developmental relationship between the acquisition of rules governing the sequence of nouns and adjectives (NA or AN) and the acquisition of rules governing basic word order (VSO, SVO, etc.) when the word orders of the native and target languages differ (cf. Luján, Minaya, and Sankoff 1984; Zobl 1986). One tendency, for example, might be for the acquisition of SVO order in English not to take place until learners have mastered the preposition-noun order, which contrasts with the noun-postposition order seen in languages such as Japanese and Turkish (3.4). Yet while the theories upon which such studies are based are indeed interesting, empirical observations do not always support them (e.g., Muysken 1984). In the discussion of negation in Section 6.3, there will be further consideration of some of the issues related to developmental sequences and word order.

6.2   Relative clauses

Branching direction in relative and adverbial clauses

Although there is no necessary connection between the position of words and phrases in a clause and the position of clauses in a sentence, some research suggests important relations. For example, Kuno (1974) has investigated the tendency in SOV languages for relative clauses to *precede* the noun they modify as opposed to the tendency in VSO (and most SVO) languages for relative clauses to *follow* the noun, as seen in the following examples from English (SVO) and Japanese (SOV):

The cheese that the rat ate was rotten

Nezumi ga	tabeta	cheese	wa	kusatte	ita[13]
rat	ate	cheese		rotten	was

These examples only begin to show how different English and Japanese syntax can be. If a relative clause modifies *rat* in the above English sentence, as in *the rat that the cat chased*, the result will be a very complex sentence with *center-embedding*, as seen in *The cheese that the rat that the cat chased ate was rotten.* The SVO order of English appears to constrain the use of relative clauses following the subject of the main clause, since a center-embedding within a center-embedding may lead to extreme comprehension difficulties.[14] In contrast, Japanese syntax does not lead to center-embedding with this type of relative clause.

---

13 The particles *ga* and *wa* in Kuno's example mark the syntactic categories of *topic* and *subject* (cf. Li and Thompson 1976).
14 Kuno's analysis makes strong claims about the relation between language structure and human perceptual capacities. Such claims are suspect, however, since there exist languages in which the degree of permissible center-embedding appears to be greater than that found in English and Japanese (cf. Hagège 1976; Gazdar and Pullum 1985). Nevertheless, it is not at all clear that such languages are numerous. If there are few of them, the problem may be similar to what typologists find in other domains. For example, a language such as Vietnamese may have an unusual eleven-vowel system, but there are many more languages that have five-vowel systems (Section 3.4). Even though the significance of some statistical patterns is often hard to interpret, it would be short-sighted to claim that such patterns have no significance just because there are counterexamples to the dominant trend.

According to Kuno, the Japanese translation equivalent of the above English sentence is quite comprehensible:

Neko ga oikaketa nezumi ga tabeta cheese wa kusatte ita
cat   chased   rat   ate   cheese   rotten was

Such differences in comprehensibility suggest that the **branching direction** favored in a language is an influence on the types of syntactic complexity likely to occur in a language. English primarily relies on a Right Branching Direction (RBD), as is seen in the above examples in which the relative clauses appear to the *right* of the head noun (*cheese*). In contrast, Japanese primarily relies on a Left Branching Direction (LBD), as is seen in the relative clause *nezumi ga tabeta cheese wa*, in which the modifying clause appears to the *left* of the head noun.

The above examples suggest that the SOV typology of Japanese more easily accommodates syntactic complexity, but there are many instances in which SOV does not allow much complexity. When a noun is in direct-object position in English, multiple embeddings of relative clauses are possible:

John read the letter that Mary wrote to the boy that Jane was in love with.

The LBD of Japanese, on the other hand, leads to a translation with a highly complex center-embedding:

John ga Mary ga Jane ga aisite iru syoonen ni kaita tegami o yonda
                          loving is boy   to wrote letter   read

There is evidence that when two languages show a difference in principal branching directions, the acquisition of complex syntax will be more difficult than when both languages show the same branching direction. In a study of Japanese-speaking and Spanish-speaking ESL students, Flynn (1984) found that Japanese speakers had more difficulty in repeating sentences with adverbial clauses, such as *The boss informed the owner when the worker entered the office*. Flynn attributed the greater success of the Spanish speakers to the fact that Spanish, like English, is an RBD language. According to her analysis, Spanish-speaking students have an advantage in repeating sentences such as the one above since the adverbial clause follows the main clause, thus conforming to an RBD pattern found in Spanish.[15] Flynn and Espinal (1985) have

15 The results of Flynn's study do not seem attributable to differences in listening comprehension or in overall proficiency, as there were controls for these factors in her experimental procedure. However, there may be other problems in her design. For example, there is an ambiguity in the sentence *The boss informed the owner when the worker entered the office* – the subordinate clause may be either an indirect question or an adverbial clause. Such ambiguity might affect comprehension. Moreover, Eubank (1988) was not able to replicate some of Flynn's results on branching direction effects.

provided further evidence that when an LBD is predominant in the native language, the acquisition of RBD patterns in English is more difficult.[16]

Aside from difficulties encountered on repetition tests, another manifestation of negative transfer is evident in one of the earliest empirical studies of relative clauses in second language research. Schachter (1974) provided evidence that differences in branching directions favored in relative clause patterns will occasion *underproduction* (Section 3.3). Consistent with the predictions of a contrastive analysis, the speakers of Japanese and Chinese (LBD languages) in Schachter's study seem to have often avoided using relative clauses in written compositions; in contrast, equally proficient students who spoke Arabic and Persian (which are, like English, RBD languages) used many more such clauses (cf. Schachter and Hart 1979). Although the Arabic and Persian speakers produced a greater number of errors in the relative clauses that they used, the similarity of patterns in the native and target languages apparently led them to attempt writing more sentences with relative constructions (cf. Section 8.1).

Relativized positions, transfer, and universals

The order of clauses in a sentence is not the only factor affecting the acquisition of complex syntax. In the case of relative clauses, another crucial factor is the grammatical *role* of nouns and pronouns. Keenan (1985) defines restrictive relativization as a construct usually having a "domain noun" and invariably having a modifying clause. For example, the sentence *The musician who played at the concert is from China* has a relative construction consisting of a domain noun (in this case, *musician*) and a clause modifying the noun (in this case, *who played at the concert*).[17] One of the most common patterns in relative clauses is to have within the clause a pronoun with the same reference as the domain noun (e.g., *who* and *musician* in the preceding example). However, one important difference between the domain noun in main clauses and the pronoun in relative clauses is that they may take different grammatical roles. While *who* functions as subject (SU) within the subordinate clause and *musician* as subject within the main clause in the preceding example, this identity of grammatical roles is not inevitable, as five of the following examples show:

16 Flynn and others who have worked on branching direction problems do not attribute to transfer all difficulties encountered by learners. Nevertheless, they do see native language influence as an important factor in many difficulties.
17 While domain nouns in a relative clause are not always the same as what grammarians often refer to as *head nouns*, this identification is valid for English and for the other languages to be discussed in this section (cf. Keenan 1985).

SU   The musician who played at the concert is from China.
DO   The musician whom we met at the concert is from China.
IO   The musician to whom we sent the message is from China.
OPREP   The musician from whom we got the message is from China.
GEN   The musician whose son played at the concert is from China.
OCOMP   The musician who George is taller than is from China.

In each of these sentences *musician* is the subject of the main clause, but in each sentence (except for the first) the relative pronoun takes a different grammatical role: direct object (DO), indirect object (IO), prepositional object (OPREP), genitive (GEN), and object of comparison (OCOMP).

Some languages mark DO, IO, and other constituents with a *resumptive* instead of a *relative* pronoun, as in the following example from Persian (Keenan 1985:146):

Man zan-i-ro ke John be u   sib-e-zamini dad mišnasam
I   woman that John to her potato   gave know

The translation of this sentence in English, *I know the woman that John gave the potato to*, uses a relative, but not a resumptive, pronoun, and a translation that would more closely represent the IO constituent in Persian (that is, *be u*) would be anomalous: *I know the woman that John gave the potato to her.*[18] The designations DO, IO, and so forth are useful even in cases where no pronoun appears in the subordinate clause, as in *The musician we met at the concert is from China.* The relative clause in that sentence is considered to have a DO position since, if there *were* a relative pronoun marking that position, it would be functioning as a direct object within the clause. Thus, whether a constituent is marked by a relative pronoun, a resumptive pronoun, or by no form, the designations of DO, IO, and so on are used to describe **relativized positions.**

Not all languages have syntactic equivalents of some of the above types of relative clauses. A cross-linguistic survey of relativization patterns by Keenan and Comrie (1977) suggests that there is an implicational relationship among relativizable positions:

SU>DO>IO>OPREP>GEN>OCOMP

For example, if OPREP is a relativized position in a given language, IO, DO, and SU will also be relativized positions. The converse is not necessarily true, however; if SU, for instance, is a relativized position, DO, IO, and the rest may or may not be relativized. Keenan and Comrie's

---

18 Persian *ke* is usually translated as *that*, but it is more of a subordinating conjunction than a pronoun (Lazard 1957). The transliteration of the Persian words presented in this chapter departs in minor ways from the transliteration given by Keenan.

survey of fifty languages indicates considerable variation in what positions may be relativized in any language.[19] While English allows relativization on all six of the above positions, Tagalog allows it only on SU. Thus, although *The musician who played at the concert is from China* could be translated easily into Tagalog, a more circuitous translation would be needed for *The musician whom we met at the concert is from China.*

Keenan and Comrie see the implicational sequence as related to comprehensibility; thus, structures incorporating SU, DO, and IO may be more easily understood than ones incorporating OPREP, GEN, and OCOMP (cf. Keenan and Bimson 1975; Fox 1987). Support for the Keenan-Comrie interpretation is seen in the fact that the implicational relationship appears to be a good predictor of how frequently the six relativized positions will appear in the discourse of a given language. In a count of relative clause types in two English novels, Keenan (1975) found that SU clauses were the most frequent, DO the next most frequent, and so forth. Still further support for the Keenan-Comrie interpretation is seen in the fact that the implicational relationship also seems to be a good predictor of which relativized positions will make use of resumptive pronouns, as in the Persian example cited above.[20] The positions on the right-hand end of the implicational sequence, OPREP, GEN, and OCOMP, are far more likely to have such pronouns than are those on the left-hand end, SU, DO, and IO. Keenan and Comrie suggest that the use of resumptive pronouns aids in comprehension by making the structure of the relative clause more transparent.

Characteristics of relative clause structure, such as pronoun retention, pose an interesting problem for second language acquisition researchers. On the one hand, the implicational hierarchy posited by Keenan and Comrie may somehow reflect language universals. On the other hand, there is considerable cross-linguistic variation in relative clause structures, and such variation may occasion language transfer. In fact, research on the acquisition of English and Swedish suggests that transfer does indeed play a role in the erroneous use of resumptive pronouns. From the results of a sentence-combining task given to ESL students with nine different native languages, Gass (1979, 1983) determined that the native language was likely to influence the frequency of resumptive

19 Comrie and Keenan (1979) have provided an updated account, but one not substantially different from what is summarized here.
20 More often than not, positions such as GEN and OCOMP require resumptive pronouns if they can be relativized. In fact, Keenan and Comrie have identified an implicational relation that seems to govern the use of resumptive pronouns. Singler (1988) has noted that cases do exist that do not conform to such an implicational relation; however, he believes such exceptions do not constitute major problems for the Keenan-Comrie analysis (cf. Joseph 1983b).

pronouns in DO, IO, and OPREP positions. Thus, sentences like *I know the woman that John gave the potato to her* were more often produced by speakers of languages such as Persian (i.e., languages in which the IO position *must* have a resumptive pronoun). The influence of transfer also appears in some of the results of a grammaticality judgment test that Gass gave to the same subjects: speakers of languages such as Persian were more likely to accept DO and IO sentences like *I know the woman that John gave the potato to her* as grammatical in comparison with speakers of languages that do not make use of pronoun retention.

Further evidence of transfer comes from a recent study by Singler (1988) of pidginized forms of Liberian English. For example, speakers of Vai rarely used resumptive pronouns in SU position, while speakers of a language called Dan used them rather frequently. As Singler observes, such tendencies reflect the fact that Vai does not allow resumptive pronouns in SU position, whereas Dan requires such pronouns in the same position. Moreover, Singler's evidence suggests that some highly unusual patterns of resumptive pronoun use in certain other West African languages are mirrored in relativization patterns in some varieties of Liberian English. As in other cases to be discussed, the social factors involved in the acquisition of these varieties of Liberian English seem to have greatly influenced patterns of transfer (Section 8.3).

The findings on English relativization have been corroborated by research on the acquisition of Swedish, a language that, like English, does not use resumptive pronouns.[21] Using a picture-description test, Hyltenstam (1984) elicited relative clauses from speakers of four different languages. Speakers of Greek and Persian, languages that allow pronominal retention, produced many more instances of resumptive pronouns than did speakers of Finnish and Spanish, languages that do not allow pronominal retention. Another result similar to Gass's findings was that the resumptive pronouns used by Greek and Persian speakers were frequently in DO, IO, and OPREP positions, whereas such pronouns were less frequently used in the same positions by speakers of Finnish and Spanish.

Drawing on evidence from grammaticality judgment tests, some researchers (Ioup and Kruse 1977; Tarallo and Myhill 1983) have offered universalist arguments that the use of resumptive pronouns does not indicate transfer. For example, in the study carried out by Tarallo and Myhill, native speakers of English studying German, Portuguese, and other languages that do not use resumptive pronouns often considered as acceptable ungrammatical sentences that had such pronouns. In a

---

21 Resumptive pronouns do occur in relative clauses in some nonstandard varieties of English (Jespersen 1954). However, the influence of such nonstandard varieties on the English of students in Gass's study is unlikely.

similar study of grammaticality judgments of French sentences, native speakers of English frequently accepted sentences with resumptive pronouns even though French, like English, does not use such pronouns (Birdsong, Johnson, and McMinn 1984). Since neither native nor target language facts account well for the performance of English ESL speakers in these studies, a universalist explanation appears highly plausible – especially since there is also some support for this explanation in the research of Gass and Hyltenstam. In the latter two studies, learner behaviors closely matched the implicational patternings predicted by the Keenan-Comrie analysis. Nevertheless, such an explanation cannot account for all the known facts about the use of resumptive pronouns. The English and Swedish studies indicate that speakers of languages not using pronoun retention were less likely to employ resumptive pronouns than were speakers of languages using pronoun retention. Thus, even though a sentence such as *I know the woman that John gave the potato to her* could come from a French speaker, it would more likely come from a Persian speaker.

Despite its inability to explain everything, a universalist explanation does account well for a number of facts. First, the studies of Gass and Hyltenstam indicate that speakers of *any* native language are likely to use resumptive pronouns in the GEN and OCOMP positions. Second, the findings of Keenan (1975) on the frequency of relative clause types are corroborated by a count of the types of relative clauses used in student compositions (Gass 1983): SU sentences were more frequent than DO sentences, which in turn were more frequent than IO sentences, and so forth. Third, although there are some discrepancies in the data (especially in Liberian English), the frequency of correct production of relative clauses generally conforms to the Keenan-Comrie implicational sequences (Gass 1979, 1983; Hyltenstam 1984). Fourth, while a contrastive analysis can predict the use of avoidance strategies, as Schachter's research indicates, the Keenan-Comrie analysis provides insights about what relative clause patterns students are most likely to avoid (Gass and Ard 1984).

Other considerations

Relative clauses show other variations in structure besides those considered so far, but the role of such variations in second language acquisition has not yet been studied in as much detail. For example, there is some evidence supporting Kuno's analysis of the difficulties that embedded relative clauses may occasion. In a study of ESL students' grammaticality judgments, Ioup and Kruse (1977) found that student judgments were less accurate for sentences with embedded relative clauses (e.g., *The dish which fell on the floor broke in half*) than for ones in which the relative clause was not embedded (e.g., *The little girl is looking for the cat which ran away*). It is not clear, however, that the results of Ioup and Kruse's study reflect universals at work in second language acquisition. In an investigation of relative clauses in first language acquisition, Sheldon (1977) found that embedding did not affect children's ability to interpret relative clauses in their native languages (English and French). More crucial were sentences having "parallel functions," for example, *The lion that pushes the horse knocks down the cow*, where both the domain noun and the relative pronoun function as subjects within their respective clauses. Even though that sentence has an embedded relative clause (i.e., *that pushes the horse*), it proved to be of a type easier to understand than nonembedded types that did not have parallel functions (e.g., *The lion knocks down the cow that pushes the horse*).

Structures that are highly language-specific are another aspect of relative clauses warranting further investigation. For example, English makes use of a somewhat unusual relative clause pattern that does not have a relative pronoun but that does have a stranded preposition marking an IO or OPREP position in a clause (for example, *I want the pencil I write with*). Birdsong, Johnson, and McMinn (1984) found that native speakers of English do not frequently accept as grammatical the French translation equivalents of such patterns: in this case, *Je veux le crayon j'écris avec*. Moreover, research by Adjemian and Liceras (1984) suggests that French learners of English and French learners of Spanish (a language with relative clause patterns more like those of French) are equally unwilling to accept as grammatical sentences with stranded prepositions. On the other hand, preposition stranding *is* transferable to some extent. In a study of English-speaking children in a French immersion program, Selinker, Swain, and Dumas (1975) cite the following case of transfer: *Un chalet qu'on va aller à* ("A cottage that we're gonna go to") (cf. White 1987). The description of the French immersion program suggests that the social context, a relaxed setting of learners speaking with each other, may well have encouraged cross-linguistic influence despite putatively universal constraints on the transferability of preposition stranding (cf. Section 8.3).

6.3   Negation

Formal dimensions of negation

The study of negation in second language acquisition has sometimes been regarded as simply a question of word order. In some languages, **negators** (i.e., forms expressing negation, such as *no* and *nicht*) may either precede a verb phrase, as in Spanish *Juan no va* ("Juan is not going"), or follow a verb phrase, as in German *Ingrid kommt nicht* ("Ingrid is not coming"). As much of the following discussion will show, the use of **preverbal** or **postverbal** negation is indeed an important clue to relations between transfer and universals in second language acquisition. Nevertheless, fundamental differences between negation and word order must be noted. Negation is fundamentally a semantic notion, whereas word order is a formal arrangement (Section 5.1). As such, word order can play a role in *expressing* negation, but such a role presupposes constructions of two or more words. Since one-word negation is possible, the need for word order is not absolute, as the following example shows:

A: Are you hungry?
B: No.

Aside from independent words, prefixes and suffixes may also serve as negators, as in *uninterested, disinterested, nonaligned,* and *thoughtless.* The boundary between words and suffixes functioning as negators is sometimes hazy. In English, negators may be either words (as in *Alice is not here*) or contracted forms that have some properties of suffixes (e.g., *Alice isn't here*). The rules for negation are not always as simple as the Spanish and German examples given above suggest. For example, English verb-phrase negators are often neither preverbal nor postverbal, strictly speaking, since in negative constructions the verb phrase usually has both an auxiliary and a main verb (e.g., *Alice hasn't come*). And multiple negation in French shows that there can be both preverbal and postverbal negators in the same clause (e.g., *Jean ne voyage pas* – "John is not traveling"), as two forms, *ne . . . pas,* function together as negators. Thus although the following discussion considers in detail preverbal and postverbal patterns, a full understanding of negation in second language acquisition involves much more.

Negation and developmental sequences

As with the other areas of syntax already reviewed in this chapter, negation shows evidence not only of transfer but also of other influences on acquisition. Negation, in fact, was one of the areas first described by researchers who maintained that transfer did not offer a fully satisfactory account of acquisition (cf. Section 2.2). For example, data from Norwegian-speaking children (Ravem 1968) show that the predictions of contrastive analysis are sometimes utterly wrong. Like German, Norwegian uses postverbal negation in main clauses having one-word verb phrases, and so a contrastive analysis would naturally predict that a Norwegian learner of English would frequently use postverbal negation in the target language. Ravem found, however, that preverbal patterns were predominant: for example, *I not like that* and *I not looking for edge*. Moreover, there were almost no examples of postverbal negation. Occurrences of preverbal negation have also been described in studies of the English spoken by speakers of other native languages, such as Spanish and Greek (summarized by Schumann 1979). In these cases the occurrence of preverbal negation is generally compatible with a transfer explanation, since Spanish and Greek (and many other languages) use preverbal negation. Yet, since transfer cannot account for *all* learners' uses of the preverbal pattern, other factors influencing acquisition might account for *any* use of preverbal negation, no matter whether an individual's native language uses preverbal or postverbal negation or some other pattern.

In attempts to compare first and second language acquisition, Wode (1981, 1983a, 1983b, 1983c) studied the use of negation in the performance of monolingual and bilingual children in terms of developmental sequences. In both types of acquisition, Wode (1981, 1983a) found evidence of a developmental sequence consisting of three major stages: (1) one-word negation; (2) two- or more word negation; and (3) intrasentential negation. From his analysis emerges a pattern of evolution in negation that is similar in both first and second language acquisition.[22]

One-word negation is somewhat like zero anaphora (Section 6.1) – a lone negator is often sufficient to signal negation and to maintain topic continuity, as seen in the question and response given earlier of *Are you hungry? No*. The formal simplicity of a single negator and the minimal need to know any other vocabulary are undoubtedly key factors in the early appearance of one-word negation in the acquisition either of one's native language or of another language. The form a learner uses need not be identical with the target form. As Wode (1983a) has noted in observations of children learning German as their native language, the pronunciation of the negator may only weakly resemble an adult's pronunciation of the form; nevertheless, the choice of negator that a child uses often seems to be modeled after adult pronunciation.

Two-word utterances that include a negator are clearly similar to ones having three or more words, although longer utterances certainly require more knowledge of vocabulary and of some kind of clause structure. In two-word negation, the negator may accompany either a verb (as in a Spanish speaker's use of *No understand* [Cancino, Rosansky, and Schumann 1978]) or some other element (e.g., *No pink* [Young 1974; cited

---

22 Despite giving one of his papers a title that suggests a four-stage model, Wode presents a tripartite analysis in which the second part (two- or more word negation) consists of two substages. Other analyses by Wode (e.g., Wode 1981) show a somewhat different approach to the developmental sequence, but the evolutionary pattern remains essentially the same.

by Schumann 1979]). As utterances grow longer and new syntactic patterns begin to emerge, the negation pattern may still be far from the target pattern, as in *No drink some milk* (Wode 1981).

Intrasentential negation presupposes the development of other syntactic structures, since in this stage the negator generally occurs within the sentence. In the sentence *I not looking for edge*, for example, the negator occurs between the subject and the predicate. According to Wode, another crucial indicator of intrasentential negation is the growing use of other negators besides those found in the earliest stages of acquisition. Thus, in English the use of the form *no* often gives way to the use of other forms such as *not* and *don't*. However, the development of alternative forms may not necessarily begin in the intrasentential stage (cf. Schumann 1979).

Wode has acknowledged that other stages are also involved in the acquisition of negation, but his findings generally concur with those of other researchers (cf. Schumann 1979; Stauble 1984). Much in his analysis supports a universalist position. Neither native- nor target-language facts can explain all of what goes on in the early stages. For example, German-speaking children's use of two-word constructions, such as *no finish* and *no cold* in English, cannot be fully explained in terms of either the structure of German or of English (Wode 1983b). And in all likelihood, the acquisition of negation in *any* language by children or by adults will often show an initial use of one-word negation followed in turn by two-word negation and then by more complex patterns. The three-stage analysis also offers insights about the use of word order in negation. Noting the frequency of preverbal negation in the second and third stages of acquisition, Wode (1983c) has speculated that universal language-processing abilities may be the ultimate explanation for the frequent appearance of preverbal negation both in language acquisition and in the syntax of many of the languages of the world (Dahl 1979b).

Although there is a clear universalist strain in his analysis, Wode (1983b) has also shown that important differences – differences related to transfer – can arise in the development of negation by children learning a second language and children learning their native language. While there are attested cases of German-speaking children using English sentences such as *I'm steal not the base*, which shows a postverbal pattern, there are few if any comparable examples of this done by children learning English as their native language. Thus, a contrastive analysis of English and German does appear to have some predictive power; for at least one stage in the acquisition of negation, German-speaking children may use postverbal negation in English.

In attempting to account for the appearance of transfer, Wode has suggested that structures in both the native and target languages must be developed to the point where a "crucial similarity" between them can occasion transfer (cf. Section 5.2). In the case of the bilingual children that he studied, for example, the syntax of learners' German and English had to be considerably developed – and similar – for there to be post-verbal negation, which did not develop until preverbal patterns had appeared (cf. Wode 1978, 1981, 1983a; Zobl 1980). Without sufficient development, structures in both languages might be too similar for a distinct native language influence to be evident. Since the earliest developmental stages in the acquisition of any language are remarkably alike and since the forms in these stages are structurally simple, some phenomena have several possible explanations, including transfer and target language influence (cf. Adiv 1984).

Developmental sequences: one or many?

Research on the acquisition of negation in other contexts shows additional evidence for the existence of developmental sequences. Hyltenstam (1977) examined the use of negation by adult learners of Swedish, which employs postverbal negation in main clauses and preverbal negation in subordinate clauses. Using a written grammar test, Hyltenstam found frequent word-order errors, such as preverbal negation in main clauses and postverbal negation in subordinate clauses. Errors in subordinate clauses were much more frequent; in fact, mastery of negation in subordinate clauses generally implied mastery of negation in main clauses, but not vice versa. In other words, a developmental sequence seems to exist in the acquisition of Swedish – learners first master postverbal order in main clauses and only then the preverbal order in subordinate clauses. A common intermediate stage in this developmental continuum was evident in the use of postverbal negation in *all* contexts, with such overgeneralization only gradually giving way to the correct use of word order in both types of clauses. Hyltenstam was able to arrive at an even finer-grained characterization of learners' negation patterns in terms of the type of verb found with the negator: there was a clear tendency in main clauses to use preverbal negation with main verbs and postverbal negation with auxiliaries.[23] While he found virtually no evidence of transfer in learners' use of negation, Hyltenstam (1984) has more re-

23 Hyltenstam's analysis has sparked some controversy. Jordens (1980) criticizes, among other things, Hyltenstam's assumptions about the role that auxiliaries play in the development of negation (cf. Hyltenstam 1982; Jordens 1982). While the claims and counterclaims go beyond the scope of this chapter, one of the questions Jordens raises is highly significant for language acquisition studies generally: how closely do the categories of a learner's developing linguistic competence match those of an adult native speaker? Since it involves problems of comparison (Section 3.2), that question is especially significant for transfer research (cf. Bley-Vroman 1983).

cently observed that any firm conclusions regarding transfer and negation in Swedish were difficult to reach in light of a number of methodological problems (cf. Section 6.2).

The negation studies of Wode and Hyltenstam have provided valuable
insights about developmental sequences, but their results do not entirely
clarify certain issues. For example, while Wode's research indicates that
the development of negation in first and second language acquisition is
not invariably the same, there remains the question of just how much
the acquisition sequences can differ. And in second language acquisition
there is also the question of just how much transfer can influence the
evolution of different sequences. A number of researchers have argued
that such influence is considerable (e.g., Schumann 1979; Zobl 1980).
Support for that position comes from a detailed comparison of the
negation patterns in the English of Spanish and Japanese speakers (Stauble 1984). Stauble's findings suggest that the paths along which the
syntax of negation develops sometimes cross but often diverge. The
Spanish and Japanese speakers least proficient in English made use of
preverbal negation, but Spanish speakers tended to employ *no* extremely
frequently whereas Japanese speakers used both *no* and *not*. Among the
more proficient individuals, the Japanese speakers tended to use a wider
variety of negators, although the most proficient individuals demonstrated relatively few differences due to transfer.

Stauble's results strongly suggest that a *lexical* similarity between two
languages can increase the likelihood of not only lexical but also *syntactic*
transfer. The Spanish negator *no* is phonologically similar to the English
form *no*, and this similarity may explain why Spanish speakers seem
more ready to employ it than to employ such forms as *not* and *can't*.[24]
Although the cross-sectional nature of Stauble's research does not allow
for firm conclusions, it may also be the case that Spanish speakers persist
longer in using *no*. A study by Schachter (1986) of a Colombian named
Jorge indicates that use of *no* persists even while other types of negators
such as *don't* and *never* are used more frequently. While the lexical
similarity between English *no* and Spanish *no* is one possible reason for
such persistence, discourse function also seems to be an important factor.
Schachter's analysis suggests that some negators are especially likely to
be used when particular speech acts are negated. For example, when
Jorge used *no* before a prepositional phrase, the negator sometimes
signaled the nonexistence of something (e.g., *No in Colombia?*), but he
preferred using *don't* to signal rejections (e.g., *I don't like*).

---

24 Another likely instance of lexical and syntactic transfer interacting is found in
Hiberno-English. Henry (1957) suggests that sentences such as *It's flat it was* were
especially likely to develop among Irish-English bilinguals because of the similarity
of the Irish copula *is* and English *it's* (cf. Section 4.3).

Aside from variations in a developmental continuum that are due to transfer, individual differences in learners may lead to somewhat different continua. This is more than just a possibility, as Clahsen (1984) has shown in a longitudinal study of Spanish and Portuguese learners of German (cf. Wode 1981). Even though, for instance, both Spanish and Portuguese have preverbal negation, not all the individuals studied by Clahsen used preverbal negation in German a great deal.[25] While Clahsen maintains that his data support the notion of developmental stages, he stresses that some learners show more of a tendency to simplify target language patterns:

it might be expected that simplifying learners will tend to use preverbal NEG placement, whereas learners who are more oriented toward use of the target norm will tend to prefer postverbal negation from the beginning of the learning process. (1984:237)

In the case of "simplifying" learners, there is likely to be more of a resemblance between first and second language acquisition. Such differences in learner behavior show the importance of taking individual variation into account in the study of transfer (Section 8.1).

6.4   Summary and conclusion

A comprehensive treatment of syntactic transfer would have to include much more than the present survey of word order, relative clauses, and negation. Nevertheless, some tendencies evident in those three areas suggest that similar tendencies will also emerge when other areas of syntax are investigated in greater detail in the future. In the acquisition of word order, relative clauses, and negation, transfer figures as an important factor, but it often occurs in conjunction with other acquisition processes, some of which show hints of typological and universal influences at work. With regard to word order, an important influence of language universals seems to be the effect that discourse has on the arrangement of basic clause constituents. With regard to relative clauses, typological factors such as the range of relativizable positions and the primary branching direction that a language shows appear to have a strong influence on the development of complex syntax, in what subordinate clauses learners first use, and how successfully they use them. And with regard to negation, there is also evidence of developmental sequences, albeit with some individual differences. Aside from the likeli-

---

25 In a study of negation patterns used by English-speaking adults learning German, Eubank (1986) found even less evidence for the use of preverbal negation. Eubank attributed such a difference to the effects of formal instruction (cf. Section 8.3).

hood that one-word negation is a universally occurring first stage of development, there appears to be a strong typological influence that favors the use of preverbal negation at an early stage of syntactic development in some languages even when neither the native nor the target language uses preverbal negation. Yet while typology and universals seem to play a role in the acquisition of negation and the other syntactic structures discussed, so does transfer. Whether syntactic transfer is as important as (for example) phonological transfer is still an open question. However, the discussion of typologies and universals in the next chapter indicates that the problem of transfer in second language pronunciation is similar to the problem of syntactic transfer, since language-specific facts are not the only data important to consider.

Further reading

A text by Givón (1984a) on syntax provides an extensive discussion of facts about word order and negation relevant to this chapter, and an article by Keenan (1985) provides a good typological survey of relative clause formation. Gass (1984) surveys much of the work on second language syntax that has led to a reconsideration of transfer by many researchers in the 1980s. A very detailed longitudinal study by Wode (1981) offers insights not only about the development of second language syntax but also many other aspects of child bilingualism.

7 *Phonetics, phonology, and writing systems*

There is little doubt that native language phonetics and phonology are powerful influences on second language pronunciation, and this chapter will consider some of the more important aspects of those influences. As with other aspects of second language performance, pronunciation often shows other influences besides cross-linguistic ones; accordingly, developmental and other factors will be examined, as well as transfer involving writing systems.

7.1 General versus specific predictions

The literature on second language acquisition and language teaching is replete with descriptions of the difficulties that learners encounter in trying to pronounce sounds in a foreign language, and contrastive explanations for such difficulties are quite common (Dechert, Brügge-meir, and Futterer 1984). As the discussion in the next section shows, there is considerable – but not total – support for specific contrastive predictions. Aside from specific predictions, general predictions are also possible. For example, one might predict that a speaker of Thai will have more difficulty in learning to pronounce English than a speaker of Persian will. In fact, some research on ESL pronunciation (Suter 1976; Purcell and Suter 1980) supports that prediction; in carefully controlled analyses of judgments of pronunciation accuracy, the pronunciation of speakers of Thai and Japanese did not receive as high ratings as did the pronunciation of speakers of Arabic and Persian. Suter (1976) acknowledges that such results do not in themselves explain what features of native language pronunciation contribute most to a high or low evaluation of pronunciation accuracy. Moreover, such results do not entirely rule out the possibility that nonstructural factors (e.g., personality factors) account for some of the differences in performance (Section 8.1). Nevertheless, detailed analyses of several possible factors showed the native language of students to be an especially good predictor of what evaluation their speech in English received as opposed to such factors as length of residence in the

United States and motivation to pronounce English correctly (Purcell and Suter 1980).

7.2   Phonetic and phonological transfer

Phonetic differences

A cross-linguistic comparison of sounds in two languages should include descriptions of the phonetics as well as the phonology of the native and target languages (cf. Brière 1968). A phonetic description is necessary since sounds in two languages often show different *physical* character-istics, including both acoustic characteristics (e.g., the pitch of a sound) and articulatory characteristics (e.g., how widely the mouth is open in producing a sound). Two languages frequently have sounds which may seem identical but which in fact are acoustically different. For example, a comparison of an American English /d/ with a Saudi Arabian Arabic /d/ shows several differences (Flege 1980). Among the differences, the duration of an English /d/ at the end of a word (e.g., in *bad*) tends to be shorter than its Arabic counterpart. As a contrastive analysis would predict, Saudi learners' pronunciation of the English /d/ tends to show a duration longer than the English norm. Nevertheless, Flege's analysis shows that learners are capable of modifying their production of sounds so that their pronunciation comes closer to the target language norms. The modifications often do not result in the attainment of target language norms, but rather in *approximations* that are neither fully nativelike nor targetlike. Thus, the "English" /d/ that some Arabic speakers produce is longer than the target language norm but is shorter than a normal Arabic /d/.[1] The development of such compromise forms shows the im-portance of learners' unconscious *judgments*. While these judgments are influenced by learners' knowledge of forms in their native language, they are also based on judgments about how phonetic material is structured in the target language.[2]

Phonemic differences

Learners' identification of the Arabic /d/ and the English /d/ illustrates the importance of phonetic similarity in **interlingual identifications,**

---

1 Although the term *interlanguage* coined by Selinker (1972) usually connotes more than simply compromise forms, the example of the /d/ in Flege's study supports Selinker's contention that second languages are systematic varieties in their own right. Trudgill (1986) has shown the usefulness of Selinker's analysis for the study of compromise forms in cases of dialect contact (cf. Section 2.1).

2 In the case of subtle phonetic differences such as those that distinguish the Arabic /d/ from the English /d/, learners' judgments of similarities and differences are likely to be unconscious (cf. Section 8.3).

which are the equivalence relations that learners establish between the native and target languages. While any resemblance between sounds creates the potential for identifications, the judgments of equivalence that learners make are affected by much more than just the acoustic properties of sounds in the native and target languages. The similarity of cognate forms, for example, may induce learners to establish correspondences between sounds that are phonetically very different (cf. Section 5.2). For instance, the uvular /r/ of Parisian French and the retroflex /r/ of American English have very different phonetic properties, but there are other acoustic, as well as orthographic, cues that may induce American learners of French to equate the French /r/ with the English /r/ in cognates such as *route*.

Another factor that influences interlingual identifications is the set of relations implicit in the **phonemic system** of a language. A study by Scholes (1968) of the perception of vowels by native and non-native speakers of English indicates that non-native speakers are likely to categorize foreign language sounds largely in terms of the phonemic inventory of the native language (cf. Liberman et al. 1957). In Scholes's study, native speakers distinguished between the vowels /e/ and /æ/ (as in the words *rain* and *ran*), whereas speakers of Russian and Greek did not. In contrast to other non-native speakers of English, speakers of Persian, which, like English, has a phonemic contrast between /e/ and /æ/, did distinguish between the two vowel sounds. Although such research clearly demonstrates the importance of native-language phonemic systems, the explanation for some perceptual confusions is a bit less straightforward. For example, Spanish has a nasal consonant /n/ phonetically similar to the English /n/ and, like the English sound, a Spanish /n/ can occur at the end of a word. One might naturally expect, then, that Spanish speakers would never have difficulty in perceiving the English /n/ at the end of a word (e.g., in *fan*). However, a study by Marckwardt (1946) showed some confusion on the part of Spanish speakers in distinguishing between /n/ and the nasal phoneme /ŋ/ in *fang*. Since the latter nasal sound exists in Spanish, but never in a phonemic contrast such as between *fan* and *fang*, the phonetic similarities of the Spanish and English nasals do not always outweigh the differences in phonemic systems for purposes of interlingual identification. In Marckwardt's study, such systemic differences appear to have encouraged hypercorrection.

While Scholes's study indicates that major differences in phonemic inventories can cause perceptual confusions in foreign language learning, the phonemic inventory of the native language does not totally impede perception of foreign language sounds. Phonetic mimicry is one kind of evidence that individuals can recognize sounds rather different from those in the native language. Flege and Hammond (1982) studied the

"Spanish accents" imitated by native speakers of English and determined that the sounds the English speakers produced were often approximations of Spanish vowels and consonants. Another kind of evidence, identification of differing accents, also indicates that individuals can recognize foreign language sounds. For example, Ioup (1984) found that native speakers of English can identify different groups of non-native speakers simply on the basis of their pronunciation (cf. Smith and Bisazza 1982).

The phonetic sensitivity needed for such identifications is evident among individuals learning a second language even when their native language seems to impede certain perceptual distinctions. The distinction between /l/ and /r/ in English is notoriously difficult for speakers of languages such as Japanese and Korean, which do not have that phonemic distinction. Frequent problems involving misperceptions and mispronunciations of these sounds in words such as *lice* and *rice* make it natural to suppose that Japanese speakers, for example, may not actually attend to the phonetic material that distinguishes these sounds. However, research by Mann (1986) indicates that Japanese speakers can attend to the differences. In one sense, such findings should not be surprising, since learners often do show success in achieving pronunciations closer and closer to target language norms (cf. Dickerson 1974; Flege 1980; Borden, Gerber, and Milsark 1983). Nevertheless, individuals differ in their perceptual acuity, and it may be that only individuals with especially high phonetic sensitivity will be able to overcome most of the inhibiting influence of phonological patterns in the native language (cf. Section 8.1).

Types of segmental errors

Although cross-linguistic differences in phonetics and phonology have important consequences for perception and comprehension, the most salient consequences of linguistic differences are production errors which result in pronunciation patterns that diverge from those found in the target language. Most attempts at classification of pronunciation errors have emphasized phonemic contrasts (e.g., Weinreich 1953/1968; Lado 1957). However, the evidence of phonetic transfer discussed earlier suggests that an adequate classificatory scheme must take into account other factors. An error taxonomy devised by Moulton (1962a) takes into account much, though not all, of the complexity found in second language pronunciation. Although many of the assumptions about phonological theory and transfer that are implicit in Moulton's classification have been challenged, his taxonomy still provides a valuable analysis of the range of second language **segmental errors** (i.e., errors involving vowels and consonants). Based mainly on a contrastive analysis of English and German, Moulton's taxonomy recognizes four types of errors: (1) phonemic errors; (2) phonetic errors; (3) allophonic errors; and (4) distributional errors.

Phonemic errors can arise when the phonemic inventories of two languages differ. For example, German has a phonemic contrast between the voiceless velar fricative /x/ and the voiceless velar stop /k/. Thus, German has minimal pairs such as /naxt/ ("night") and /nakt/ ("naked"). While the latter consonant has phonemic status in English, the former does not (except in some dialects in the British Isles). In fact, many native speakers of English have difficulty pronouncing /x/ and often fail to distinguish minimal pairs such as /naxt/ and /nakt/. An analogous problem in ESL is the /r/–/l/ distinction in English discussed earlier, which results in frequent pronunciation confusions among speakers of Chinese, Japanese, and Korean.

Phonetic errors in Moulton's classification involve cases of cross-linguistic equivalence at the phonemic but not the phonetic level. Thus, while the German uvular /r/ and the English retroflex /r/ are corresponding consonants in cognate forms such as German *rar* and English *rare*, their acoustic properties differ considerably. Moreover, speakers of American English are normally not accustomed to using the uvula, whereas speakers in many regions of Germany are.[3] The /r/ sounds that English speakers are likely to produce will thus differ considerably from the target language consonant.

Allophonic errors can arise in cases of interlingual identifications of phonemes in two languages. A particular sound or allophone that is a manifestation of a native language phoneme is not always an accepted manifestation of a corresponding target language phoneme. For example, both English and German have a voiceless alveolar stop /t/. When the American English /t/ occurs between vowels, however, it is not always voiceless; thus, the sound of /t/ in words such as *writer* and *whiter* is acoustically quite similar to the sound of /d/ in *rider* and *wider*. The German /t/, on the other hand, remains essentially voiceless when it occurs between vowels. Americans learning German are thus liable to use a voiced consonant between vowels in words such as *bitter* ("bitter").[4]

Distributional errors sometimes resemble allophonic errors, but they may involve combinations of sounds. For example, German has a pho-

---

3 As discussed earlier, the equation of transfer and "old habits" is misleading (Section 3.1). However, articulatory problems that English learners of German have with uvulars suggest that a theory of habit formation may be applicable to certain types of phonetic transfer.

4 Allophonic and other types of errors in Moulton's classification might also be described in terms of rules such as those in generative phonology (e.g., Schane 1973).

neme /ts/ which is acoustically similar to the consonant cluster found at the end of English words such as *its* and *bits*. While speakers of English have no difficulty in pronouncing the German phoneme when it occurs at the end of words, as in *Sitz* ("seat"), they do often have difficulty in pronouncing it at the beginning of words, as in *zu* (/tsu/, "to"). Thus the *position* of a sound within a word or syllable can affect how easy a sound is to pronounce. When there are distributional differences in the sounds of two languages, transfer errors may occur.

Suprasegmental patterns

Although cross-linguistic influences on pronunciation frequently involve segmental contrasts, the influences are also frequently evident in **suprasegmental** contrasts involving stress, tone, rhythm, and other factors. Stress patterns are crucial in pronunciation since they affect syllables and the segments that constitute syllables, as seen in the stress alternation in English between certain nouns and verbs, such as between *COMbine* and *comBINE*. The first syllable in these two words has a different vowel sound, with the sound varying according to the acoustic prominence of the syllable. Such interactions have important implications not only for speech production but also for comprehension. Research reviewed by Cutler (1984) indicates that stress patterns play a crucial role in listeners' recognition of words. When non-native speakers do not use a stress pattern that is a norm in the target language, vowels and consonants may also vary from the target pattern, and this can result in a total misperception by listeners. Bansal (1976) argues that errors in stress are the most important cause of unintelligibility in Indians' pronunciation of English, and gives examples of misidentifications by listeners. For instance, *diVIsions* was sometimes pronounced *DIvisions* and was consequently misperceived by British listeners as *REgions*, and *talking among themSELVES* was sometimes pronounced as *talking among THEMselves* and was consequently misperceived as *talking among DAMsels*.

Stress errors such as those noted by Bansal do not necessarily reflect native language influence. However, a somewhat similar study by Tiffin (1974) found differences in the intelligibility of Nigerian English that were related both to stress errors and to native language. According to Tiffin, Yoruba speakers in the study tended to make more errors involving stress than Hausa speakers did, and as a result British listeners had more difficulty in identifying what the Yoruba speakers had said. The greater intelligibility of the Hausa speakers seems to have been due mainly to a somewhat greater similarity between the suprasegmental system of Hausa and that of English. Other evidence of cross-linguistic influences related to stress is found in a study by Andrews (1984). French speakers, for example, tended to accent syllables at the end or close to the end of English words; that tendency accords with stress patterns in French, and it proved to be different from the stress patterns of speakers of other languages. Such a tendency suggests that cognate forms (e.g., *motor* and *moteur*) might often be unrecognizable when listeners (whether native or non-native speakers) do not take into account differences in stress patterns.

One of the most important typological distinctions between languages involves tone and intonation (cf. Section 3.4). In tone languages, pitch levels have phonemic significance. A common example of the phonemic status of tone in certain languages involves the Mandarin Chinese syllable *ma*, which, among other denotations, represents "mother" when it is used with a high level tone, and "horse" with a low rising tone (Bloomfield 1933). Such a system uses pitch levels quite differently from what is encountered in most European languages.

The ease of acquisition of the phonology of tone languages may depend very much on the typological similarity between the native and target languages. Research by Gandour and Harshman (1978) suggests that knowledge of one tone language (e.g., Yoruba) can aid learners in identifying the significant suprasegmental units in another tone language (e.g., Thai). Thus, it is likely that speakers of a language such as Yoruba would have less difficulty than would speakers of English, which is not a tone language, in mastering the suprasegmental system of a language such as Thai. There is evidence that speakers of English do have considerable difficulty in learning to identify and use tones in Mandarin (Chiang 1979; Broselow, Hurtig, and Ringen 1987). However, it also appears to be true that speakers of tone languages encounter difficulties in learning another closely related tone language; Leung (1978) notes that Cantonese speakers often have difficulties with Mandarin and that such difficulties are due in part to the tone system of the native language.

While tone languages such as Chinese and Yoruba are found in many parts of the world, intonational languages such as English are also quite common. Pitch in English does not signal phonemic distinctions as it does in Chinese, but it does convey important information about speakers' attitudes and emotional states. As such, pitch and other suprasegmental features, including stress, rhythm, and loudness, play a role in discourse similar to that of gestures and other paralinguistic signals (cf. Section 4.1). A study by Rintell (1984) suggests that speakers of Chinese have special difficulty in identifying the emotional states of speakers of English; in contrast to speakers of Spanish and Arabic, Chinese speakers' judgments of the emotional tone of conversations often diverged from the judgments of native speakers of English. While intonation may be only one of the factors accounting for the difference between Chinese and other ESL students in Rintell's study, it does seem significant that Spanish and Arabic are, like English, intonational languages, whereas Chinese is not.

Intonational signals have other functions besides suggesting speakers' attitudes and emotions; they also help to structure conversation by providing signals for openings and closings, for the managing of turns, and for other functions (Brazil, Coulthard, and Johns 1980). Moreover, intonation often interacts with discourse and syntactic structures. There do seem to be some universal tendencies in the functions that suprasegmental units will have in phrases and clauses. For example, Bolinger (1978) observes that a rising intonation is characteristic of *yes-no questions* in many languages (e.g., *Are you coming?*, which can have either an affirmative or a negative reply). Nevertheless, there is considerable cross-linguistic variation in suprasegmental systems, and the effects of similarities and differences in systems are evident in second language acquisition.

A similarity in the suprasegmental patterns of two languages can give a learner important advantages in learning the syntax of the target language according to a study by Keller-Cohen (1979). In a comparison of the acquisition of English by children who spoke Japanese, Finnish, and German, Keller-Cohen found that the similarity between the question intonation patterns of English and those of German and Japanese aided speakers of those languages in acquiring the syntax of questions in English. In contrast, the absence of rising intonation in yes-no questions in Finnish appears to delay the acquisition of English question patterns.

Similarity or dissimilarity between native- and target-language intonation patterns can also affect production in other ways. Adams (1979) attributes much of the divergence of ESL speakers' speech rhythms to the rhythmic systems in their native languages (in her study, Vietnamese, Cambodian, and other languages). Contrastive studies of intonation in German, Dutch, English, and other languages also point to native language influence (Pürschel 1975; Willems 1982; Van Els and De Bot 1987); indeed, one of the surest clues to the specific "foreign accent" of an individual appears to be the ensemble of characteristics of sentence rhythm and pitch in the native language.

The effects of suprasegmental (or segmental) transfer may often be relatively unimportant. When speaking English, a German may "sound German" and a Korean may "sound Korean," but they may still succeed in communicating gracefully, fluently, and accurately in most respects (cf. Chapter 10). Nevertheless, non-native speakers may at times risk giving offense simply from the use of intonation patterns that signal one emotional state in the native language and a different one in the target language (cf. Kasper 1981; Loveday 1982b).

7.3 Pronunciation, language universals, and typologies

The cross-linguistic frequency of phonemes

Although the native language has a major influence on the phonetic and phonological patterns evident in second language acquisition, research in the last decade or so has raised important questions about the independence of native language influence from other factors. One factor that many contrastive analyses have unfortunately not taken into account is the cross-linguistic frequency of the sounds being contrasted. Languages tend to have a mix of sounds, some found in many languages and some not so commonly found. While there is no particular vowel or consonant phoneme found in every language of the world, some sounds are extremely common. For instance, in a controlled sample of 317 languages, the vowels /i/, /u/, and /a/ all appeared in the phonemic inventories of over 250 languages; similarly, the bilabial nasal /m/ appeared in almost 300 languages, and the voiced bilabial stop /b/ in almost 200 languages (Maddieson 1984). In contrast, some sounds in Maddieson's survey were somewhat rarer: for example, the German /x/ appeared in 76 languages and the German /ts/ in 46 (cf. Section 7.2). Some sounds were rarer still. One such example is a voiceless pharyngeal fricative /ħ/ in Kurdish that appeared in only 12 other languages in Maddieson's survey.

The significance of such cross-linguistic facts for second language acquisition is that there seems to be a rough correlation between the frequency of a sound and its difficulty for adults learning a second language.[5] For example, a study by Brière (1968) suggests that American students will have considerably more trouble in learning the rarest sounds: /ħ/ as opposed to /x/, for instance. The significance of such experimental results for contrastive analysis is great. A comparison of Kurdish and English, for example, shows that the former language has both /ħ/ and /x/, whereas the latter has neither. Any contrastive analysis is likely to predict that both sounds will cause difficulty for English-speaking learners of Kurdish, but the facts of cross-linguistic frequency suggest that /ħ/ will cause far more difficulty.

Common phonological rules

As with the cross-linguistic frequency of particular sounds, the frequency of phonological rules can be an important clue to what will be easy or

5 The relative ease that children may have in learning target language sounds is discussed in the next chapter (Section 8.2).

difficult in acquisition. One rule that has proved to be especially interesting involves consonant **devoicing**; in some languages certain consonants at the ends of words become voiceless. In German, for instance, the final consonant of *Rad* ("wheel") is pronounced the same as the final consonant in *Rat* ("advice"), although the plural form of *Rad*, which is *Räder*, has a voiced consonant (/d/). Linguists often interpret the voiceless consonant in words such as *Rad* as evidence of a devoicing rule by which a voiced consonant becomes voiceless whenever it appears at the end of words. In the sense that similar rules appear in many other languages, this German rule is a very "natural" rule, and this "naturalness" leads to predictions rather different from those of traditional contrastive analyses (Eckman 1977). Even though English does not have such a devoicing rule, English speakers have little difficulty, according to Moulton (1962b), in learning to pronounce *Rad* and *Rat* identically despite the fact that the plural form of *Rad* (i.e., *Räder*) has a voiced consonant. In contrast, German speakers learning English will have, Moulton claims, considerable difficulty in suppressing the native language devoicing rule, and thus will find it difficult to avoid pronouncing words such as *nod* the same way as *not*.[6] The presence of the devoicing rule in German and its absence in English therefore do *not* imply that English learners and German learners will have comparable difficulty in acquiring the rule, on the one hand, and suppressing the rule on the other.[7] It is highly likely that cross-linguistic contrasts frequently entail such asymmetrical patterns of difficulty (cf. Section 7.4).

The relative lack of difficulty of the devoicing rule for English learners seems to be related to the cross-linguistic frequency of the rule, which is found in many other languages. There is other evidence of the naturalness of the rule. Eckman (1981a, 1981b) has documented cases of speakers of Cantonese and Spanish devoicing word-final stops in English even though such a rule does not exist in either the native or target languages. For example, Cantonese speakers may pronounce *pig* like *pick* even though Cantonese does not have a devoicing rule like that found in German (Eckman 1981a). Thus, in some acquisition contexts

---

6 Eckman develops his analysis in terms of *markedness*, a frequently discussed concept in the study of linguistic typologies and universals. Scholars generally agree that the more marked a structure is, the more unusual it is, and the more difficult it will be to learn. Beyond that consensus, however, there is considerable uncertainty about how markedness is best defined (cf. Moravcsik and Wirth 1986). In the interest of terminological simplicity, the term *markedness* has been avoided in this and other chapters where it is relevant (e.g., the discussion of relative clauses in Chapter 6).

7 Hecht and Mulford (1987) claim that consonant devoicing occurs in some dialects of English. While devoicing may occur, the importance of this rule in English is probably negligible in comparison with its importance in German.

the devoicing rule has an existence somewhat independent of both the native and target languages (cf. Eckman 1984).

Syllable structure

The relative independence of the devoicing rule from the structure of the native and target languages might suggest that transfer is not a factor in, for example, Cantonese speakers' pronunciation of *pig* and *pick*. Nevertheless, native-language phonological rules do appear to interact with rules such as the devoicing rule. The pronunciation errors of Cantonese speakers described by Eckman (1981a) differ considerably from those of Japanese speakers in the same study. The Japanese speakers never devoiced final consonants; thus, words such as *pig* were not pronounced like *pick* but instead often had a vowel added to create a second syllable as in [pigǝ]. Eckman attributes such errors to syllable structure typology – Japanese is one of many languages that allow very few consonants to occur at the end of a word. The addition of a vowel to words such as *pig* therefore seems to be a consequence of a typological preference in Japanese for **open syllables**, syllables that do not end in consonants, as in the consonant-vowel (CV) sequence in *pa*. Even though the vowel-insertion rule posited by Eckman does not exist either in Japanese or English, it reflects a possible influence of native language syllable structure (cf. Anderson 1987).

According to Eckman's analysis, the preference of Japanese speakers for open syllables arises from the influence of the native language. There is, however, a possibility that this preference is related to language universals. Tarone (1980) compared the English pronunciation errors of native speakers of Cantonese, Portuguese, and Korean and found that while many errors could be attributed to language transfer, not all could. Many of the errors, according to Tarone, suggest a universal preference for open syllables of the CV type. For example, even though Korean allows for nasal consonants such as /n/ at the end of words, speakers of Korean did not always pronounce that consonant at the end of English words such as *then* and thus produced words with a CV syllable structure. In light of the observation of Hyman (1975) and others that CV is the most widespread syllable type, the errors documented by Tarone suggest that speakers of all languages may be predisposed to using CV syllables in a second language (cf. Greenberg 1983).

If there is such a predisposition, however, it interacts with other factors. The Cantonese speakers studied by Eckman (1981a) often produced syllables with a final consonant (e.g., CVC), and frequent use of CVC syllables is also evident in data obtained from studying Spanish speakers (Eckman 1981b). Moreover, Sato (1984) has argued that Vietnamese speakers prefer CVC syllables to CV. For example, Vietnamese speakers appear less likely to pronounce *next* (/nekst/) as [ne] than as [ne?], where the final consonant is a **glottal stop**. Other research on Vietnamese speakers' pronunciation, however, suggests that some universal factors are at work. Benson (1986) was able to use an implicational analysis of Greenberg (1965) to predict what syllable types Vietnamese speakers would find most difficult. Greenberg's analysis indicates, for example, that languages are more likely to have syllables ending in two voiceless consonants (e.g., /-ps/ as in *tops*) than to have syllables ending in two voiced consonants (e.g., /-bd/ as in *rubbed*). Benson's findings very clearly indicate that Vietnamese speakers did indeed have far more difficulty pronouncing consonant clusters such as /-bd/.

Transfer and developmental factors

The evidence presented so far in this section has suggested that studies in language universals and linguistic typology are relevant to research on second language pronunciation in a number of ways, including the cross-linguistic frequency of phonemes, the naturalness of phonological rules, and preferences for certain syllable structure types. In all of these areas, the evidence points to influences on second language acquisition that are not due solely to native language patterns of pronunciation. As in the case of syntactic patterns such as negation, the acquisition of sound patterns appears to involve *developmental* factors both in first and in second language learning (cf. Section 6.3). A very probable example of a developmental influence is the consonant devoicing rule investigated by Eckman and others. As noted, the devoicing of final consonants at the end of words can occur in the ESL pronunciation not only of speakers of languages in which the rule operates (e.g., German) but also of speakers of languages in which the rule does not operate (e.g., Cantonese). Some evidence from child language acquisition also suggests that consonant devoicing is a developmental rule. Edwards (1979) found that children acquiring English as their native language tend to devoice word-final consonants such as the /z/ in *shoes*.

The relative importance of transfer and of developmental processes such as consonant devoicing has been the object of some investigations. In a study of a child from Iceland in the United States, Hecht and Mulford (1987) have provided interesting evidence that transfer and developmental factors may affect learners' pronunciation in different ways. They found that developmental errors were especially common with fricatives (e.g., /v/), whereas transfer errors were more common with other types of consonants and with vowels. Major (1986, 1987) has hypothesized that transfer errors will be more evident in the earlier stages of acquisition and that developmental errors will not be common until learners have made considerable progress; his hypothesis is similar to others that have been made about syntactic errors (Section 8.1). While such analyses are provocative and are supported by some evidence, the relation between transfer and developmental factors is probably as complex in phonology as it is in other areas.

7.4 Writing systems

In contrast to other systemic aspects of language, such as phonology and syntax, writing systems are unique. Since writing systems do not exist in every language, cross-linguistic comparisons of such systems will not always be possible. Furthermore, in cases where writing systems do exist in both the native and target language, contrastive analyses of those systems will not be applicable to the performance of learners who never learn the target language writing system or who have not learned the system of their own language (cf. Section 8.1). However, many acquisition contexts do involve cases of learners who are literate in one language and who seek to become literate in another. In this section, the focus will be on such cases since they are the only ones eligible for contrastive analyses of writing systems and since transfer involving such systems can play an important role in acquisition.

Contrasts in writing systems

Any consideration of transfer involving writing systems must take into account the relation that frequently exists between pronunciation and writing. As suggested at the beginning of the chapter, writing systems often reflect the sound patterns in a language, and therefore a contrastive analysis of writing systems often presupposes some familiarity with the phonetics and phonology of the languages being compared. Much of the negative transfer evident in misspellings has its origins not in native language orthography but in native language pronunciation (as discussed later). Thus, even in cases in which learners do not read or write any language except the target language there can be native language influences on second language literacy.

There is no question that literacy involves much more than just the ability to encode and decode the symbols used in a writing system. Coming to terms with the meanings intertwined in rhetorical, lexical, and syntactic patterns surely constitutes much of the challenge of learning to read and write in a new language. However, successful reading and writing also presuppose a certain mastery of encoding and decoding skills. Such skills involve not only individual symbols but also *systems* of symbols. To become literate in an *alphabetic* system, one must come to recognize the correspondence (however rough) between letters and phonemes. To become literate in a *syllabic* system such as the Vai script used in West Africa, one must recognize correspondences between written symbols and syllables (Scribner and Cole 1981). And to become literate in a so-called *ideographic* system such as Chinese, one must recognize the correspondences between written symbols and morphemes (Coulmas 1983). The most widespread orthographies function exclusively on an alphabetic, or on a syllabic, or on an ideographic principle, although some languages, such as Japanese, make important use of more than one principle (cf. Gelb 1963; Sampson 1985).

Pedagogical practice reflects the fact that the more similar the writing systems of two languages are, the less time learners will need to develop basic encoding and decoding skills. Spanish and English, for example, are extremely similar in their writing systems, whereas Chinese and English are not. Textbooks that introduce Spanish to English speakers therefore need not – and generally do not – devote much space to the writing system of the target language, whereas introductory texts on written Chinese for English speakers obviously must devote a great deal of space to the ideographic system. The Spanish writing system does show some differences from English in spelling and handwriting conventions, but what differences there are are differences between alphabetic systems.[8] While such differences can occasion spelling difficulties, the similarities that arise from two languages having essentially the same alphabet are so great as to reduce considerably the time needed to become literate in the target language (cf. Section 3.3).

The overlap between alphabetic systems is not always as great as in the case of Spanish and English. The Cyrillic alphabet of Russian, for example, has some letters in common with English (e.g., the printed uppercase letters *M* and *T*), but many of the letters will not be familiar to an English reader even when they represent phonemes that are functionally equivalent in Russian and English. Empirical work on readers' processing of the Cyrillic and Roman alphabets used in Yugoslavia suggests that when students learn an alphabet having some correspondences with the one they have already mastered, they make interlingual identifications of familiar letters and thus begin their mastery of the new alphabet on the basis of the similarities of the two writing systems (Lukatela et al. 1978). With some alphabets there is little or no overlap in the writing systems of two languages except for the alphabetic principle itself. For example, the Persian and the English alphabet have

---

8 Vachek (1964) has argued that there are important reasons to distinguish between *written language* and *printed language*. Such a distinction might have implications for studies of transfer, but there seems to be little research on transfer and handwriting or on related issues.

virtually no letters in common and they use opposite directional principles, that is, the Persian alphabet is written from right to left and the English alphabet is written from left to right. Since the two languages only share the alphabetic principle, there is little if any positive transfer aiding the acquisition of English by Persian speakers or the acquisition of Persian by English speakers, though there is probably some advantage arising from having already learned to encode and decode written language (cf. Section 8.1).[9]

Spelling problems

A similarity in writing systems doubtlessly can reduce the amount of time needed to learn to encode and decode written symbols in a second language. Yet, as in other cases of linguistic similarity, there may arise difficulties due to partial but not complete overlap in writing conventions. For example, Oller and Ziahosseiny (1970) cite instances of misspellings that are clearly due to the cognate status of words in English, which was the target language in their study, and words in the native language of students. Thus, speakers of Spanish, Italian, and Portuguese all spelled *comfort* as *confort* (the cognate form in all three languages uses *n* instead of *m*).

Even in words that are not cognates there may be spelling errors due to the influence of spelling conventions in the native language, as in the case of *traied*, the spelling of *tried* used by a Spanish speaker (Oller and Ziahosseiny 1970). Another important influence besides spelling conventions can be pronunciation. For example, English makes a phonemic distinction between /p/ and /b/, but Arabic does not, and accordingly Ibrahim (1978) attributes the following ESL spelling errors of Jordanian students – *blaying, bicture,* and *bombous* – to phonological influence from Arabic.[10]

As with other systemic errors, not all spelling problems can be attributed to native language influence. Although the categorizations differ, the results of a number of investigations make clear that sources such as overgeneralization also account for many errors (Kamratowski and Schneider 1969; Oller and Ziahosseiny 1970; Ibrahim 1978; Bebout 1985). In the case of languages such as English, which has an orthog-

---

9 In a description of the reading skills of Persian-English bilinguals, Cowan and Sarmad (1976) suggest that some of the problems evident in the bilinguals' skills are attributable to the very different alphabets used in the two languages.

10 While such evidence suggests that native language pronunciation can have an effect on spelling, "spelling pronunciations" that reflect imperfections in the target language orthography can lead to pronunciation errors. Altenberg and Vago (1983) give some interesting examples of spelling pronunciations interacting with native language phonology.

raphy notoriously difficult for native as well as non-native speakers, the variety of errors reflects in large measure the idiosyncrasies of the system; thus, the errors made by ESL students are often identical to those made by native speakers, as *tought* (instead of *taught*) and *sleaping* (instead of *sleeping*) (Ibrahim 1978).

The difficulties of the English spelling system provide further evidence that whatever proves difficult for native speakers can also prove difficult for non-native speakers. This fact is crucial for understanding the asymmetry of linguistic systems, which any thorough contrastive analysis must take into account (cf. Section 7.3). The differences between the Spanish and English spelling systems, for example, are not likely to lead to symmetrical patterns of difficulty. The letter-phoneme correspondences in Spanish are far more straightforward than the correspondences in English are, and it seems improbable that spelling in Spanish will prove as difficult for English speakers as spelling in English will for Spanish speakers. In the case of Chinese, a language with a writing system far more intricate than the English system, the consequences for acquisition are even more evident: most books in English consist of various combinations of only twenty-six letters, whereas books in Chinese consist of combinations of hundreds and often thousands of different characters (cf. Ong 1982). Chinese speakers find the system difficult and English speakers are likely to find it even more so.

7.5 Summary and conclusion

Native language influence is an important factor in the acquisition of target language phonetics and phonology. The importance of transfer is evident in studies of specific pronunciation contrasts and also in research comparing the overall pronunciation accuracy of speakers of different native languages. As with syntax and other language subsystems, transfer is not the only factor affecting the ease or difficulty of reproducing target language sounds. Typological and apparently universal factors sometimes operate independently of transfer and sometimes operate together with it. Thus, the study of developmental patterns is as important in investigations of second language pronunciation as it is in investigations of other subsystems. Similarities and differences in writing systems can result in positive or negative transfer. Learners have tremendous advantages in learning a language with a writing system similar to that of their native language. As with pronunciation, transfer is not the only factor that must be considered in the study of encoding and decoding written symbols in a second language.

This and the previous three chapters have considered the question of transfer in specific subsystems. While the evidence in all four chapters argues for the importance of cross-linguistic influences, the problem of transfer cannot be understood only through reference to *system-internal* factors. With regard to the probability (or improbability) of transfer in particular contexts, *who* the learners are and what their environment is can be just as important as the languages they speak. Chapter 8 therefore considers factors usually not discussed in contrastive analyses.

Further reading

A collection edited by Ioup and Weinberger (1987) not only has many important articles on second language pronunciation but also provides a glossary. Schane (1973) provides a short, readable introduction to modern phonology.

8 Nonstructural factors in transfer

In the preceding chapters on semantics, syntax, and pronunciation, the focus of discussion was on cross-linguistic differences in language *structure* and the consequences that those differences have for acquisition. Any study of transfer must naturally provide a detailed consideration of cross-linguistic differences in structure. However, as the discussion of discourse in Chapter 4 noted, a purely structural analysis of discourse will not suffice to account for cross-linguistic influences in conversation and writing. Nonstructural factors relevant to transfer involve not only discourse but also pronunciation, vocabulary, and grammar.

A comprehensive review of nonstructural factors in second language acquisition is beyond the scope of this book, but mention of a couple should make it clear that structural factors are not the only influence on acquisition. *Motivation* surely plays a major role. Even though, for example, the smaller number of structural differences between Spanish and English in comparison with Chinese and English can give Spanish speakers a considerable head start in their acquisition of English, a highly motivated Chinese speaker will probably learn more English – and learn it faster – than will a poorly motivated Spanish speaker. *Class size* may also have an important effect. Sixty Spanish-speaking students in an English class will not likely receive as much individual attention as will four Chinese speakers who comprise another English class, and so in aspects of second language acquisition where individual attention is extremely important (e.g., writing), a Chinese speaker may acquire a greater mastery of English. Factors such as motivation and class size have an obvious potential to influence acquisition no matter what native or target languages are involved. Nonstructural factors may thus operate *independently* of transfer. However, there are other factors which are not structural yet which *interact* with transfer. Those factors are the subject of this chapter.

Chapter 8 reviews not only the widest range of nonstructural factors affecting transfer – those related to individual variation – but also single factors that affect transfer: the age of the learner, and human awareness of language, especially as it exists in social contexts. Individual variation, age, and language awareness interact with each other in various ways, and some of these interactions will be discussed.

8.1   Individual variation

Variation is one of the most important characteristics of language. Not only the existence of different languages, but also the differences seen within languages in dialects and speech styles provide evidence of the staggering range of possible variation. Moreover, the potential diversity extends to individual behavior. No two people speak exactly the same: differences in voice quality, intonation, and vocabulary choice are among the most common distinguishers of individual speech, and there are other distinguishers as well. The existence of such differences poses an important problem for the study of transfer. Contrastive analysis, the structural basis for predictions of transfer, normally relies on comparisons of *collective*, not *individual*, linguistic behavior (cf. Section 3.2). While one could compare, for instance, the English of one American with the Sindhi of one Pakistani, a contrastive analysis of English and Sindhi would more likely consist of idealized descriptions of both languages. Such descriptions might or might not allow for regional and social variation in English and Sindhi, but in either case they still would only be approximations of the speech of any single American and any single Pakistani.[1]

As descriptions of collective behavior, contrastive analyses may frequently give rise to inaccurate predictions of individual performances (Sections 2.2, 3.3). Even while some kind of transfer is likely in the second language performance of most learners, the manifestations of transfer can vary from one learner to the next. In this section, the following kinds of individual variation will be considered: (1) personality; (2) aptitude for phonetic mimicry; (3) linguistic proficiency; and (4) literacy.

Personality

While individuals can vary in any number of ways, personality differences are among the most obvious distinguishers, and some of those differences probably increase or decrease the likelihood of transfer. There is, however, a major problem that complicates the study of personality and transfer: the uncertain status of theories of personality (Littlewood 1983). Personality traits such as aggressiveness and friendliness figure

---

1 The problem of individual variation is even more complex since, among other reasons, individual speech changes over time.

importantly in many theories of personality, but there is no certainty about how consistent any individual's personality traits will be in a wide array of contexts. Despite this and other problems, there are enough hints in the literature on second language acquisition which point to traits that may make transfer more likely or less likely.

In her research on avoidance of relative clauses by Chinese and Japanese students, Schachter (1974) noted the probability that many learners experience *anxiety* about using unfamiliar structures (cf. Section 6.2). In another study of avoidance, Kleinmann (1977) sought empirical verification of the relation between anxiety and cross-linguistic differences. Some results of Kleinmann's study suggest that students especially susceptible to certain forms of anxiety are more likely to avoid structures that a contrastive analysis would predict to be difficult.

Personality factors may also account for the varying degrees of success that individuals have in approximating pronunciation patterns in the target language. Guiora (1972:145) hypothesized that "individual differences in the ability to approximate native-like pronunciation should reflect individual differences in the flexibility of psychic processes, or more specifically, in the empathetic capacity." Considering pronunciation to be the most concrete manifestation of a "language ego," Guiora and colleagues have sought to show that the more permeable an individual's "ego boundary" is (i.e., the more empathetic an individual's disposition is), the more attainable a nativelike pronunciation of foreign language sounds will be. There is some experimental evidence supporting the notion of ego permeability and empathy. Individuals given moderate amounts of alcohol or Valium have been able to improve their pronunciation of foreign language sounds (Guiora et al. 1972; Guiora et al. 1980). By Guiora's interpretation, such altered states of consciousness are analogous to the empathetic state of mind believed to facilitate the acquisition of nativelike pronunciation (cf. Taylor et al. 1969). If his interpretation is correct, individuals more susceptible to feeling emotionally "inside" the target language speech community are more likely to overcome their foreign accent. Accordingly, there is a probable inverse relation between individual empathy and transfer: the less an individual learner can feel emotionally "inside" the target language speech community, the more pervasive the influence of native language pronunciation will be.[2]

Anxiety and empathy are two personality characteristics that appear to interact with transfer, and there are probably others as well. Identifying all such characteristics, however, presupposes a thorough under-

---

2 As discussed earlier, not every characteristic of a foreign accent can be attributed to native language influence (Section 7.3). Nevertheless, much evidence does point to the importance of phonetic and phonological transfer (Sections 7.1, 7.2).

standing of relations between societies and individuals. The personality that any learner seems to have may be as much a reflection of socio-linguistic norms in the native-language speech community as it is of an individual self. For example, in a study of introversion and extroversion in Japanese students, Busch (1982) suggested that the norms for class-room behavior in Japanese schools often encourage the development of introverted behavior. If this and similar observations accurately char-acterize the influence of native-language speech communities on second language behavior, much of an individual's apparent personality may say more about a native language community than about the individual. As Scollon and Scollon (1981) and others have suggested, community norms may lead to unfortunate stereotypes of individual speakers, but in many acquisition contexts two mitigating influences may come into play. First, the norms of a native-language speech community may be rather flexible and may thus overlap with norms of the target language community. Second, individuals do not always wish to adhere to the norms of their native-language speech community and may there-fore find it relatively easy to adapt to a new set of norms (cf. Paulston 1978).

Aptitude for phonetic mimicry

In some societies, individuals are believed to have or not have "an ear" for foreign languages, and research on adult capacities has led to detailed characterizations of the concept of foreign language apti-tude. Several abilities seem to underlie that aptitude. Among the most important is a "phonetic coding ability," which Carroll (1981:105) defines as "an ability to identify distinct sounds, to form associations between these sounds, and symbols representing them, and to retain these associations." A related ability, Carroll notes, is an aptitude for phonetic mimicry. Individuals vary considerably in their capacity to mimic sounds in a foreign language (Pike 1959), and research by Purcell and Suter (1980) indicates that this capacity is a significant predictor of pronunciation accuracy.

Part of the aptitude for mimicry is probably related to the capacity for empathy discussed earlier. However, there is no logically compelling reason to suppose that an aptitude for mimicry is entirely attributable to empathy. Just as the capacity for rote memorization (which Carroll considers to be another component of foreign language aptitude) prob-ably has little to do with individual personality, so the capacity for mimicry may not simply reflect a personality trait (such as empathy). No matter what their personality characteristics are, individuals with little aptitude for mimicry are likely to show the effects of phonetic and phonological influence from their native languages.

Proficiency

The notion of second language proficiency is somewhat controversial; many problems attend its definition and measurement, and there is no consensus among language testers about what test or combination of tests would constitute a thoroughly adequate index of proficiency. It is nevertheless undeniable that learners' abilities differ vastly, with much (though not all) of the individual variation reflecting different degrees of second language skill. Some evidence suggests that there is a relation between proficiency and transfer.

Taylor (1975) has argued that less proficient learners will rely more on transfer. Much of his evidence comes from the results of a translation test given to Spanish-speaking students at an American university. Students placed in less advanced classes were especially likely to produce translations with errors reflecting Spanish-language influence: for example, *Can the director to speak with me now?*, which reflects the probable influence of a verb phrase rule in Spanish. Students placed in more advanced classes were more likely to produce translations with errors reflecting overgeneralizations, such as *Does Gilbert don't speak French?*, which seems to reflect confusion about English question and negation patterns more than it does any influence from Spanish (cf. Sections 2.2, 6.3). Taylor argues that the apparent differences in reliance on transfer mainly reflect the differences in the knowledge base that less advanced and more advanced learners have to work with. More advanced learners know much more about the target language and can more often make analogies on the basis of that information. Since less advanced learners have less such information, they will, by Taylor's analysis, tend to draw more on their native language (or some other source language) for analogies that appear relevant. As Taylor observes, this interpretation of the effects of previous knowledge is consistent with claims made about the general nature of human learning (Ausubel 1968).

Taylor's analysis has a great deal of intuitive appeal, and other evidence supports his position. For example, the studies of word order transfer discussed earlier indicate that the transfer of basic word order is most probable among learners with little proficiency in the target language (Section 6.1). In phonology, moreover, studies by Major (1986) and others suggest that transfer is especially prevalent in the earlier stages of proficiency. Nevertheless, there are reasons to be cautious about claiming a strong relation between transfer and proficiency level. Most important, as a study in error analysis, Taylor's research speaks only to negative transfer. When one considers the facilitating effects of some cross-linguistic similarities, such as cognate vocabulary, the likelihood seems great that positive transfer will occur at the advanced stages just as much as at the beginning stages of second language acquisition. Another problem with taking Taylor's claim as unequivocally true is that certain kinds of negative transfer *cannot* occur until learners have reached a certain level of proficiency (cf. Kellerman 1984). For example, the existence of transfer errors made with resumptive pronouns in relative clauses presupposes that learners can form relative clauses, and that capacity often takes a long time to develop (cf. Section 6.2). Since there is evidence that the use of resumptive pronouns is sometimes affected by cross-linguistic influence (as in the case of Liberian English), it is probable that transfer can occur whenever a structure seems new, and therefore problematic, to a learner. While Taylor's study is an important indicator that proficiency may interact with transfer, the relation between target language ability and native language influence is likely to be a complex one.[3]

Literacy

Literacy can have a major impact on second language acquisition, and a modest amount of evidence suggests that literacy interacts with transfer. There is no logically necessary connection between literacy in one language and successful acquisition of another language; one can read and write in one language without being able to read and write in another (cf. Section 7.4). Nevertheless, several studies reviewed by Cummins (1979) indicate that bilinguals highly literate in one language tend to find easier the acquisition of many second language skills, including literacy skills.[4] A word of caution is necessary here, however. The comparative success of literate bilinguals does not as clearly indicate the importance of language transfer in the sense of native language influence as it indicates the importance of transfer of training. That is, literate

3 Another problem with Taylor's analysis is that the evidence he uses presupposes a classification of errors into mutually exclusive categories of transfer and overgeneralization (along with a few other categories). Even if that classification correctly suggests the relative importance of transfer and overgeneralization – and that assumes that all errors were properly classified – such a taxonomy discounts the possibility of interactions between transfer and overgeneralization (cf. Section 3.3).

4 Defining the term *literacy* is problematic. While virtually everyone would agree that literacy requires certain abilities to read and write, there is some controversy over just what those abilities are. Part of the problem of studying literacy is that different cultures have different uses for reading and writing (cf. Scribner and Cole 1981; Heath 1983). Moreover, there is some controversy over what the differences are – if any – between spoken and written language (cf. Biber 1986; Shuman 1986). Any thorough understanding of discourse transfer will have to account for these and other problems. Despite such problems, however, some facts about literacy relevant to transfer are not controversial. One is that literate adults tend to have a wider range of literacy skills (or, a "higher degree of literacy") than children do. Another fact is that people differ in their abilities to read and write certain types of texts. In light of such facts, it is meaningful to discuss literacy in developmental terms (i.e., degrees of literacy) in relation to language transfer.

bilinguals may have an advantage not just because of their linguistic skills but also because of problem-solving skills that they may have acquired in the course of their education. Yet there does appear to be a specifically linguistic factor in bilingual literacy, as Genesee (1979) indicates in a discussion of the reading skills of Canadian children who were literate in three languages: French, English, and Hebrew. Genesee notes that tests of literacy in the three languages yielded higher correlations between French and English reading skills than between English and Hebrew reading skills. As discussed earlier, differences in writing systems can make the acquisition of a second language more difficult (Section 7.4). Since Hebrew uses a writing system very different from those of French and English, it is not surprising that there would be less of a relation between reading in Hebrew and reading in English. By virtue of the great similarity in the writing systems of French and English, reading in the one language would be rather comparable to reading in the other.

A high degree of literacy in one's native language can increase the likelihood of positive transfer in recognizing cognate vocabulary (cf. Section 5.2). A relation between transfer and native language vocabulary development is evident in a study by Limper (1932) of the French vocabulary known by American high school and college students – having a better knowledge of English vocabulary, the college students were much more successful in identifying cognate forms. Limper's research thus supports the intuition that individuals unable to read a wide range of texts in their native language will not be in a good position to take advantage of cognate forms in a second language (cf. Stendahl 1972). If an English speaker does not understand *ambitious*, for example, the similarity to it of French *ambitieux* will be of little help in understanding the French word.

Native language literacy also seems to be a factor in success in learning to write in a second language. One particular area in which native language literacy might make an immense difference is the ability to compose for the needs of a specific audience. Scribner and Cole (1981) found that literate individuals who generally had experience in writing letters were able to compose more usable descriptions of the rules for playing a board game than were nonliterate individuals. While Scribner and Cole's research does not address directly the problem of literacy in a second language, it does suggest that individuals literate in their native language will have a head start on some second-language writing tasks.

There is also reason to believe that individuals with more developed native-language literacy skills will perform better in second language writing. Linnarud (1978) asked native speakers of English to judge ESL writing by students in Sweden, and she asked native speakers of Swedish to judge writing by the same students in their native language. She found a considerable consistency in both sets of native speaker judgments: the most favorably judged essays in English and Swedish were generally written by the same students, and the least favorably judged essays in English were written by the students whose Swedish essays were also judged least favorably.[5] Using a rather different approach, Masny and d'Anglejan (1985) found that the native-language reading skills of French-speaking students in Canada correlated significantly with their skills in ESL, including writing.

Other factors

Aside from characteristics such as literacy, other aspects of learners' backgrounds may prove to be important factors in how much transfer affects any individual's acquisition of a second language. Social and pedagogical factors are especially likely to interact with transfer. There is considerable evidence that the social background of learners can and does affect their reliance on transfer, and some of that evidence will be discussed later in this chapter (Section 8.3). Along with social factors, a number of pedagogical factors may have an important effect. For example, teachers who know the native language of their students may provide information about native–target-language contrasts that other teachers cannot provide. Similarly, textbooks and other materials that present analogies between the native and target languages may promote or inhibit some kinds of transfer. Pedagogical practices such as the use of translation tests may also encourage transfer, as Dulay, Burt, and Krashen (1982) argue.

Factors such as schooling, literacy, personality, and so forth surely account for much of the individual variation affecting transfer. Yet even if all those factors were better understood, there would still be the possibility that seemingly idiosyncratic characteristics of learners could affect their reliance on transfer. The differences among individual learners described by Fillmore (1979) and others make clear how wide the range of possible acquisition behaviors is.

8.2   Transfer and age of acquisition

The population of most speech communities shows considerable variation in the age of community members, and to that extent chronological

5 Although Linnarud's sample size is quite small (eight students), her hypothesis about native and second language skills receives additional support from the fact that she edited the English papers so that native speaker judgments would be independent of the grammatical accuracy of the writers.

age is one more manifestation of individual variation. However, the inevitability of the aging process makes the relation between language and age special. It is not inevitable that an adult will have an empathetic personality, a high aptitude for mimicry, or any skill in reading or writing. It *is* inevitable, however, that an adult will have experienced childhood and the sequence of developmental changes that accompany growing up. If the common belief is true that "younger is better" for the acquisition of a second language, there may be a definite relation between transfer and aging. Younger learners may be more receptive to transfer, or they might be less receptive. Not all second language researchers subscribe to the "younger is better" position, but even if that position is incorrect, the apparent relation between aging and foreign accents warrants consideration. Moreover, there is other evidence for a relation between child-adult differences and transfer that also merits consideration.

Aging and foreign accents

Although non-native pronunciation shows influences besides those of the native language, the importance of phonetic and phonological transfer has considerable empirical support (Sections 7.1, 7.2). The relation between such transfer and the age of learners, however, is not very clear. In the large body of literature on age and second language acquisition, a number of studies indicate that *younger* children are more likely to achieve nativelike pronunciation (e.g., Asher and Garcia 1969; Seliger, Krashen, and Ladefoged 1975; Oyama 1976). Such studies thus support the notion that the older the learner, the more important the influences of native language pronunciation will be. Other studies have shown very different results, however. Some indicate that *older* learners are likely to have just as good or better pronunciation than younger (e.g., Olson and Samuels 1973; Snow and Hoefnagel-Höhle 1977; Neufeld 1978); moreover, age has not always proved to be a significant factor when compared with related factors, such as the length of residence in an area in which the target language is spoken (Purcell and Suter 1980).

To a large extent the conflicting views on the relation between age and pronunciation reflect disagreements about the overall relation between age and second language learning. Several studies of the acquisition of morphology and syntax support the "younger is better" position (e.g., Krashen, Long, and Scarcella 1979), yet the evidence has not convinced all scholars (e.g., McLaughlin 1981; Hatch 1983). Some research suggests that neither the "younger is better" nor the "older is better" position is entirely correct. In a study of the acquisition of Thai by native speakers of English, Ioup and Tansomboon (1987) found that younger learners were better able to control pitch contrasts in Thai, which is a tone language (Section 7.2). On the other hand, adults showed a greater ability to master some segmental contrasts. It is entirely possible that such differences in ability also exist in the acquisition of morphology and syntax. Moreover, it is possible that differing abilities that have been observed in adults and children are related to differences in their literacy skills, their use of the target language, their manner of learning the target language, their social background, their social attitudes, and many other factors as well.

While the pronunciation-age issue is part of a larger debate, some aspects of that issue involve questions specific to phonetics and phonology. One explanation for the nontargetlike sounds so commonly found in adult second language speech is an alteration in the motor control program governing speech organs (Scovel 1969). With the passing of years, the argument goes, the program will change and no longer allow the vocal tract to form sounds that learners can nevertheless perceive. Another (and possibly related) explanation is that speakers who have learned one language much earlier than another will tend to make interlingual identifications resulting in a target language sound being categorized in terms of phonetic norms of the native language (cf. Section 7.2). Flege (1981) suggests that the simultaneous acquisition of two languages in childhood may be the only situation in which such identifications can be avoided; by establishing early two distinct sets of phonetic norms, young bilingual children may have an advantage over older children and adults learning a second language (cf. Flege 1987). Whatever the merits of these and other explanations, it does seem that pronunciation is more likely than other aspects of linguistic performance to show age-related differences. Studies of dialect contact in the English-speaking world also suggest that there is something unique about pronunciation. Trudgill (1986) discusses research indicating that American adults in Britain and British adults in the United States rarely lose their accents completely. As in the case of language contact, the reasons for this preservation of native-dialect features appear to be numerous: perceptual, articulatory, and affective factors are all probably among those involved.

Other evidence

In the debate on age and second language acquisition, there has been relatively little attention given to the source of various learner errors, although in the case of pronunciation, native language influence is probably the most important source. Aside from research on pronunciation, there is evidence that age and native language also interact in the lexical and syntactic development of second language learners.

Analyzing data from several studies of first and second language acquisition, Zobl (1983) argues that word order transfer varies with the chronological age in which a second language is acquired. Up to about age three, the second-language word orders used by children are quite variable, with the variation being governed, according to Zobl, by discourse considerations analogous to those that govern languages with flexible word order (cf. Section 6.1). For example, a three-year-old child whose native language was French produced the following sentence: *Elephant plane is this* ("This is the plane elephants fly on"). The sentence reflects, in Zobl's analysis, an interaction between the relatively flexible word order of French and the tendency of young children to use word orders determined by discourse factors. From about age four up to about age ten, a period of "syntactic conservatism" develops. In that period, children are more inclined to stick with one word order, which may or may not be that of the target language (cf. Harley 1984). This decrease in word order variability is consistent with first-language acquisition studies showing a preference for consistency in syntactic patterns in middle childhood. In contrast to children, French-speaking adults and adolescents do not show as much "conservatism" in their use of word order, although they seem to avoid employing most French word-order patterns in their English sentences (Trévise 1986).

In very young bilingual children an extreme sort of language mixing is quite common. For example, in the speech of Danny, a two-year-old whose mother spoke English and whose father spoke German, English and German words and phrases were often mixed:

Mehr books ("More books")
Guck, alle Auto on the ship ("Look, all auto on the ship")
With the cars rauf ("With the cars on top")
(Redlinger and Park 1980:343)

Studies by Redlinger and Park (1980), Vihman (1985), and others indicate the usual period in which such mixing occurs ranges from about a year and a half up till about three. At the age of three, mixing begins to taper off. Although mixing is common in child bilingualism, the extent of mixing varies considerably. Children in some settings do very little mixing, yet in other settings mixing may continue into adulthood (cf. Taeschner 1983; Fantini 1985; Le Page and Tabouret-Keller 1985).

Although such language mixing and code-switching are often equated in discussions of bilingualism, code-switching is only one possible type of mixing. Switching is superficially similar to the language mixing of young bilinguals, since words, phrases, and sentences of two (or more) languages may appear in juxtaposition, as seen in the following English-Spanish switch:

Why make Carol SENTARSE ATRAS PA'QUE ("sit in the back so")
everybody has to move PA'QUE SE SALGA ("for her to get out")? (Poplack 1980:589)

However, the conditions under which adult code-switching and infant language mixing take place are often quite different. For example, young children who mix languages may not always be aware of the existence of two separate languages, but individuals who code-switch do have such an awareness. Other characteristics of mixing and code-switching will be discussed in the next section.

8.3   Transfer, linguistic awareness, and social context

The difference between "knowing" and "knowing about" a language has long been recognized, and in the general increase of study of second language acquisition that difference has received considerable attention. Opinions vary greatly about the role of linguistic awareness (i.e., "knowing about"), especially as to how helpful such awareness is (cf. Krashen 1981; McLaughlin, Rossman, and McLeod 1983). Whatever the exact nature of the role that linguistic awareness plays, such awareness is a nonstructural factor that interacts with cross-linguistic influences.[6]

Linguistic awareness can be either conscious or unconscious. When awareness is conscious, people frequently give a name to the object of their awareness. The designation that people give may be imprecise from the standpoint of the descriptive linguist (cf. Odlin 1986). For example, many speakers of English mistakenly believe that the pronunciation represented with an apostrophe in such words as *nothin'* is a case of "dropping a *g*." Yet, while the expression "dropping a *g*" is misleading (the pronunciation of *nothin'* does not involve any "dropping"), the expression does show that listeners with no background in phonetics have some conscious awareness of the difference between two nasal consonants (i.e., /n/ and /ŋ/). Even if individuals do not know the phrase "dropping a *g*" or show any other conscious awareness of that difference, they may be unconsciously aware that the pronunciation of *nothin'* is not an example of the prestigious "Network Standard" spoken by newscasters.

However aware people are of various formal units, their awareness is frequently as much social as it is linguistic. The attention that English speakers pay to "dropping a *g*" reflects the fact that in English some uses of nasal consonants have more social prestige. In second language acquisition the linguistic awareness that learners show frequently reflects social considerations. Thus in much of the following discussion of the

---

6 The term *metalinguistic awareness* is frequently used to describe individuals' awareness of language. In the interest of terminological simplicity, it is not used in this chapter.

relation between linguistic awareness and transfer, the importance of social context will loom large.

Multilingualism and learners' perceptions,

Through most of this book, discussions of transfer have focused on *bilingual* situations in which influence from the native language has important consequences for the acquisition of a second language (Section 3.1). This emphasis on bilingual situations reflects the preponderance of situations described in research and perhaps also the preponderance of actual cases of language contact. However, individuals learning a new language may already know two, three, or even more languages.[7] Therefore no study of transfer can neglect the importance of trilingual and other multilingual situations. One of the most interesting kinds of evidence obtainable in multilingual settings is that regarding language distance. Studies of trilingualism indicate that the more similar linguistic structures in two languages are, the greater the likelihood of transfer. However, studies of language awareness indicate that the importance of language distance depends very much on the *perceptions* of that distance by learners.

A study by Vildomec (1963) of writing errors shows the difficulties that researchers encounter in attempting to detect negative transfer in multilingual situations. The range of possible explanations for errors is certainly greater in multilingual than in bilingual situations. Nevertheless, credible evidence of transfer is found in some multilingual situations. Todd (1983) briefly describes an area of West Africa where speakers' use of English is often influenced by knowledge of French as a second language. Todd notes that the sentence *At the bottom he is a naughty somebody* probably reflects influences not from any African language but instead from French, as in the use of the phrase *at the bottom*, for which there is a clear parallel in French, *au fond*. Some less direct evidence of transfer comes from the results of a grammaticality judgment test of French sentences given to students in the same part of Africa: The judgments students gave indicate that English can have a considerable influence on their acquisition of French (Ahukana, Lund, and Gentile 1981). While those results also indicate that knowledge of Igbo, the native language of the students, influenced some judgments, knowl-

---

7 Vildomec (1963) notes some claims of extraordinary multilingual ability. For example, biographers of a Cardinal Giuseppe Mezzolini attributed to him a knowledge of as many as seventy-eight languages and fluency in thirty of them! While such claims are dubious, as Vildomec suggests, the importance of positive transfer may increase in rough proportion to the number of languages an individual learns. There are obvious problems, however, in seeking empirical verification of such a prediction.

edge of English, which was a second language for the students, influenced many more judgments. Thus, even though all subjects in the study knew both Igbo and English, the greater typological similarity between French and English seems to have been an especially strong influence on learner judgments (cf. Singleton 1987). Further evidence of the importance of typological similarity appears in a study of reading (Singleton and Little 1984) that indicates that knowledge of a second language can provide considerable help in the reading of a closely related third language (Section 3.3).

Such research justifies the efforts of contrastive analysts to determine language distance. However, some evidence suggests that an *objective* estimation of language distance can sometimes be misleading about the likelihood of transfer: in some cases, the *subjective* estimation of distance by learners can override an objective measure. In any learner's attempt to acquire a new language, language distance is ultimately in the eye of the beholder. Research indicates that when everything else is equal, transfer will most likely result from a learner's judgment (made consciously or unconsciously) that particular structures in a previously learned language are quite like – if not the same as – structures in the target language.

Studies by Kellerman (1977, 1978) of Dutch and English vocabulary provide interesting evidence for the importance of judgments about language distance. In light of the evidence on lexical transfer discussed earlier, it is not surprising that Dutch students learning English (and English students learning Dutch) will find the acquisition of vocabulary somewhat easier since the two languages have many cognates, such as *hoe* and *how*, *dat* and *that*, and *breken* and *break* (cf. Section 5.2). Yet, while Dutch students learning English often use – and sometimes misuse – such cognate forms, they show some wariness about using certain forms (cf. Lightbown and Libben 1984). Idioms also seem to incur a great deal of suspicion: "I have often noted the amazement on our students' faces when they do discover the existence of Dutchlike idioms in English" (Kellerman 1977:102). Kellerman found empirical support for his observations in the form of acceptability tests. Dutch students frequently judged as unacceptable idioms that are actually parallel in the two languages, such as *to have the victory in the bag, to lay it on thick*, and *dyed-in-the-wool* (Kellerman 1977). In a study of various uses of the verb *break*, Kellerman (1978) found a systematic preference for "transparent" uses. Senses of *breken* that are closer to the "core meaning" of the verb were seen as more transferable into English than other forms were (with the core meaning being determined through an experimental procedure). For example, high school and university students frequently accepted *She broke his heart* as a possible translation from Dutch into English, but less often accepted *Some workers have broken the strike*, even though there is nothing anomalous about either sentence or their translation equivalents. The importance of transparency is evident in other research. Word association studies by Osgood, May, and Miron (1975) suggest that form-meaning relations commonly found in the lexicons of many languages are highly transparent (cf. Section 5.2). Moreover, certain (possibly universal) relations between syntax and semantics suggest that transparency is relevant to other domains of linguistic structure besides the lexicon (e.g., Jordens 1977; Gass and Ard 1984).

Semantic transfer and social context

As the discussion in the preceding section indicates, Kellerman believes that there are fairly strong constraints on what is transferable. He has claimed, for example, that "idioms are one class of language items that are generally *not* transferred" (Kellerman 1977:101–02, emphasis in the original). Yet, while Kellerman has acknowledged that his claims are based primarily on research on the intuitions of students in Dutch high schools and universities, other researchers (e.g., Krashen and Terrell 1983) have interpreted his findings much more broadly. Some of these interpretations are *universalist* (cf. Section 3.4). That is, some researchers believe that Kellerman's work has identified constraints on semantic transfer in *any* second language context. In one sense, such interpretations are not surprising given claims made by Kellerman (1978, 1983) about semantic transparency. According to his analysis, transparent idioms are more "transferable," and there is little question that the notion of transparency presupposes universal form-meaning relations (cf. Cooper and Ross 1975; Friedrich 1979; Kellerman 1983; Slobin 1985).

Although Kellerman's work has important implications for second language research, it cannot provide very much support for universalist analyses. While some expressions that he cites, such as *to break someone's heart* and *to talk behind someone's back*, are undeniably good examples of transparent expressions, often what should or should not be considered transparent is unclear. Ease of comprehension would seem an essential criterion in any definition of transparency, but if that is so, there are characteristics of semantic transfer that Kellerman's analysis may not explain well. The following sentences from Hiberno-English cited by Henry (1977) suggest one of the problems: *Did-ya hear of anna wan bein' on road?* and *He was fallin' back wit' a while.* Both were used by English speakers in a bilingual region of Ireland and both have Irish translation equivalents, yet in neither case is the idiomatic sense likely to be clear to individuals unfamiliar with Hiberno-English.[8] An

---

8 The standard English versions of these idioms given by Henry are: "Have you heard

expression in Malaysian English based on a Malay idiom illustrates a similar problem: *to shake legs* means "to be idle," just the opposite of the meaning of the common English idiom *to shake a leg* (Platt, Weber, and Ho 1984). Are both idioms transparent? If so, one has to make the dubious argument that an idiom can be transparent but also ambiguous. If the Malay idiom is not transparent, the occurrence of semantic transfer in *to shake legs* is a counterexample to Kellerman's claims.

Although the existence of such idioms may not invalidate Kellerman's analysis, it does suggest a need to look closely at the social contexts in which people speak second languages. Perhaps bilinguals in Ireland and Southeast Asia countenance a greater amount of semantic transfer in comparison with Dutch high school and college students. There is no reason to believe that social constraints on transfer are uniform everywhere. In fact, there is evidence suggesting that the importance of transfer in any situation varies largely according to the social context.

Linguistic focusing

A number of distinctions of types of social contexts are relevant to transfer, such as formal versus informal settings and academic versus nonacademic environments. Another distinction, however, is especially useful: **focused** versus **unfocused** contexts. Le Page and Tabouret-Keller (1985:116) see the notion of focusing as applicable to any social context:

[B]y means of individual adjustments in response to feedback, both "languages" and "groups" may become more highly focused in the sense that the behavior of members of a group may become more alike.

Linguistic focusing presupposes the existence of linguistic awareness, since focusing involves: (1) some awareness of belonging to a group; (2) considerable awareness of linguistic and other norms that distinguish one group from another; and (3) adherence to and enforcement of such norms. Focusing most typically occurs in the development of standard languages. When individuals feel a strong sense of belonging to a group, they are frequently concerned about preserving the linguistic forms believed to characterize the group and such concern often leads to attempts to standardize usage. In many cases standardization involves minimizing

---

of anyone going matchmaking?" and "His health was declining for some time." One might argue that these idioms perhaps came into Hiberno-English from another variety of English. However, in investigating these and other Hiberno-English idioms, I have not found any evidence suggesting that another dialect of English is the source of these sayings (cf. Odlin 1988). One might also argue, of course, that the two Hiberno-English idioms cited would be understandable in some discourse contexts. However, little or no context is necessary to understand such undeniably transparent idioms as *to break someone's heart* and *to talk behind someone's back*.

the influence from other languages. For example, there have been recent campaigns in France to discourage the use of English loanwords such as *cocktail, software,* and *drugstore,* all of which are used in French (cf. Hagège 1987). Governments and educational authorities in France and some other nations advocate "pure" forms (usually words with a long history of use in the language) to minimize borrowing transfer (cf. Section 2.1).

The standard languages promoted by governments and schools are not, however, the only instances of focused varieties. In the Vaupés region of South America, multilingualism in various Indian groups is quite common, and even though schools did not exist in the 1960s and early 1970s, anthropologists noted a concern among Indians to keep each language as distinct as possible (Sorenson 1967; Jackson 1974). Another type of focusing is evident in the efforts of some parents to discourage their bilingual children from mixing languages. As discussed above, two-year-old bilinguals frequently mix languages (Section 8.2); however, there have been cases in which such mixing was minimal (e.g., Ronjat 1913; Pavlovitch 1920). What seems to have mattered in these cases was the avoidance of language mixing by parents (e.g., where Ronjat spoke to his child exclusively in French while his wife spoke exclusively in German). Even when parents do not make such efforts, however, children are likely to reduce the amount of mixing during the course of acquisition – provided there is some focusing in the language of adults and older children (cf. Redlinger and Park 1980; Vihman 1985).

Although the language mixing of young children is similar to the negative transfer seen in the performance of older learners, there are important differences in terms of the amount of available linguistic awareness. Older learners will more often be aware of the existence of two (or more) distinct languages, typically their native language and the target language. With such an awareness, older learners may try to use only what they believe to be structures of the target language (e.g., Fantini 1985). Negative transfer can occur, however, on either a conscious or unconscious plane. When older learners cannot think of any other way to express what they want to say, they may have conscious recourse to forms in their native language (or some other source language), or they may inadvertently resort to native language forms without any awareness that transfer is occurring. The case cited earlier of the Swedish-speaking student who used the Swedish word *bort* ("away") in the sentence *But sometimes I must go bort* could involve either conscious or unconscious transfer (Section 3.3). With very young children, on the other hand, there may be little awareness that two distinct languages are spoken in their environment; if only one linguistic code seems to exist, nothing can transfer (Taeschner 1983). As their awareness of the objective existence of two languages grows, children tend to develop a sense of focusing comparable to the focusing practiced by adults.[9] As linguistic development continues, then, a largely unconscious mixture of languages will give way to acquisition patterns liable to show the conscious and unconscious forms of negative transfer found with older learners.

As suggested earlier, code-switching is distinct from the language mixing of young bilinguals (Section 8.2). It is also different from transfer. Fluent adult bilinguals frequently code-switch, and numerous studies concur on some basic characteristics of such switching (e.g., Huerta 1978; Poplack 1980; Gumperz 1982; Bentahila and Davies 1983). First, such switching is often *intentional* and can serve a variety of purposes. For example, two Mexican-Americans speaking in English can remind each other of their common ethnic background by occasionally switching into Spanish. Second, code-switching is similar to conscious negative transfer, but is more *augmentative* than *compensatory*. That is, fluent bilinguals usually know how to say in either language what they want to convey, and in such cases switching is not a falling-back on the native language. Third, unconscious transfer seems to be rare in the switches of highly proficient bilinguals. There may be some mutual influence of the sound systems, but even the pronunciation patterns tend to conform to the norms of each of the languages being switched. Fourth, the most fluent bilinguals seem to have the greatest repertory of switching skills. For example, Poplack (1980) found a wider variety of syntactic structures in the switching patterns of fluent bilinguals. Finally, even though switching might seem to be completely the opposite of focusing, the language mixture created in switching can result in a focused variety. In the Middle Ages and Renaissance, educated people developed a taste for "macaronic" verse, in which Latin and vernacular languages (e.g., French and Italian) were mixed, and such verse became a recognized genre for many years (Lazzerini 1982). A more complex case of mixing and focusing is seen in Yiddish, which incorporated elements of German, Hebrew, and other languages and which eventually developed into a focused variety acquiring considerable literary prestige (Weinreich 1980).

Focusing seems to discourage most kinds of language mixing, including negative transfer. Unlike positive transfer, which stems from similarities between languages, any manifestation of negative transfer may be stigmatized. Classrooms and other environments promoting the use of focused language will normally encourage learners to develop an awareness of the differences between their native language and the target language. Sometimes specific materials and teaching strategies are de-

---

9 Vihman (1985) contends that the developing awareness of two languages by bilingual toddlers parallels their growing self-awareness.

veloped to promote such awareness; for example, lists of *faux amis* ("false friends" – erroneous French-English cognates) warn Francophone ESL students not to consider French vocabulary too similar to English vocabulary (cf. Section 5.2). Overt instruction may not always prevent negative transfer, and when the instruction is poorly conceived, it may even encourage such transfer. However, there is reason to believe that instruction can often diminish negative transfer. In a detailed analysis of the English used in Ghana, Sey (1973:6) claims that educated speakers are

aware, in varying degrees depending on their standard of education of the dangers of possible interference, and are therefore on guard against this. The assertion . . . that in West Africa there is the belief that one language may be translated into another word for word is a truism which is applicable only to those second language learners who lack sufficiently well informed tuition.

There is support for Sey's contention in a study by Singler (1988) of Liberian English, in which cross-linguistic influences appear to have an important effect on relative clause patterns (cf. Section 6.2). Singler was somewhat skeptical of the importance of educational factors in explaining relativization patterns. Nevertheless, adult speakers of Mande languages tended to use more resumptive pronouns in relative clauses if they had less than ten years of school, whereas adults who had ten or more years made much less use of such pronouns.

In unfocused contexts, the constraints on negative transfer may be weak, as there is generally less concern about heeding target language norms and less linguistic awareness on the part of learners who often have little schooling and minimal literacy skills. Detailed evidence for this possibility appears in a study by Muysken (1984) of Ecuadorean Spanish. Individuals whose Spanish showed the greatest influence from Quechua tended to be peasants or unskilled laborers with little or no schooling; these individuals were at a considerable social distance from middle-class Spanish speakers and had little economic incentive to speak standard Spanish.

Transfer and social prestige

In formal situations, highly focused language is quite common. Sociolinguists have amply documented how varying language activities affect the formality of pronunciation (e.g., Labov 1972). For example, the reading of lists typically induces more self-conscious pronunciation than other types of reading do: the forms used in list reading often indicate the pronunciation that people believe is "good," whether or not they normally use such forms. Such contextual variations in linguistic form are as evident in second language acquisition as in other situations. In a study of the pronunciation of certain English consonants by Japanese speakers, Dickerson (1974) found that the reading of lists led to pronunciations considerably closer to target language norms than did the reading of dialogues. The consonants studied were, significantly, among those that a contrastive analysis of Japanese and English would predict to be difficult.

Most of the discussion of focusing so far has been with respect to sociolinguistic norms that define prestige in the *target* language. There is evidence, however, that norms in the *native* language can also affect transfer. Schmidt (1987) describes Egyptian students' varying pronunciations of the English consonants /ð/ and /θ/ (as in *then* and *thin*). While classical Arabic consonants /ð/ and /θ/ are used by educated Egyptians, these consonants are often pronounced the same as the phonemes /z/ and /s/ in informal contexts. Schmidt found that the variation in Arabic usage substantially influenced the pronunciation of English /ð/ and /θ/. Less educated Egyptians, who do not frequently use classical Arabic /ð/ and /θ/, tended to mispronounce English /ð/ and /θ/ more frequently. Moreover, the variations seen in the amount of transfer were predictable in terms of the formality of the language tasks, which included the reading of lists and passages, as in the Japanese English research of Dickerson.

While the evidence in this section generally suggests that negative transfer will be more frequent in unfocused situations, there are important exceptions to that tendency. If a particular form has great prestige in the native language, speakers may use it more in focused second-language situations, no matter whether the form is acceptable in the target language. Beebe (1980) studied the variations in the pronunciation of American English /r/ produced by speakers of Thai, a language in which certain pronunciations of /r/ have considerable social prestige. Transfer from Thai was more evident when the subjects read lists than when they engaged in conversation: that is, their pronunciations of /r/ tended to have more Thailike variants, which were quite different from the English variants, in a more formal context.

The motivation of the Thai speakers in Beebe's study was probably similar to that of the Arabic speakers in Schmidt's: both groups were probably unaware of cross-linguistic influences on what they considered to be prestigious forms in English. In other situations, however, non-native speakers may be well aware that their speech shows native language influence and they may take pride in that fact. In former colonies of Britain such as Singapore and India, where English has the status of an official or quasi-official language, the English spoken and written often shows the influence of local languages (Braj Kachru 1983; Platt, Weber, and Ho 1984). The social significance of transfer seems to be greater in these contexts than it does in countries where English has not had a long tradition of widespread use. In a survey of a large number of university students, Shaw (1981) reports that in comparison with Thai students, Singaporean and Indian students were much more willing to consider the way they spoke English as a legitimate variety (cf. Lowenberg 1986). Similarly, the differences between Hiberno-English and British English became a source of nationalist pride for some leading literary figures in Ireland (Garvin 1977). What is usually considered negative transfer can thus persist sometimes and achieve a favorable social status.[10]

The importance of demographic factors

The social context of transfer involves factors besides those directly related to linguistic awareness and focusing. The focusing – or lack of it – in any contact situation depends in part on demographic factors. For example, the relative number of native and non-native speakers in a community can greatly influence the type of language that learners will hear. In the case of the Ecuadorean community described by Muysken, one's chances of hearing highly variable, Quechua-influenced Spanish would be very high – even when the Spanish speakers have no command of Quechua. Similarly, Irish-English bilingualism was quite widespread in Ireland during the nineteenth century, when many people began to use English, and at the same time there were few monolingual speakers of English in certain counties. Thus, in some parts of Ireland, people learning English probably heard dialects of English showing the effects of transfer more often than they heard any other dialect (Bliss 1977; de Fréine 1977).

Within some classroom settings, transfer can be just as evident as in Ecuador and Ireland. Selinker, Swain, and Dumas (1975) noted frequent instances of native language influence on the French of native speakers of English who were in a bilingual immersion program in Canada (cf. Section 6.2). Students were encouraged to speak frequently with each other, and thus the French that they heard was often different from what their teacher used.[11] As Selinker, Swain, and Dumas note, the effects of

10 The more favorable status can be ambiguous, however. The results of Shaw's survey indicate that Indians may never come to a complete acceptance of a uniquely Indian variety of English. Similarly, Barry (1983) believes that Hiberno-English has changed in the twentieth century, with many of the changes reflecting the influence of the standard English spoken in Britain.

11 Some skeptics about transfer (e.g., Dulay, Burt, and Krashen 1982) seem to assume that some social contexts, such as bilingual immersion programs, are somehow "abnormal" since learners have little contact with native speakers of the target language. Such assumptions about normal and abnormal contexts do not, however, take into account the fact that in many language-contact situations, monolingual native speakers may either be totally absent or a minority whose own

peer communication resembled the effects of second language acquisition in language contact situations in which few monolingual native speakers of the target language could serve as models for learners.

Further reading

Harley (1986) offers a detailed look at the problem of age differences in second language acquisition. A recent paper by Schmidt (1988) surveys much of the research on linguistic awareness in second language acquisition.

speech is little different from that of bilinguals. In western Ireland, for example, children a century ago probably heard similar varieties of Hiberno-English from monolingual speakers as well as from Irish-English bilinguals (cf. Odlin 1988).

9 *Looking back and looking ahead*

The preceding chapters have discussed the evidence for the probability or improbability of transfer in specific subsystems and specific acquisition contexts. It is now appropriate to consider some of the limitations in transfer research, to review some of the most important tendencies seen in that research, and to discuss some of the areas in which more study of transfer would be useful.

9.1 Some caveats

There has been considerable progress in the study of transfer during the last hundred or so years, especially during the years since World War II. Yet the controversies that have accompanied this progress make it clear that the findings of transfer research must be interpreted cautiously. Viewing transfer as the single most important reality of second language acquisition is clearly risky – though no more so than viewing transfer as a negligible factor in acquisition.

In this book there has been relatively little discussion of the individuals studied or of the methods used in the research. A brief look at the studies cited will show considerable variation in the numbers of subjects, in the backgrounds of the subjects, and in the empirical data, which come from tape-recorded samples of speech, from student writing, from various types of tests, and from other sources. Without question, every study has limitations, and virtually every elicitation technique used in the studies has its partisans and its critics (e.g., Tarone 1979; Kohn 1987). In some of the studies discussed there are problems related to linguistic descriptions, statistics, small sample sizes, reporting procedures, and so forth, and improvements in data gathering would be highly desirable. Yet the likelihood is high that future research will reproduce the results in many (and perhaps most) of the studies cited. Despite the problems evident in some research, the importance of transfer is clear in light of the considerable agreement among conclusions drawn from different types of studies.

As suggested in Chapter 3, a thorough understanding of transfer depends a great deal on progress in other areas of linguistics. Opinions vary as to how much progress there has been in the last thirty or so years, and there is probably even less of a consensus about how much progress is likely in another thirty years. Nevertheless, there is confidence among a good many linguists, including many who study second language acquisition, about the growth of the empirical record. The accumulation of better, more detailed information has led many to feel that they are now asking some of the right questions.

9.2   Some conclusions

Uncertainties in research leave many questions about transfer still unanswered (cf. Section 9.3). However, a number of conclusions seem warranted:

1.   *Transfer occurs in ALL linguistic subsystems.* Much of the skepticism about transfer has been with regard to cross-linguistic influences involving morphology and syntax as opposed to influences involving phonetics, phonology, and lexical semantics. While it does seem to be true that bound morphology is less susceptible to transfer, there are known cases of it (Section 5.2). In syntax, cross-linguistic influence is evident in a number of areas, including word order, relative clauses, articles, and verb phrases (Sections 2.1, 3.2, 6.1, 6.2). Sometimes this influence may interact with influences from other subsystems, including discourse and lexicon. For example, Spanish speakers seem to rely more than Japanese speakers on the form *no*, which is a cognate of a Spanish negator (Section 6.3).

2.   *Transfer occurs both in informal and formal contexts.* The evidence for transfer comes not only from second language investigations in school settings but also from naturalistic studies of individuals who have acquired what they know of a second language without any schooling. Negative transfer may be less likely in focused contexts, those situations which foster a considerable awareness of language (cf. Section 8.3). On the other hand, positive transfer is probably more likely in focused contexts.

3.   *Transfer occurs among children as well as among adults.* Although there have occasionally been claims that adults are more susceptible to transfer than children are, evidence from several studies suggests that transfer is common, though not inevitable, in child second language acquisition (e.g., Keller-Cohen 1979; Wode 1981; Appel 1984; Luján, Minaya, and Sankoff 1984; Hecht and Mulford 1987). It may well be true that children have certain advantages that help them to minimize negative transfer in their pronunciation. Nevertheless, the exact relation between age and transfer is still far from clear (Section 8.2).

4. *Language distance is a factor that affects transfer.* While similarity between languages can create special problems, such as errors involving false cognates, similarity often confers important advantages. The greater similarity in vocabulary between Spanish and English as opposed to that between Arabic and English, for example, makes the acquisition of English vocabulary relatively easy for Spanish-speaking students (Section 5.2). Moreover, language distance is most probably a major determinant of the amount of time students will need in order to become highly proficient in a language (Section 3.3).

5. *Typological factors can affect the likelihood of transfer.* Transfer is likely to be common when the native language influence involves typologically common patterns, such as preverbal negation or resumptive pronouns in relative clauses (Sections 6.2, 6.3). In these cases, transfer effects may be especially likely to persist. The use of some patterns can also occur, however, even when the native language does not employ such patterns.

6. *Transfer can sometimes involve unusual structures.* Native language influences can involve structures that are not typologically common, such as preposition stranding in relative clauses (e.g., *Un chalet qu'on va aller à* – "A cottage that we're gonna go to") as well as other structures (Section 6.2). Transfer of these structures, however, seems less likely in comparison with cases involving typologically common structures such as resumptive pronouns (Section 6.2).

7. *Nonstructural factors can affect the likelihood of transfer.* Some individual differences, as in linguistic proficiency and literacy, can affect how often cross-linguistic influences have an impact (Section 8.1). The linguistic awareness of learners can also increase or decrease the probability of transfer (Section 8.3). And in some settings, for example in contemporary Ecuador, demographic and other social factors can make transfer especially likely (Section 8.3).

While these findings suggest that transfer is a reality in second language acquisition, the question remains as to just how important cross-linguistic influences are. In an assessment that no doubt reflects the views of many second language researchers, Ellis (1985:40) asserts that while the learner's native language is an important determinant of second language acquisition, it

is not the only determinant, however, and may not be the most important. But it is theoretically unsound to attempt a precise specification of its contribution or even try to compare its contribution with that of other factors.

Given the many uncertainties of second language research, Ellis's caution is doubtlessly warranted. However, certain language contact studies suggest that it is not premature to assess the *potential* that transfer has for affecting acquisition. Among the relevant cases discussed in this book are Japanese Pidgin English, Hiberno-English, and the Spanish spoken in Peru and Ecuador. The evidence from these cases suggests that transfer has very important effects on acquisition. Moreover, the social conditions in these examples seem especially favorable for transfer to have its maximum possible impact (Sections 2.1, 8.3). Yet even in classrooms or other social situations not especially conducive to cross-linguistic influence, transfer can have distinct effects on the acquisition patterns of distinct groups of learners (e.g., Ringbom 1976, 1987).

These social considerations do not, however, tell all of what is interesting about transfer. There are also psychological issues of considerable importance. In one respect, transfer is not a phenomenon extremely different from what occurs in child language acquisition, since cross-linguistic influence involves the use of old knowledge in new situations, and no one disputes that children must also use old knowledge in new situations. The language of four-year-old children normally differs from that of two-year-olds, but four-year-olds use a great deal of the phonological and lexical and other kinds of knowledge that they had at the age of two. If one defined transfer as simply the use of old knowledge in new situations, it would be tempting to argue that transfer is just as characteristic of first as of second language acquisition. Yet such a wide definition of transfer is unsatisfactory, even though similar psychological mechanisms may well be involved in the ability of second language learners to use knowledge of their native language and in the ability of children to use old forms and functions in new contexts with socially appropriate adjustments. There are fundamental differences in the *knowledge base* available to first and second language learners. The knowledge base in monolingual contexts (including child language acquisition) is much smaller than the knowledge base available in bilingual contexts simply because bilinguals can draw on not one but *two* languages.

Transfer is relevant to differences between first and second language acquisition in still other ways (cf. Schachter, in press). For example, transfer can give adults (and sometimes older children) tremendous advantages in achieving a useful knowledge of another language even though second language acquisition does not often result in the kind of proficiency that native-speaker children may acquire. For example, a well-prepared and highly motivated student of English literature can readily take advantage of the considerable similarities in vocabulary, syntax, writing systems, and so forth between English and other Germanic languages to become a competent reader of German literature in a rather short time. Over the long run, of course, children who grow up speaking German in a German-speaking country will be better prepared to understand the linguistic and cultural nuances of a story by

Kafka or a poem by Rilke. Nevertheless, it does seem highly significant that an adult speaker of English might learn to understand rather simple texts in German (e.g., the fairy tales collected by the Brothers Grimm) in a year or so – much less time than the four or so years needed by German-speaking children to understand the same texts.

9.3   Some areas for further research

There are many areas in which further work on transfer is desirable. Among the most important are the following:

1. *Social context.*   If it is true, as suggested in the previous section, that transfer can be an enormous influence under certain sociolinguistic conditions, those conditions warrant much more study. Thomason and Kaufman (1988) have presented a number of cogent examples of where demography and other social factors seem to affect borrowing and substratum transfer just as much as structural factors do. The range of possible social and linguistic variation is enormous, and a great deal of research will be necessary to achieve a better understanding of the sociolinguistic dimensions of transfer.

2. *Subsystem effects.*   In virtually every linguistic subsystem (discourse, syntax, phonology, etc.), there is evidence not only of transfer but also of developmental and other factors. As Wode (1981) and others have suggested, there may well be general acquisition principles – including principles governing transfer – that will affect all subsystems. Investigations of such principles may help linguists to understand such problematic aspects of transfer as the apparent infrequency of cross-linguistic influence on bound morphology (Section 5.2).

3. *Longitudinal comparisons.*   These comparisons could help clarify relations between transfer and developmental processes (cf. Section 2.2). For example, it would be useful to have longitudinal studies comparing speakers of languages using resumptive pronouns (e.g., Persian) and speakers of languages not using such pronouns (e.g., Swedish). If Zobl (1980) and others are correct in their analyses of the relation between transfer and developmental errors, one might accurately predict that Persian speakers will persist much longer in producing errors like *I know the man that John gave the book to him* (Sections 6.2, 6.3). Moreover, longitudinal studies could establish more definitively that a language such as Chinese will require a longer time for English speakers to master than will a language such as Spanish.

4. *Subsystem interactions.*   The effects of native language discourse on the development of target language lexicon and syntax are among the areas well worth further investigation. For example, Loveday (1982a) has suggested that rules of politeness in Japan induce Japanese speakers

to try to avoid using negative forms in both their native language and in English. Since avoidance of English relative clauses seems to be common among Japanese learners (Section 6.2), avoidance of some types of negators might also affect the development of syntax.

5. *Bidirectionality.* Gass (1986) has compared difficulties encountered by Italian speakers learning English with difficulties encountered by English speakers learning Italian. There is a need for more such work, which might compare, for example, the difficulties encountered by English speakers learning Russian and by Russian speakers learning English. Such comparisons could provide a better idea of the general structural principles that affect transfer.

6. *Borrowing and substratum transfer.* Thomason and Kaufman (1988) describe important social and structural differences between these types of transfer. Nevertheless, both involve cross-linguistic influences and further comparative work might provide insights about the fundamental nature of such influence. For example, a comparison of the effects of Irish on English and the effects of English on Irish in regions where the latter language is still spoken might show interesting parallels (cf. Section 2.1).

7. *Acquisition of non-European languages.* Most of the research discussed in this book concerned the acquisition of European languages, especially English. Hopefully, more studies in the future will focus on target languages with very different typological properties. Many questions will remain unanswered until such research is carried out. Sohn (1980) has claimed, for example, that Koreans find it easier than English speakers do to learn to use particles in Japanese signaling discourse topics. If this claim is true, it might prove highly significant for a better general understanding of the acquisition of syntax.

8. *Comprehension and production.* It is possible, but not certain, that transfer is more important as an influence on comprehension than on production. To the extent that listening and reading comprehension are prerequisites for fluent speaking and writing, positive transfer may play an especially important role in the beginning stages of acquisition of one language by speakers of another language that happens to be rather similar.

9. *Child bilingualism.* There is, as suggested earlier, considerable evidence for the existence of transfer among children learning a second language. It appears, however, that such influence is related to the relative awareness or lack of awareness that children have of the differences between languages (Sections 8.2, 8.3). Further research on the relationship between transfer and linguistic development in childhood would certainly be useful for an understanding of such issues as constraints on transfer and the role of linguistic awareness in bilingualism.

10 *Implications for teaching*

The preceding chapters touched only occasionally on the pedagogical implications of studies of transfer. In comparison with research twenty or thirty years ago, second language studies now tend to show more caution about what conclusions teachers should draw from any particular set of findings. This caution reflects a growing awareness of the complexity of transfer and other topics in second language research. Accordingly, many researchers would now hesitate in dispensing prescriptions for the classroom, especially since very little of the advice one might give has been thoroughly tested. Yet despite the commendable caution seen more and more in second language studies, some of the research on transfer does have implications for teaching that merit discussion.

The most important implication is that cross-linguistic influence has considerable potential to affect the course of second language acquisition both inside and outside the classroom (cf. Section 9.2). As Schachter (in press) observes, there is far too much evidence for anyone who looks closely at the empirical record to be skeptical about the significance of transfer. It is true that much uncertainty remains about many issues related to cross-linguistic influences, and it is undeniably true that researchers are far from able to predict with full accuracy when transfer will occur (cf. Section 9.3). However, it is also true that skeptics are far from able to predict when transfer will *never* occur.

Transfer is thus an important, though incompletely understood, factor in acquisition. This chapter discusses what pedagogical concerns the existence of transfer warrants and what steps teachers can take to understand transfer as it occurs in their classrooms.

Attitudes

The research discussed in this book suggests that negative transfer is quite possible – and often probable – in the pronunciation, grammar, and so forth of second language learners. Given the existence of that influence, there remains the question of just how much of a problem teachers ought to take such influence to be. Negative transfer should be a cause for concern in light of the social significance of foreign accents (including not only pronunciation but also grammar, vocabulary, etc.); as noted earlier, there seems to be a widespread, though probably not universal, belief that language mixing is a kind of linguistic corruption (Section 2.1). To the extent that second language speech shows such mixing in the form of a foreign accent, there is a possible negative reaction on the part of listeners. In fact, some evidence suggests that the more heavily accented a person's pronunciation is, the more likely it is that listeners *will* have negative reactions. In one case, Ryan, Carranza, and Moffie (1977) presented native speakers of American English with tape-recorded examples of English read by Spanish-English bilinguals. The readers with the strongest accents tended to be judged the least pleasant and the least friendly (cf. Brennan and Brennan 1981). While this attitudinal research primarily involves language and society in the United States, there is a strong likelihood that similar research in many other countries would yield similar results (cf. Kalmar, Zhong, and Xiao 1988).[1]

Negative transfer does not always prompt negative attitudes: that is, a foreign accent will not always provoke distrust or hostility. Even though a prejudice against speakers with foreign accents exists in the United States, many individuals with accents have been highly successful in American society. Despite a noticeable German accent, Henry Kissinger achieved distinction in public affairs, and partly *because* of a very noticeable French accent, Charles Boyer became a beloved celebrity in the United States and other English-speaking countries. Friendliness, intelligence, and other positive personality traits can often charm people into cultivating a liking for a certain accent – or at least into ignoring its "foreignness" (cf. Orth 1982). A look at the history of nearly any country is likely to show cases of talented foreigners who achieve success even though their command of the local language differed considerably from that of native speakers.

Yet the success that non-native speakers may achieve rarely if ever comes easily. Xenophobia or a dislike of particular ethnic groups can jeopardize a non-native speaker's chances to gain respect, make friends, get an education, or make a living, and a foreign accent can trigger

---

1 As discussed earlier, not all pronunciation problems can be attributed to native language influence (Section 7.3), but there is little doubt that if the sound patterns produced by an individual sound "foreign," transfer will have been a major determinant of that individual's pronunciation. A similar claim might also be made for grammar and vocabulary problems. Some research has suggested that grammatical transfer does not contribute to the distinctiveness of a foreign accent and that grammatical errors cannot aid listeners in identifying foreign accents (Ioup 1984). However, the conclusions of such research are questionable since stereotypical representations of accents may involve syntactic features, as noted in Chapter 1.

hostile attitudes. It might go without saying that teachers should do what they can to eliminate the prejudices in a society. In an ideal society, one might dream, any use of language that was polite, clear, and well thought out would achieve the same amount of respect regardless of the accent of the speaker (cf. Giles 1973). However, the elimination of many negative attitudes is likely to take a very long time, and in the meanwhile students in a language classroom have a right to any instruction that can help them to produce speech or writing that will minimize the threat of a society's prejudices.[2]

Comprehensibility

In some contexts, students may not wish or need to change the way they speak. For example, many Indian students believe that the varieties of English spoken in their country are as respectable as varieties of British or American English (Section 8.3). Whether instructors in India them-selves have an Indian, a British, or some other accent, they would do well to consider carefully how much they insist that students imitate their own way of speaking (cf. Kachru 1987). If students are planning to stay in India and use their English primarily with other Indians, there is little sense in forcing students to adopt a pronunciation or vocabulary not widely used in India. On the other hand, if students are planning to study or work in areas where no one – or almost no one – is familiar with Indian pronunciation or vocabulary choices (e.g., most of the South in the United States), they could profit a great deal from becoming familiar with features of non-Indian varieties of English. Comprehensible language should be the goal no matter what dialect is learned, and the comprehensibility of people can vary in different contexts (cf. Smith and Rafiqzad 1979; Smith and Bisazza 1982).

The study of comprehensibility involves complex issues. A great deal of work in psycholinguistics indicates that many factors besides struc-tural ones contribute to the comprehensibility of speech and writing (cf. Clark and Clark 1977; Foss and Hakes 1978). Among the factors that can contribute to the comprehensibility of any discourse are the context in which the speaking (or writing) is produced, the cultural assumptions that speakers and listeners share, and universals of language and cog-nition. Thus, it would be mistaken to assume that a foreign accent will necessarily cause misunderstandings. Yet even with the contribution of nonlinguistic factors to comprehensibility, structural factors can make

2 Even if it ever becomes an attainable goal, the total eradication of a foreign accent in favor of, for example, an American or a British accent is a questionable pedagogical aim. Sociolinguists have often commented on the risks of outsiders speaking a language "too well" with native speakers (cf. Loveday 1982b).

a big difference in whether an individual is understood or not. For example, a study by Bansal (1976) of the intelligibility of speakers of Indian English indicates that pronunciation errors had a crucial effect on how much British listeners were able to understand (cf. Section 7.2). While further research is needed on the relation between errors and comprehensibility, there seems little doubt that a large number of errors – whether due to transfer or to other sources – can seriously affect comprehension.

The discussion of comprehensibility so far has focused on how well non-native speakers may be understood. However, transfer studies are also relevant to the question of how well non-native speakers understand the target language. Research indicates that when two languages share a large number of similar words, learners will have a considerable head start in their efforts to read another language (Sections 3.3, 5.2). Conversely, learners speaking a language with few lexical similarities to the target language will be more likely to experience incomprehension or miscomprehension. Since vocabulary plays a crucial role in all uses of language, teachers should take special care to monitor what words individual students may find easy or difficult in reading materials or in spoken language in the classroom.[3]

The issues of language attitudes and of comprehensibility are by no means completely separate. Some misunderstandings in cross-cultural communication seem to involve differences in standards of linguistic politeness (Section 4.1) and expectations about discourse coherence (Section 4.2). As discussed in Chapter 4, misunderstandings involving politeness and coherence are especially likely to cause bad feeling, and so discourse differences are a matter of particular concern. Since languages directly or indirectly encode some cultural differences, instruction pointing out those differences is also appropriate, as Lado and many others have recognized (Section 2.2). While it would be naive to think that all cases of ethnic tensions within a nation or of conflict between nations are due primarily to linguistic or cultural differences, a fundamental goal of language instruction should be to minimize any misunderstandings due to such differences.

3 This point may seem obvious to many teachers, but the following anecdote suggests that not everyone is aware of the importance of lexical similarities. An American engineer asked an Algerian technician, "Is it up to you whether or not your family comes here?" The technician did not understand the question, and the engineer repeated the question a number of times, with more and more frustration. When the technician was asked by another person, "Does it depend on you whether or not your family comes here?", he understood and was able to answer the question satisfactorily. The Algerian technician was fluent in French (as well as in Arabic), and *depend* and *dépendre* are cognate forms in English and French.

Process

One criticism of contrastive analysis has been that it emphasizes *product* over *process*: that is, comparisons of languages focus more on static forms and functions in two languages than on the way people learn a second language. Without question, teachers must be concerned not only with forms and functions but also with the learning process. Although transfer is only one aspect of that process, it is a crucial one. Any fully adequate theory of second language acquisition must also be able to account for the role of language universals in the acquisition process, and the role of universals will never be fully understood until researchers can account for the occurrence or nonoccurrence of cross-linguistic influence in second language contexts (cf. Sections 3.1, 3.4). To some extent, the product-process distinction reflects the uneasy alliance of linguistics and psychology. While their comments are about the general stance of that alliance, the words of two eminent psycholinguists suggest well the specific value of contrastive research: "It is highly profitable to know the product before studying the process by which it [the product] is arrived at" (Clark and Clark 1977:8).

Materials

One of the most important pedagogical questions concerning the study of transfer is how specific to each language group any classroom materials should be. Fries, Lado, and other contrastive theoreticians believed that Spanish-speaking students, for example, needed textbooks and other materials very different from those needed by Chinese-speaking students. While error research and other investigations did much to undermine the credibility of contrastive approaches, comparisons between structures in the native language of students and in the target language are still quite common in textbooks in certain countries.[4] However popular such materials may be, there is little empirical support for the effectiveness (or ineffectiveness) of contrastive approaches. Such approaches may well be effective, as the long use of contrastive materials suggests (Section 2.2), but their effectiveness is likely to remain unverified for a considerable period of time largely because of the uncertainty about the effectiveness of teaching linguistic structure. While most teachers and researchers would agree that the teaching of structure has *some* effect, no consensus exists about its exact nature. Research on the ef-

4 Among other reasons for the continuing use of contrastive presentations is the fact that such comparisons are difficult to avoid if there is no transparent relation between a native and target language structure.

fectiveness of contrastive materials is certainly feasible, but it would have to be related to questions such as what methods of teaching are most effective, what types of learners are most likely to benefit from particular methods, and what periods in acquisition are especially favorable to introduce particular structures to learners (cf. Pica 1984; Pienemann 1984).

Whatever the merits of contrastive materials in some contexts, it is clear that such materials are not always feasible. For example, when an ESL class consists of speakers of Chinese, Persian, Spanish, Tamil, and Yoruba, there is not likely to be any textbook that contrasts English verb phrases with verb phrases in all of those languages – and even if there were, teachers could not profitably spend the class time necessary to illuminate so many contrasts. Yet even in such classes, one type of contrastive information is frequently available: bilingual dictionaries. Although the comparisons are sometimes restricted to words in the native and target languages, the most carefully prepared dictionaries often provide some comparisons of pronunciation and grammar as well. If the class size allows it, teachers can help individual students in using any contrastive information that their dictionaries provide.

Information

Apart from dictionaries and other materials suitable for classroom use, a great deal of other information about language contrasts is available and may help teachers to see more clearly some of the problems that their students encounter. Bibliographies of contrastive studies (e.g., Sajavaara and Lehtonen 1981; Dechert, Brüggemeir, and Futterer 1984) are a useful place to begin looking, and the studies themselves commonly have many useful references. Some of the contrastive research not only describes the structures in contrast but also provides quantitative evidence for their relative ease or difficulty (e.g., Andersen 1977; Flynn 1984). While many second language studies are written primarily for other researchers, some books and articles are written primarily for teachers, as in the case of a recent collection of contrastive descriptions (Swan and Smith 1987).

As with classroom materials, contrastive descriptions have their weaknesses, and teachers who read these descriptions should use them with a certain wariness. For example, a contrastive sketch by Coe (1987) suggests that such errors as *Do you can swim?* result from differences between the verb system of English and the systems of Spanish and Catalan. While a contrastive explanation is possible, such an error seems more likely to involve overgeneralization (cf. Sections 2.2, 8.1). Another problem that teachers should be alert to is that students may speak their native language differently from what is seen in a contrastive description.

For example, if the native language of students is English, a contrastive account of pronunciation difficulties of American students may not jibe with what British teachers of French or German notice in their classes. Furthermore, it may not be the case that students speak a standard or even a near-standard variety of the native language depicted in a contrastive description (Section 3.2).

One limitation of contrastive descriptions now available is their incompleteness. As noted earlier, even languages such as English have not been thoroughly described, and for many languages information is quite scarce (Section 3.2). The lack of information (or its inaccessibility to teachers in certain parts of the world) should not be an insurmountable problem to well-prepared teachers, however. It is always possible to learn the language of students or at least enough about a student's language to develop contrastive descriptions. Anthropological linguists often teach themselves languages that have never been described, and the techniques they use in their fieldwork are not beyond the reach of professional language teachers (cf. Gudschinsky 1967).

Becoming familiar with the culture as well as the language of their students should be a goal for teachers, just as students usually have to become somewhat familiar with the culture in which the target language is used. Discourse and vocabulary are areas where such familiarity is no doubt necessary, yet hopefully a teacher's curiosity would also extend to any culture for its own sake, to the history, the religion, the arts, the literature, the cuisine, and all other aspects of life in any student's native land. Few language teachers would dispute the need to treat students as individuals, and individual attention is difficult – and at times even impossible – without an understanding of a person's linguistic and cultural background. Even though language and culture are the common property of many people in a society, they say a great deal about how different people can be. As such, language and culture are extremely important distinguishers of, for example, Greek students and Japanese students. A strong interest in those distinguishers will, more often than not, lead to a strong mutual respect between teachers and students.

Glossary

The numbers at the end of each gloss refer to the sections which introduce the glossed term or which discuss it at greater length.

borrowing transfer: In bilingual contexts, the influences found in the use of a person's native language that are due to the subsequent acquisition of another language. (Section 2.1)

bound morphemes: Forms that cannot stand alone, as in the case of prefixes and suffixes in English. Thus, while *buy* is a free form, the suffix on *buying* is not since it must always occur with a free form. (Section 5.2)

bound morphology: The system of bound morphemes in a language. (Section 6.1)

branching direction: A serial relation between two constituents in a sentence. In the case of restrictive relative clauses, a *right branching direction* results from a relative clause following the noun modified and a *left branching direction* from a clause preceding the noun modified. (Section 6.2)

calques: Literal translations from one language into another, including cases where such translations are unacceptable: for example, a learner's literal translation of *put the fire out* into Spanish as *poner el fuego afuera* instead of as *extinguir el fuego.* (Section 3.3)

code-switching: A systematic interchange of words, phrases, or sentences taken from two or more languages. (Sections 2.1, 8.2)

comment: Most typically, information that elaborates upon a previously established **topic.** (Section 6.1)

contrastive analysis: Systematic comparison of two or more languages. (Chapter 1)

creole: A more developed form of a **pidgin.** It is typically learned by children growing up in a community where use of a pidgin is an everyday occurrence. (Section 2.1)

cross-sectional studies: Studies in which an individual's language is observed at only one interval. Such studies typically compare different groups of individuals at one time period (cf. **longitudinal studies**). (Section 2.2)

developmental errors: Errors that are normal occurrences in the course of learning either a first or a second language. (Section 2.2)

developmental sequence: A succession of phases in learning to master new linguistic structures. (Sections 2.2, 6.3)

devoicing: The cessation of the vibrating motion of the vocal cords. For example, if *tab* is changed to *tap*, there is no vibration in the production of the final consonant. (Section 7.3)

error analyses: Investigations that seek to determine the types and causes of errors (and often the frequency of the various error types). (Section 2.2)

focused: Describes linguistic behavior that tends to show a great deal of uniformity among different individuals. (Section 8.3)

Foreigner Talk: Adjustments in speech made by native speakers so that non-native speakers can understand what is said to them. Repetition, the use of simple words, and a slow rate of speech are among the most frequent characteristics of Foreigner Talk. (Section 2.1)

genitive: A frequent formal marking, often signaled by **morphological case** but sometimes by prepositions, that most typically indicates possession, as the *'s* in the phrase *Mary's book*. (Section 5.1)

glottal stop: A consonant produced by a rapid constriction of the region near the vocal cords. In American English, glottal stops often follow the first occurrence of the nasal consonant /n/ in such words as *fountain* and *mountain*. (Section 7.3)

hypercorrection: An inappropriate use of a form due to excessive concern over the use of another form: for example, Arabic speakers spelling *habit* as *hapit* as a reaction to **substitutions** of the letter *b* for the letter *p*. (Section 3.3)

implicational: Describes any relation in which the existence of one structure implies the existence of another. For example, languages in which verbs occur at the beginning of sentences usually have prepositions; thus verb-initial word order implies the use of prepositions. (Sections 3.4, 6.2)

interlingual identification: A judgment made by learners about the identity or similarity of structures in two languages. (Section 7.2)

language distance: The relative degree of similarity between two languages. (Sections 3.2, 8.3)

language mixing: The merging of forms or functions of two or more languages. Transfer is only one type of mixing; other types include **code-switching** (Sections 2.1, 8.2) and the **unfocused** mixing found in the speech of very young bilingual children. (Section 8.3)

left dislocation: A word order rule by which a linguistic constituent appears to the left of its normal position in a written sentence (in spoken language the same constituent occurs earlier than it normally does). For example, the sentence *John bought the car* shows *car* in a normal object position while *The car, John bought it* shows the same constituent in a left dislocation. Left dislocations frequently signal new topics or referents accorded special emphasis. (Section 6.1)

longitudinal studies: Studies that compare the language of the same individual (or individuals) over at least two intervals of time. For example, one might compare an ESL student's use of articles after two and after eight months of instruction (cf. **cross-sectional studies**). (Section 2.2)

morphological case: An overt, formal marking of nouns, pronouns, or other word classes to indicate the syntactic roles of noun phrases, such as subject and object, or to indicate a **semantic case**. For example, the *'s* on *Mary's* indicates the **genitive** case relation evident in *Mary's book*. Some languages such as Russian make very great use of morphological case, while others such as English make very little use, and other languages such as Thai make virtually no use of it (cf. **semantic case**). (Section 5.1)

negative face: Claims that a person has to privacy and autonomy. (Section 4.1)

negative politeness: Strategies that reduce threats to the **negative face** of another person. (Section 4.1)

negative transfer: Cross-linguistic influences resulting in errors, overproduction, underproduction, miscomprehension, and other effects that constitute a divergence between the behavior of native and non-native speakers of a language. (Sections 3.1, 3.3)

negator: Any form used to signal negation. (Section 6.3)

open syllable: Any syllable that ends with a vowel instead of a consonant. (Section 7.3)

overgeneralizations: Uses of a linguistic rule that go beyond the normal domain of that rule. For example, the use of the **bound morpheme** represented by *-s* on English nouns frequently signals pluralization, but *mans* and *mouses* are overgeneralizations of the pluralization rule. (Section 2.2)

phonemic system: The system of *phonemes*, that is, the smallest sound units that can distinguish meanings of words. For example, the consonants /s/ and /z/ are part of the phonemic system of English since there are contrasts in meaning that depend on such sounds: thus *sip* and *zip* do not mean the same thing. Although Spanish (as well as some other languages) makes some use of the *z* sound, there are no meaning contrasts such as between *sip* and *zip*, and therefore, while /z/ is part of the phonemic system of English, it is not part of the phonemic system of Spanish. (Section 7.2)

pidgin: A new language that develops as a result of language contact between speakers of different languages. Pidgins typically develop among speakers who need to talk about trade, work, and so forth, but who are unable to learn the native language(s) of their interlocutors. Pidgins usually show a great deal of structural **simplification** and sometimes a great deal of **substratum transfer** (cf. **creole**). (Section 2.1)

positive face: A person's self-image and self-respect. (Section 4.1)

positive politeness: Strategies that reduce threats to the **positive face** of another person. (Section 4.1)

positive transfer: Any facilitating effects on acquisition due to the influence of cross-linguistic similarities. Unlike **negative transfer**, positive transfer results in a convergence of behaviors of native and non-native speakers of a language. (Section 3.1)

postverbal negation: Any construction in which the **negator** follows the verb, as in *Ingrid kommt nicht* ("Ingrid comes not" = Ingrid isn't coming), where *nicht* is the negator. (Section 6.3)

preverbal negation: Any construction in which the **negator** precedes the verb, as in *Juan no va* ("Juan not goes" = Juan isn't going), where *no* is the negator. (Section 6.3)

proposition: The meaning of statements represented by sentences and sometimes by other linguistic forms. (Sections 4.2, 5.1)

relativism: In linguistics, the belief that knowing a particular language can induce one to adopt a particular worldview. (Sections 3.4, 5.1)

relativized position: The syntactic constituent in a relative clause that may be marked by a relative pronoun. (Section 6.2)

resumptive pronoun: In relative clauses, nonrelative pronouns that help to identify a referent, as in the case of *him* in *The musician that I saw him is from China*. While resumptive pronouns are not allowed in relative clauses in standard English, they are normal in relative clauses in many languages. (Sections 3.2, 6.2)

right dislocation: A word order rule by which a linguistic constituent appears to the right of its normal position in a written sentence (in spoken language the same constituent occurs later than it normally does). For example, the sentence *John bought the car* shows *John* in a normal subject position while *He bought the car, John did* shows the same constituent in a right dislocation. Right dislocations often signal a speaker's "afterthoughts," expressed to make the identity of a referent clear. (Section 6.1)

segmental errors: Pronunciation errors involving individual vowels or consonants. (Section 7.2)

semantic case: Some role that might be ascribed to a person or thing denoted by a noun phrase (and sometimes by other grammatical structures). For example, in the sentences *The sailor broke the window with a rock* and *A rock broke the window*, the noun *rock* is in *instrumental case* even while it is a prepositional object in one sentence and a subject in the other. (Section 5.1)

simplification: Any reduction resulting in a linguistic structure simpler than what is considered to be the target language norm. For example, *two boy* instead of *two boys* and *I very good fellow* instead of *I'm a very good fellow* are cases of simplification (that may or may not be a result of cross-linguistic differences). Some linguists consider **over-generalization** to be a type of simplification. (Sections 2.1, 3.3)

speech act: Purposive uses of language, such as requests, apologies, promises, and so forth. (Section 4.1)

substitutions: Errors due to the substitution of one form (often a form in the native language) for a form in the target language: for example, a Swedish speaker's use of *bort* instead of *away* in the sentence *I must go bort.* (Section 3.3)

substratum transfer: In bilingual contexts, the influences found in the use of a second language that are due to the native language. (Sections 2.1, 3.1)

suprasegmental: Describes such characteristics as word stress, rhythm, and tone. (Sections 3.2, 7.2)

topic: The focus of information in a discourse. According to Givón (1983b), important topics in a discourse tend to be frequently mentioned and to persist through relatively long stretches of discourse. Grammatical signals of topics include word order, intonation, and (in some languages) special "topic markers" (cf. **comment**). (Sections 4.2, 6.1)

transfer of training: Influences on the production or comprehension of a second language that are due to the ways learners have been taught (or to ways learners have taught themselves). (Section 2.2)

tree model: A characterization of language change as divergences from an ancestral language. The branches on the model represent new languages or dialects. Such change is not due to language contact (cf. **wave model**). (Section 2.1)

typology: Classification of languages according to structural or other characteristics. Any such classification may reflect historical relations between languages, but two languages having a common typological characteristic are not always historically related. (Section 3.4)

unfocused: Describes linguistic behavior that tends to show relatively little uniformity among different individuals (cf. **focused**). (Section 8.3)

wave model: A characterization of language change as a process due to contact between speakers of different dialects or different languages (cf. **tree model**). (Section 2.1)

zero anaphora: The absence of a form under special conditions, usually when the referent of the form can be guessed through some previous mention. For example, in *George took the money and ran*, the verb *ran* has a "zero" subject: that is, neither a noun nor a pronoun such as *he* appears as subject. Nevertheless, the referent associated with the verb (i.e., George) can be inferred. (Section 6.1)

References

Adams, Corinne. 1979. *English Speech Rhythm and the Foreign Learner*. The Hague: Mouton.

Adiv, Ellen. 1984. Language learning strategies: the relationship between L1 operating principles and language transfer in L2 development. In *Second Languages: A Cross-Linguistic Perspective*, ed. by Roger Andersen. Rowley, Mass.: Newbury House.

Adjemian, Christian. 1983. The transferability of lexical properties. In *Language Transfer in Language Learning*, ed. by Susan Gass and Larry Selinker. Rowley, Mass.: Newbury House.

Adjemian, Christian, and Juana Liceras. 1984. Accounting for adult acquisition of relative clauses: Universal Grammar, L1, and structuring the intake. In *Universals of Second Language Acquisition*, ed. by Fred Eckman, Lawrence Bell, and Diane Nelson. Rowley, Mass.: Newbury House.

Ahukana, Joshua, Nancy Lund, and J. Richard Gentile. 1981. Inter- and intra-lingual interference effects in learning a third language. *Modern Language Journal* 65:281–87.

Albert, Ethel. 1964. "Rhetoric," "logic," and "poetics" in Burundi. *American Anthropologist* 66(6) part 2, Special Publication: The Ethnography of Communication, ed. by John Gumperz and Dell Hymes.

Albert, Martin, and Loraine Obler. 1979. *The Bilingual Brain*. New York: Academic Press.

Altenberg, Evelyn, and Robert Vago. 1983. Theoretical implications of an error analysis of second language phonology. *Language Learning* 33:427–47.

Andersen, Roger. 1977. The impoverished state of cross-sectional morpheme acquisition/accuracy methodology (Or: The leftovers are more nourishing than the main course). In *Proceedings of the Los Angeles Second Language Research Forum*. Los Angeles: Department of English, University of California at Los Angeles.

1979. The relationship between first language transfer and second language overgeneralization. In *The Acquisition and Use of Spanish and English as First and Second Languages*, ed. by Roger Andersen. Washington, D.C.: TESOL.

Andersen, Roger, ed. 1983a. *Pidginization and Creolization as Language Acquisition*. Rowley, Mass.: Newbury House.

Andersen, Roger. 1983b. Transfer to somewhere. In *Language Transfer in Language Learning*, ed. by Susan Gass and Larry Selinker. Rowley, Mass.: Newbury House.

1984. The one to one principle of interlanguage construction. *Language Learning* 34:77–95.

Anderson, Janet. 1987. The markedness differential hypothesis and syllable structure difficulty. In *Interlanguage Phonology*, ed. by Georgette Ioup and Steven Weinberger. Rowley, Mass.: Newbury House.

Andrews, Geoffrey. 1984. English stress rules in adult second language acquisition. Unpublished Ph.D. dissertation, Boston University.

Anthony, Edward. 1952–53. The teaching of cognates. *Language Learning* 4:79–82.

Appel, René. 1984. *Immigrant Children Learning Dutch*. Dordrecht: Foris Publications.

Appel, René, and Pieter Muysken. 1987. *Language Contact and Bilingualism*. London: Edward Arnold.

Applegate, Richard. 1975. The language teacher and the rules of speaking. *TESOL Quarterly* 9:271–81.

Ard, Josh, and Taco Homburg. 1983. Verification of language transfer. In *Language Transfer in Language Learning*, ed. by Susan Gass and Larry Selinker. Rowley, Mass.: Newbury House.

Asher, James, and Ramiro Garcia. 1969. The optimal age to learn a foreign language. *Modern Language Journal* 38:334–41.

Au, Terry Kit-Fong. 1983. Chinese and English counterfactuals: the Sapir-Whorf hypothesis revisited. *Cognition* 15:155–87.

Ausubel, David. 1968. *Educational Psychology: A Cognitive View*. New York: Holt, Rinehart, and Winston.

Bailey, Charles J. N. 1973. *Variation and Linguistic Theory*. Washington, D.C.: Center for Applied Linguistics.

Bailey, Nathalie, Carolyn Madden, and Stephen Krashen. 1974. Is there a "natural sequence" in adult second language learning? *Language Learning* 24:235–43.

Bamgbose, Ayo. 1982. Standard Nigerian English: issues of identification. In *The Other Tongue*, ed. by Braj Kachru. Urbana: University of Illinois Press.

Bammesberger, Alfred. 1983. *An Outline of Modern Irish Grammar*. Heidelberg: Carl Winter.

Bansal, R. K. 1976. *The Intelligibility of Indian English*. Hyderabad: Central Institute of English and Foreign Languages. ERIC Report ED 177849.

Barkowski, Hans, Ulrike Harnisch, and Sigrid Krumm. 1976. Sprachhandlungstheorie und "Deutsch für ausländische Arbeiter." *Linguistische Berichte* 45:42–54.

Barry, Michael. 1983. The English language in Ireland. In *English as a World Language*, ed. by Richard Bailey and Manfred Görlach. Ann Arbor: University of Michigan Press.

Bartelt, H. Guillermo. 1982. Apachean English metaphors. In *Essays on Native American English*, ed. by H. Guillermo Bartelt, Susan Penfield Jasper, and Bates Hoffer. San Antonio: Trinity University.

———. 1983. Transfer and variability of rhetorical redundancy in Apachean English interlanguage. In *Language Transfer in Language Learning*, ed. by Susan Gass and Larry Selinker. Rowley, Mass.: Newbury House.

Bartlett, Frederic. 1954. *Remembering: A Study in Experimental and Social Psychology*. Cambridge: Cambridge University Press.

Bates, Elizabeth. 1976. *Language and Context: The Acquisition of Pragmatics*. New York: Academic Press.

Bates, Elizabeth, and Brian MacWhinney. 1981. Second-language acquisition from a functionalist perspective. In *Annals of the New York Academy of Sciences*, ed. by Harris Winitz. New York: New York Academy of Sciences.

1982. Functionalist approaches to grammar. In *Language Acquisition: The State of the Art*, ed. by Eric Wanner and Lila Gleitman. Cambridge: Cambridge University Press.

Bebout, Linda. 1985. An error analysis of misspellings made by learners of English as a first and as a second language. *Journal of Psycholinguistic Research* 14:569–93.

Beebe, Leslie. 1980. Sociolinguistic variation and style shifting in second language acquisition. *Language Learning* 30:337–51.

Beeman, William. 1976. Status, style, and strategy in Iranian interaction. *Anthropological Linguistics* 18:305–22.

Benson, Bronwen. 1986. The markedness differential hypothesis: implications for Vietnamese speakers of English. In *Markedness*, by Fred Eckman, Edith Moravcsik, and Jessica Wirth. New York: Plenum Press.

Bentahila, Abdelali, and Eirlys Davies. 1983. The syntax of Arabic-French code-switching. *Lingua* 59:301–30.

Berlin, Brent, and Paul Kay. 1969. *Basic Color Terms*. Berkeley: University of California Press.

Biber, Douglas. 1986. Spoken and written textual dimensions of English. *Language* 62:384–414.

Bickerton, Derek. 1981. *Roots of Language*. Ann Arbor: Karoma.

Bickerton, Derek, and Talmy Givón. 1976. Pidginization and syntactic change: from SXV and VSX to SVX. In *Papers from the Parasession on Diachronic Syntax*, ed. by Sanford Stever, Carol Walker, and Salikoko Mufwene. Chicago: Chicago Linguistic Society.

Birdsong, David, Catherine Johnson, and John McMinn. 1984. Universals versus transfer revisited. Paper presented at the 9th Boston University Language Development Conference.

Birdsong, David, and Terence Odlin. 1983. If Whorf was on the right track: a review essay of "The Linguistic Shaping of Thought: A Study in the Impact of Language and Thinking in China and the West" by Alfred H. Bloom. *Language Learning* 33:401–12.

Bley-Vroman, Robert. 1983. The comparative fallacy in interlanguage studies: the case of systematicity. *Language Learning* 33:1–17.

Bliss, Alan. 1977. The emergence of modern English dialects in Ireland. In *The English Language in Ireland*, ed. by Diarmaid Ó'Muirithe. Dublin: Mercier Press.

1978. *Spoken English in Ireland, 1600–1740*. Dublin: Dolmen Press.

1984. English in the south of Ireland. In *Language in the British Isles*, by Peter Trudgill. Cambridge: Cambridge University Press.

Bloom, Alfred. 1981. *The Linguistic Shaping of Thought: A Study in the Impact of Language and Thinking in China and the West*. Hillsdale, N.J.: Lawrence Erlbaum.

1984. Caution – the words you use may affect what you say: a response to Au. *Cognition* 17:275–87.

Bloomfield, Leonard. 1933. *Language*. New York: Holt, Rinehart, and Winston.

Blum, Shoshana, and E. A. Levenston. 1978. Universals of lexical simplification. *Language Learning* 28:399–415.

1980. Lexical simplification in second language acquisition. *Studies in Second Language Acquisition* 2:43–63.

Blum-Kulka, Shoshana. 1982. Learning to say what you mean: a study of speech act performance of learners of Hebrew as a second language. *Applied Linguistics* 3:29–59.

Bock, J. Kathryn. 1982. Toward a cognitive psychology of syntax: information processing contributions to sentence formulation. *Psychological Review* 89:1–47.

Bolinger, Dwight. 1975. *Aspects of Language.* New York: Harcourt, Brace, and Jovanovich.

1978. Intonation across languages. In *Universals of Language,* ed. by Joseph Greenberg. Stanford: Stanford University Press.

Bolinger, Dwight, and Donald Sears. 1981. *Aspects of Language.* New York: Harcourt, Brace, and Jovanovich.

Borden, Gloria, Adele Gerber, and Gary Milsark. 1983. Production and perception of the /r/–/l/ contrast in Korean adults learning English. *Language Learning* 33:499–526.

Borkin, Ann, and Susan Reinhart. 1978. Excuse me and I'm sorry. *TESOL Quarterly* 12:57–69.

Brazil, David, Malcolm Coulthard, and Catherine Johns. 1980. *Discourse Intonation and Language Teaching.* London: Longman.

Brennan, Eileen, and John Brennan. 1981. Accent scaling and language attitudes: reactions to Mexican American English speech. *Language and Speech* 24:207–21.

Brière, Eugene. 1968. *A Psycholinguistic Study of Phonological Interference.* The Hague: Mouton.

Broselow, Ellen. 1983. Nonobvious transfer: on predicting epenthesis errors. In *Language Transfer in Language Learning,* ed. by Susan Gass and Larry Selinker. Rowley, Mass.: Newbury House.

Broselow, Ellen, Richard Hurtig, and Catherine Ringen. 1987. The perception of second language prosody. In *Interlanguage Phonology,* ed. by Georgette Ioup and Steven Weinberger. Rowley, Mass.: Newbury House.

Brown, Gillian, and George Yule, 1983. *Discourse Analysis.* Cambridge: Cambridge University Press.

Brown, Penelope, and Stephen Levinson. 1978. Universals in linguistic usage: politeness phenomena. In *Questions and Politeness,* ed. by Esther N. Goody. Cambridge Papers in Social Anthropology. Cambridge: Cambridge University Press.

Brown, Roger. 1973. *A First Language.* Cambridge, Mass.: Harvard University Press.

Brown, Roger, and Albert Gilman. 1960. The pronouns of power and solidarity. In *Style in Language,* ed. by Thomas Sebeok. Cambridge, Mass.: MIT Press.

Busch, Deborah. 1982. Introversion-extraversion and the EFL proficiency of Japanese students. *Language Learning* 32:109–32.

Butterworth, Guy, and Evelyn Hatch. 1978. A Spanish-speaking adolescent's acquisition of English. In *Second Language Acquisition: A Book of Readings,* ed. by Evelyn Hatch. Rowley, Mass.: Newbury House.

Bynon, Theodora. 1977. *Historical Linguistics.* Cambridge: Cambridge University Press.

Callary, Robert. 1975. Phonological change and the development of an urban dialect in Illinois. *Language in Society* 4:155–69.

Cancino, Herlinda, Ellen Rosansky, and John Schumann. 1978. The acquisition of English negatives and interrogatives by native Spanish speakers. In *Second Language Acquisition: A Book of Readings*, ed. by Evelyn Hatch. Rowley, Mass.: Newbury House.

Carrell, Patricia. 1982. Cohesion is not coherence. *TESOL Quarterly* 16:479–88.

Carrell, Patricia, and Beverly Konneker. 1981. Politeness: comparing native and nonnative judgments. *Language Learning* 31:17–30.

Carroll, John. 1968. Contrastive linguistics and interference theory. In *Report of the Nineteenth Annual Round Table Meeting on Linguistics and Language Studies*, ed. by James Alatis. Monograph Series on Languages and Linguistics, Georgetown University. Washington, D.C.: Georgetown University Press.

———. 1981. Twenty-five years of research on foreign language aptitude. In *Individual Differences and Universals in Language Learning Aptitude*, ed. by Karl Diller. Rowley, Mass.: Newbury House.

Celce-Murcia, Marianne, and Diane Larsen-Freeman. 1983. *The Grammar Book*. Rowley, Mass.: Newbury House.

Chafe, Wallace. 1970. *Meaning and the Structure of Language*. Chicago: University of Chicago Press.

Chambers, J. K., and Peter Trudgill. 1980. *Dialectology*. Cambridge: Cambridge University Press.

Chaudron, Craig. 1983. Research on metalinguistic judgments: a review of theory, methods, and results. *Language Learning* 33:343–77.

Chiang, Thomas. 1979. Some interferences of English intonations with Chinese tones. *IRAL: International Review of Applied Linguistics* 17:245–50.

Chomsky, Noam. 1957. *Syntactic Structures*. The Hague: Mouton.

———. 1965. *Aspects of the Theory of Syntax*. Cambridge, Mass.: MIT Press.

———. 1981. *Lectures on Government and Binding*. Dordrecht: Foris Publications.

Clahsen, Harald. 1982. *Spracherwerb in der Kindheit*. Tübingen: Gunter Narr.

———. 1984. The acquisition of German word order. In *Second Languages: A Cross-Linguistic Perspective*, ed. by Roger Andersen. Rowley, Mass.: Newbury House.

Clark, Eve. 1973. What's in a word: on the child's acquisition of semantics. In *Cognitive Development and the Acquisition of Language*, ed. by Timothy Moore. New York: Academic Press.

———. 1982. The young word-maker: a case study of innovation in the child's lexicon. In *Language Acquisition: The State of the Art*, ed. by Eric Wanner and Lila Gleitman. Cambridge: Cambridge University Press.

Clark, Eve, and Herbert Clark. 1979. When nouns surface as verbs. *Language* 55:767–811.

Clark, Herbert, and Eve Clark. 1977. *Psychology and Language*. New York: Harcourt, Brace, and Jovanovich.

Clarke, Mark, Ann Losoff, Margaret McCracken, and JoAnn Still. 1981. Gender perception in Arabic and English. *Language Learning* 31:159–69.

Coe, Norman. 1987. Speakers of Spanish and Catalan. In *Learner English: A Teacher's Guide to Interference and Other Problems*, ed. by Michael Swan and Bernard Smith. Cambridge: Cambridge University Press.

Cohen, Andrew, and Elite Olshtain. 1981. Developing a measure of sociocultural competence: the case of apology. *Language Learning* 31:113–34.

Comrie, Bernard. 1981. *Language Universals and Linguistic Typology.* Chicago: University of Chicago Press.

———. 1984. Why linguists need language acquirers. In *Universals in Second Language Acquisition,* ed. by William Rutherford. Amsterdam: John Benjamins.

Comrie, Bernard, and Edward Keenan. 1979. Noun phrase accessibility revisited. *Language* 55:649–64.

Connor, Ulla, and Peter McCagg. 1983. Cross-cultural differences and perceived quality in written paraphrases of English expository prose. *Applied Linguistics* 4:259–68.

———. 1987. A contrastive study of English expository prose. In *Writing Across Languages: Analysis of L2 Text,* ed. by Ulla Connor and Robert Kaplan. Reading, Mass.: Addison-Wesley.

Cooper, William, and John Ross. 1975. World order. In *Papers from the Parasession on Functionalism.* Chicago: Chicago Linguistic Society.

Corbett, Edward. 1971. *Classical Rhetoric for the Modern Student.* New York: Oxford University Press.

Corder, S. Pit. 1983. A role for the mother tongue. In *Language Transfer in Language Learning,* ed. by Susan Gass and Larry Selinker. Rowley, Mass.: Newbury House.

Coulmas, Florian, ed. 1981a. *A Festschrift for Native Speaker.* The Hague: Mouton.

Coulmas, Florian. 1981b. "Poison to your soul": thanks and apologies contrastively viewed. In *Conversation Routine,* ed. by Florian Coulmas. The Hague: Mouton.

———. 1983. Writing and literacy in China. In *Writing in Focus,* ed. by Florian Coulmas and Konrad Ehlich. The Hague: Mouton.

Cowan, J. Ronayne, and Zohreh Sarmad. 1976. Reading performance of bilingual children according to type of school and home language. *Language Learning* 26:353–76.

Crystal, David, and Derek Davy. 1969. *Investigating English Style.* Bloomington: Indiana University Press.

Cummins, James. 1979. Linguistic interdependence and the educational development of bilingual children. *Review of Educational Research* 49:222–51.

Cutler, Anne. 1984. Stress and accent in language production and understanding. In *Intonation, Accent, and Rhythm,* ed. by Dafydd Gibbon and Helmut Richter. Berlin: de Gruyter.

Dahl, Östen. 1979a. Review article of John Lyons' *Semantics. Language* 55:199–206.

———. 1979b. Typology of sentence negation. *Linguistics* 17:79–106.

Dawkins, R. M. 1916. *Modern Greek in Asia Minor.* Cambridge: Cambridge University Press.

Dechert, Hans, Monika Brüggemeir, and Dietmar Futterer. 1984. *Transfer and Interference in Language: A Selected Bibliography.* Amsterdam: John Benjamins.

De Fréine, Sean. 1977. The dominance of the English language in the nineteenth century. In *The English Language in Ireland,* ed. by Diarmaid Ó'Muirithe. Dublin: Mercier Press.

Dehghanpisheh, Elaine. 1978. Language development in Farsi and English: implications for the second language learner. *IRAL: International Review of Applied Linguistics* 16:45–61.

Derbyshire, Desmond. 1986. Comparative survey of morphology and syntax in Brazilian Arawakan. In *Handbook of Amazonian Languages*. ed. by Desmond Derbyshire and Geoffrey Pullum. Berlin: Mouton de Gruyter.

De Villiers, Jill, and Peter de Villiers. 1973. A cross-sectional study of the development of grammatical morphemes. *Journal of Psycholinguistic Research* 2:267–78.

1978. *Language Acquisition*. Cambridge, Mass.: Harvard University Press.

Dickerson, Lonna. 1974. Internal and external patterning of phonological variability in the speech of Japanese learners of English: toward a theory of second language acquisition. Unpublished Ph.D. dissertation, University of Illinois at Champaign-Urbana.

Di Pietro, Robert. 1971. *Language Structures in Contrast*. Rowley, Mass.: Newbury House.

Dulay, Heidi, and Marina Burt. 1973. Should we teach children syntax? *Language Learning* 23:245–57.

1974. Natural sequences in child second language acquisition. *Language Learning* 24:37–53.

1974/1983. Goofing: an indicator of children's second language strategies. In *Language Transfer in Language Learning*, ed. by Susan Gass and Larry Selinker. Rowley, Mass.: Newbury House.

Dulay, Heidi, Marina Burt, and Stephen Krashen. 1982. *Language Two*. New York: Oxford University Press.

Dundes, Alan. 1964. *The Morphology of North American Indian Folktales*. Folklore Fellows Communication, 195. Helsinki: Academia Scientiarum Fennica.

Dušková, Libuše. 1969. On sources of errors in foreign language teaching. *IRAL: International Review of Applied Linguistics* 7:11–36.

Eckman, Fred. 1977. Markedness and the contrastive analysis hypothesis. *Language Learning* 27:315–30.

1981a. On predicting phonological difficulty in second language acquisition. *Studies in Second Language Acquisition* 4:18–30.

1981b. On the naturalness of interlanguage phonological rules. *Language Learning* 31:195–216.

1984. Universals, typologies, and interlanguages. In *Universals in Second Language Acquisition*, ed. by William Rutherford. Amsterdam: John Benjamins.

Edwards, Mary. 1979. Phonological processes in fricative acquisition. *Papers and Reports on Child Language Development* 17:98–105.

Eggington, William. 1987. Written academic discourse in Korean: implications for effective communication. In *Writing Across Languages: Analysis of L2 Text*, ed. by Ulla Connor and Robert Kaplan. Reading, Mass.: Addison-Wesley.

Ekman, Paul. 1972. Universals and cultural differences in facial expressions of emotion. In *1971 Nebraska Symposium on Motivation*, ed. by James K. Cole. Lincoln: University of Nebraska Press.

Ellis, Rod. 1985. *Understanding Second Language Acquisition*. Oxford: Oxford University Press.

Emeneau, Murray, 1980. *Language and Linguistic Area*. Stanford: Stanford University Press.

Eubank, Lynn. 1986. Formal models of language learning and the acquisition of German word order and negation by primary and non-primary language learners. Unpublished Ph.D. dissertation, University of Texas at Austin.

1988. Parameters in L2 learning: Flynn revisited. Presented at the Second Language Research Forum, University of Hawaii at Manoa.

Fantini, Alvino. 1985. *Language Acquisition of a Bilingual Child*. Clevedon, U.K.: Multilingual Matters.

Fathman, Ann. 1975. Language background, age, and the order of acquisition of English structures. In *On TESOL '75*, ed. by Marina Burt and Heidi Dulay. Washington, D.C.: TESOL.

1977. Similarities and simplification in the interlanguage of second language learners. In *Actes du 5ème colloque de linguistique appliquée de Neuchâtel*, ed. by S. P. Corder and E. Roulet. Neuchâtel: Faculté des Lettres.

Felix, Sascha. 1981. The effect of formal instruction on second language acquisition. *Language Learning* 31:87–112.

Ferguson, Charles. 1975. Toward a characterization of English Foreigner Talk. *Anthropological Linguistics* 17:1–14.

1981. The structure and use of politeness formulas. In *Conversation Routine*, ed. by Florian Coulmas. The Hague: Mouton.

Fillmore, Charles. 1968. The case for case. In *Universals of Linguistic Theory*, ed. by Emmon Bach and Robert Harms. New York: Holt, Rinehart, and Winston.

Fillmore, Lily Wong. 1979. Individual differences in second language acquisition. In *Individual Differences in Language Ability and Language Behavior*, ed. by Charles Fillmore, Charles Kempler, and William Wang. New York: Academic Press.

Filppula, Marku. 1986. *Some Aspects of Hiberno-English in a Functional Sentence Perspective*. University of Joensuu Publications in the Humanities, 7. Joensuu, Finland: University of Joensuu.

Flege, James. 1980. Phonetic approximation in second language acquisition. *Language Learning* 30:117–34.

1981. The phonological basis of foreign accent: a hypothesis. *TESOL Quarterly* 15:443–45.

1987. The production of "new" and "similar" phones in a foreign language: evidence for the effect of equivalence classification. *Journal of Phonetics* 15:47–65.

Flege, James, and Robert Hammond. 1982. Mimicry of non-distinctive phonetic differences between language varieties. *Studies in Second Language Acquisition* 5:1–17.

Flynn, Suzanne. 1984. A universal in L2 acquisition based on a PBD typology. In *Universals of Second Language Acquisition*, ed. by Fred Eckman, Lawrence Bell, and Diane Nelson. Rowley, Mass.: Newbury House.

Flynn, Suzanne, and I. Espinal. 1985. Head-initial/head-final parameter in adult Chinese L2 acquisition of English. *Second Language Research* 1/2:93–117.

Foreign Service Institute. 1985. Schedule of Courses, 1985–1986. Washington, D.C.: U.S. Department of State.

Foss, Donald, and David Hakes. 1978. *Psycholinguistics: An Introduction to the Psychology of Language*. Englewood Cliffs, N.J.: Prentice-Hall.

Fox, Barbara. 1987. The noun phrase accessibility hierarchy revisited. *Language* 63:856–70.

Friedrich, Paul. 1979. The symbol and its relative non-arbitrariness. In *Language, Context, and the Imagination: Essays by Paul Friedrich*, ed. by Anwar Dil. Stanford: Stanford University Press.

Fries, Charles. 1945. *Teaching and Learning English as a Foreign Language.* Ann Arbor: University of Michigan Press.

—— 1949. The Chicago investigation. *Language Learning* 2:89–99.

—— 1952. *The Structure of English.* New York: Harcourt, Brace, and Company.

Fromkin, Victoria, and Robert Rodman. 1983. *An Introduction to Language.* New York: Holt, Rinehart, and Winston.

Gandour, Jackson, and Richard Harshman. 1978. Crosslanguage differences in tone perception: a multidimensional scaling investigation. *Language and Speech* 21:1–33.

Garvin, John. 1977. The Anglo-Irish idiom in the works of major Irish writers. In *The English Language in Ireland*, ed. by Diarmaid Ó'Muirithe. Dublin: Mercier Press.

Gass, Susan. 1979. Language transfer and universal grammatical relations. *Language Learning* 29:327–44.

—— 1983. Second language acquisition and language universals. In *The First Delaware Symposium on Language Studies*, ed. by Robert DiPietro, William Frawley, and Albert Wedel. Newark, Del.: University of Delaware Press.

—— 1984. A review of interlanguage syntax: language transfer and language universals. *Language Learning* 34:115–32.

—— 1986. The resolution of conflicts among competing systems: a bidirectional perspective. Unpublished manuscript.

Gass, Susan, and Josh Ard. 1984. Second language acquisition and the ontology of language universals. In *Universals in Second Language Acquisition*, ed. by William Rutherford. Amsterdam: John Benjamins.

Gass, Susan, and Larry Selinker, eds. 1983. *Language Transfer in Language Learning.* Rowley, Mass.: Newbury House.

Gazdar, Gerald, Ewan Klein, Geoffrey Pullum, and Ivan Sag. 1985. *Generalized Phrase Structure Grammar.* Cambridge, Mass.: Harvard University Press.

Gazdar, Gerald, and Geoffrey Pullum. 1985. Computationally relevant properties of natural languages and grammars. *New Generation Computing* 3:273–306.

Gelb, I. J. 1963. *A Study of Writing.* Chicago: University of Chicago Press.

Genesee, Fred. 1979. Acquisition of reading skill in immersion programs. *Foreign Language Annals* 12:71–77.

Gilbert, Glenn. 1980. Introduction. In *Pidgin and Creole Languages: Selected Essays by Hugo Schuchardt*, ed. by Glenn Gilbert. London: Cambridge University Press.

—— 1983. Transfer in second language acquisition. In *Pidginization and Creolization as Language Acquisition*, ed. by Roger Andersen. Rowley, Mass.: Newbury House.

Giles, Howard. 1973. Communicative effectiveness as a function of accented speech. *Speech Monographs* 40:330–31.

Gilsan, Eileen. 1985. The effect of word order on listening comprehension and pattern retention: an experiment in Spanish as a foreign language. *Language Learning* 35:443–72.

Givón, Talmy. 1979. *On Understanding Grammar.* New York: Academic Press.

Givón, Talmy, ed. 1983a. *Topic Continuity in Discourse: A Quantitative Cross-Language Study.* Amsterdam: John Benjamins.

Givón, Talmy. 1983b. Topic continuity in discourse: an introduction. In *Topic Continuity in Discourse: A Quantitative Cross-Language Study,* ed. by Talmy Givón. Amsterdam: John Benjamins.

1984a. *Syntax: A Functional/Typological Introduction.* Vol. 1. Amsterdam: John Benjamins.

1984b. Universals of discourse structure and second language acquisition. In *Universals in Second Language Acquisition,* ed. by William Rutherford. Amsterdam: John Benjamins.

Godard, Daniele. 1977. Same setting, different norms: phone call beginnings in France and the United States. *Language in Society* 6:209–19.

Gonzo, Susan, and Mario Saltarelli. 1983. Pidginization and linguistic change in immigrant languages. In *Pidginization and Creolization as Language Acquisition,* ed. by Roger Andersen. Rowley, Mass.: Newbury House.

Granfors, Tom, and Rolf Palmberg. 1976. Errors made by Finns and Swedish-speaking Finns at a commercial college level. In *Errors Made by Finns and Swedish-Speaking Finns in the Learning of English,* ed. by Hakan Ringbom and Rolf Palmberg. Abo, Finland: Department of English, Abo Akademi. ERIC Report ED 122628.

Greenberg, Cindy. 1983. Syllable structure in second language acquisition. *CUNY Forum* 9:41–63.

Greenberg, Joseph. 1965. Some generalizations concerning initial and final consonant sequences. *Linguistics* 18:5–32.

1966. Some universals of grammar with particular reference to the order of meaningful elements. In *Universals of Language,* ed. by Joseph Greenberg. Cambridge, Mass.: MIT Press.

Gregg, Kevin. 1984. Krashen's monitor and Ockham's razor. *Applied Linguistics* 5:79–100.

Gudschinsky, Sarah. 1967. *How to Learn an Unwritten Language.* New York: Holt, Rinehart, and Winston.

Guiora, Alexander. 1972. Construct validity and transpositional research: toward an empirical study of psychoanalytic concepts. *Comprehensive Psychiatry* 10:139–50.

Guiora, Alexander, and William Acton. 1979. Personality and language: a restatement. *Language Learning* 29:193–204.

Guiora, Alexander, William Acton, Robert Erard, and Fred Strickland. 1980. The effects of benzodiazepine (Valium) on permeability of language ego boundaries. *Language Learning* 30:351–63.

Guiora, Alexander, Benjamin Beit-Hallahmi, Robert Brannon, Cecelia Dull, and Thomas Scovel. 1972. The effects of experimentally induced changes in ego states on pronunciation ability in a second language: an exploratory study. *Comprehensive Psychiatry* 10:421–28.

Gumperz, John. 1982. *Discourse Strategies.* Cambridge: Cambridge University Press.

Gumperz, John, and Robert Wilson. 1971. Convergence and creolization. In *Pidgins and Creoles,* ed. by Dell Hymes. Cambridge: Cambridge University Press.

Hagège, Claude. 1976. Relative clauses, center-embedding, and comprehensibility. *Linguistic Inquiry* 7:198–201.

1987. *Le français et les siècles*. Paris: Éditions Odile Jacob.

Hakuta, Kenji. 1976. A case study of a Japanese child learning English as a second language. *Language Learning* 26:321–51.

1986. *Mirror of Language: The Debate on Bilingualism*. New York: Basic Books.

Hamill, James. 1978. Transcultural logic: testing hypotheses in three languages. In *Discourse and Inference from Cognitive Psychology*, ed. by M. D. Loflin and J. Silverberg. The Hague: Mouton.

Harley, Birgit. 1984. Age as a factor in the acquisition of French as a second language in an immersion setting. In *Second Languages: A Cross-Linguistic Perspective*, ed. by Roger Andersen. Rowley, Mass.: Newbury House.

1986. *Age in Second Language Acquisition*. San Diego: College Hill Press.

Harris, Jesse. 1948. German language influences in St. Clair County, Illinois. *American Speech* 23:106–10.

Harris, John. 1984. Syntactic variation and dialect divergence. *Journal of Linguistics* 20:303–27.

Hartmann, Reinhard. 1980. *Contrastive Textology*. Heidelberg: Julius Groos.

Hatch, Evelyn. 1983. *Psycholinguistics: A Second Language Perspective*. Rowley, Mass.: Newbury House.

Haugen, Einar. 1953. *The Norwegian Language in America*. Philadelphia: University of Pennsylvania Press.

Hawkins, John. 1983. *Word Order Universals*. New York: Academic Press.

Heath, Shirley. 1983. *Ways with Words*. Cambridge: Cambridge University Press.

Hecht, Barbara, and Randa Mulford. 1987. The acquisition of a second language phonology: interaction of transfer and developmental factors. In *Interlanguage Phonology*, ed. by Georgette Ioup and Steven Weinberger. Rowley, Mass.: Newbury House.

Henry, P. L. 1957. *An Anglo-English Dialect of North Roscommon*. Dublin: Department of English, University College.

1977. Anglo-Irish and its background. In *The English Language in Ireland*, ed. by Diarmaid Ó'Muirithe. Dublin: Mercier Press.

Herman, Lewis, and Marguerite Herman. 1943. *Foreign Dialects: A Manual for Actors, Directors, and Writers*. New York: Theatre Arts Books.

Hillocks, George. 1986. *Research on Written Composition*. Urbana, Ill.: National Conference on Research in English and ERIC Clearinghouse on Reading and Communication Skills.

Hinds, John. 1975. Third person pronouns in Japanese. In *Language in Japanese Society*, ed. Fred C. C. Ping. Tokyo: University of Tokyo Press.

1983. Contrastive rhetoric: Japanese and English. *Text* 3:183–95.

1984. Retention of information using a Japanese style of presentation. *Studies in Language* 8:45–69.

1987. Reader versus writer responsibility: a new typology. In *Writing Across Languages: Analysis of L2 Text*, ed. by Ulla Connor and Robert Kaplan. Reading, Mass.: Addison-Wesley.

Hockett, Charles. 1954. Chinese versus English: an exploration of the Whorfian theses. In *Language in Culture*, ed. by Henry Hoijer. Chicago: University of Chicago Press.

Hocking, B.D.W. 1973. Types of interference. In *Focus on the Learner*, ed. by John Oller and Jack Richards. Rowley, Mass.: Newbury House.

Holmes, Glyn. 1977. The problem of anglicized French at the university. *Canadian Modern Language Review* 33:520.

Homburg, Taco. 1984. Holistic evaluation of ESL compositions: can it be validated objectively? *TESOL Quarterly* 18:87–107.

Hornby, A. S. 1974. *Oxford Advanced Learner's Dictionary of Current English*. Oxford: Oxford University Press.

House, Juliane, and Gabriele Kasper. 1981. Politeness markers in English and German. In *Conversation Routine*, ed. by Florian Coulmas. The Hague: Mouton.

Huang, Joseph, and Evelyn Hatch. 1978. A Chinese child's acquisition of English. In *Second Language Acquisition: A Book of Readings*, ed. by Evelyn Hatch. Rowley, Mass.: Newbury House.

Huebner, Thom. 1983. *A Longitudinal Analysis of the Acquisition of English*. Ann Arbor: Karoma.

Huerta, Ana. 1978. Code-switching among Spanish-English bilinguals: a sociolinguistic perspective. Unpublished Ph.D. dissertation, University of Texas at Austin.

Hutchins, Edwin. 1981. Reasoning in Trobriand discourse. In *Language, Culture, and Cognition*, ed. by Ronald Casson. New York: Macmillan.

Hyltenstam, Kenneth. 1977. Implicational patterns in interlanguage syntax variation. *Language Learning* 27:383–411.

    1982. On descriptive adequacy and psychological plausibility: a reply to Jordens. *Language Learning* 32:167–73.

    1984. The use of typological markedness conditions as predictors in second language acquisition. In *Second Languages: A Cross-Linguistic Perspective*, ed. by Roger Andersen. Rowley, Mass.: Newbury House.

Hyman, Larry. 1975. *Phonology: Theory and Analysis*. New York: Holt, Rinehart, and Winston.

Ibrahim, Muhammad. 1978. Patterns in spelling errors. *English Language Teaching* 32:207–12.

Ijaz, I. Helene. 1986. Linguistic and cognitive determinants of lexical acquisition in a second language. *Language Learning* 36:401–51.

Ioup, Georgette. 1984. Is there a structural foreign accent? A comparison of syntactic and phonological errors in a second language. *Language Learning* 34:1–17.

Ioup, Georgette, and Anna Kruse. 1977. Interference and structural complexity as a predictor of second language relative clause acquisition. In *Proceedings of the Los Angeles Second Language Acquisition Research Forum*, ed. by Carol Henning. Los Angeles: Department of English, University of California at Los Angeles.

Ioup, Georgette, and Amara Tansomboon. 1987. The acquisition of tone: a maturational perspective. In *Interlanguage Phonology*, ed. by Georgette Ioup and Steven Weinberger. Rowley, Mass.: Newbury House.

Ioup, Georgette, and Steven Weinberger, eds. 1987. *Interlanguage Phonology*. Rowley, Mass.: Newbury House.

Itoh, Harumi, and Evelyn Hatch. 1978. Second language acquisition: a case study. In *Second Language Acquisition: A Book of Readings*, ed. by Evelyn Hatch. Rowley, Mass.: Newbury House.

Jackson, Jean. 1974. Language identity of the Colombian Vaupés Indians. In

Explorations in the Ethnography of Speaking, ed. by Richard Bauman and Joel Sherzer. Cambridge: Cambridge University Press.

James, Carl. 1971. The exculpation of contrastive linguistics. In *Papers in Contrastive Linguistics*, ed. by Gerhard Nickel. Cambridge: Cambridge University Press.

1980. *Contrastive Analysis*. London: Longman.

Jansen, Bert, Josien Lalleman, and Pieter Muysken. 1981. The alternation hypothesis: acquisition of Dutch word order by Turkish and Moroccan foreign workers. *Language Learning* 31:315–36.

Jespersen, Otto. 1912. *How to Teach a Foreign Language*. London: George Allen.

1929. *The Philosophy of Grammar*. London: Allen and Unwin.

1954. *A Modern English Grammar on Historical Principles*. Part 3. London: Allen and Unwin.

Johansson, Faith. 1973. *Immigrant Swedish Phonology*. Lund, Sweden: Gleerup.

Jordens, Peter. 1977. Rules, grammatical intuitions, and strategies in foreign language learning. *Interlanguage Studies Bulletin* 2:5–76.

1980. Interlanguage research: interpretation or explanation. *Language Learning* 30:195–207.

1982. How to make your facts fit: a response from Jordens. *Language Learning* 32:175–81.

Joseph, Brian. 1983a. *The Synchrony and Diachrony of the Balkan Infinitive*. New York: Cambridge University Press.

1983b. Relativization in Greek: another look at the accessibility hierarchy constraints. *Lingua* 60:1–24.

Kachru, Braj. 1969. English in South Asia. In *Current Trends in Linguistics 5*, ed. by Thomas Sebeok. The Hague: Mouton.

1983. English in South Asia. In *English as a World Language*, ed. by Richard Bailey and Manfred Görlach. Ann Arbor: University of Michigan Press.

1987. *The Alchemy of English*. New York: Pergamon Press.

Kachru, Yamuna. 1983. English and Hindi. In *Annual Review of Applied Linguistics, 1982*, ed. by Robert Kaplan. Rowley, Mass.: Newbury House.

Kalmar, Ivan, Zhong Yong, and Xiao Hong. 1988. Language attitudes in Guangzhou, China. *Language in Society* 16:499–508.

Kamratowski, Joachim, and Joachim Schneider. 1969. Zum Problem der englischen Rechtschreibung. *Englisch* 4:69–74.

Kaplan, Robert. 1966. Cultural thought patterns in intercultural education. *Language Learning* 16:1–20.

Kasper, Gabriele. 1981. *Pragmatische Aspekte in der Interimsprache*. Tübingen: Gunter Narr.

Keenan, Edward. 1975. Variation in Universal Grammar. In *Analyzing Variation in Language*, ed. by Ralph Fasold and Roger Shuy. Washington, D.C.: Georgetown University Press.

1976. Towards a universal definition of "subject." In *Subject and Topic*, ed. by Charles Li. New York: Academic Press.

1978. The syntax of subject-final languages. In *Syntactic Typology*, ed. by Winfred Lehmann. Austin: University of Texas Press.

1985. Relative clauses. In *Language Typology and Syntactic Description*, Volume 2, ed. by Timothy Shopen. Cambridge: Cambridge University Press.

Keenan, Edward, and Kent Bimson. 1975. Perceptual complexity and the cross-language distribution of relative clause and NP-question types. In *Papers from the Parasession on Functionalism*, ed. by Robin Grossman, L. James San, and Timothy Vance. Chicago: Chicago Linguistic Society.

Keenan, Edward, and Bernard Comrie. 1977. Noun phrase accessibility and Universal Grammar. *Linguistic Inquiry* 8:63–99.

Keller-Cohen, Deborah. 1979. Systematicity and variation in the non-native child's acquisition of conversational skills. *Language Learning* 29:27–44.

Kellerman, Eric. 1977. Toward a characterisation of the strategy of transfer in second language learning. *Interlanguage Studies Bulletin* 2:58–145.

1978. Transfer and non-transfer: where we are now. *Studies in Second Language Acquisition* 2:37–57.

1983. Now you see it, now you don't. In *Language Transfer in Language Learning*, ed. by Susan Gass and Larry Selinker. Rowley, Mass.: Newbury House.

1984. The empirical evidence for the influence of L1 on interlanguage. In *Interlanguage*, ed. by Alan Davies, C. Criper, and A.P.R. Howatt. Edinburgh: Edinburgh University Press.

Kellerman, Eric, and Michael Sharwood Smith. 1986. Crosslinguistic influence in second language acquisition: an introduction. In *Crosslinguistic Influence in Second Language Acquisition*, ed. by Eric Kellerman and Michael Sharwood Smith. New York: Pergamon Press.

Kelly, Louis. 1969. *25 Centuries of Language Teaching*. Rowley, Mass.: Newbury House.

Kempf, Margaret. 1975. A study of English proficiency level and the composition errors of incoming foreign students at the University of Cincinnati 1969–1974. Unpublished Ph.D. dissertation, The Ohio State University.

Kinneavy, James. 1971. *A Theory of Discourse*. Englewood Cliffs, N.J.: Prentice-Hall.

Kintsch, Walter, and Edith Greene. 1978. The role of culture-specific schemata in the comprehension and recall of stories. *Discourse Processes* 1:1–13.

Klein, Wolfgang. 1986. *Second Language Acquisition*. Cambridge: Cambridge University Press.

Kleinmann, Howard. 1977. Avoidance behavior in adult second language acquisition. *Language Learning* 27:93–107.

Koch, Barbara Johnstone. 1983. Presentation as proof: the language of Arabic rhetoric. *Anthropological Linguistics* 25:47–60.

Kohn, Kurt. 1987. The analysis of transfer. In *Crosslinguistic Influence in Second Language Acquisition*, ed. by Eric Kellerman and Michael Sharwood Smith. New York: Pergamon Press.

Krashen, Stephen. 1978. Some issues relating to the Monitor Model. In *On TESOL '77*, ed. by H. Douglas Brown, Carlos Yorio, and Ruth Crymes. Washington, D.C.: TESOL.

1981. *Second Language Acquisition and Second Language Learning*. Oxford: Pergamon Press.

1983. Newmark's "Ignorance Hypothesis" and current second language acquisition theory. In *Language Transfer in Language Learning*, ed. by Susan Gass and Larry Selinker. Rowley, Mass.: Newbury House.

Krashen, Stephen, Michael Long, and Robin Scarcella. 1979. Age, rate and eventual attainment in second language acquisition. *TESOL Quarterly* 13:573–82.

Krashen, Stephen, and Tracy Terrell. 1983. *The Natural Approach*. Oxford: Pergamon/Alemany Press.

Kuno, Susumo. 1974. The position of relative clauses and conjunctions. *Linguistic Inquiry* 5:117–36.

Labov, William. 1972. *Sociolinguistic Patterns*. Philadelphia: University of Pennsylvania Press.

——— 1975. *What Is a Linguistic Fact?* Lisse, The Netherlands: Peter de Ridder.

Lado, Robert. 1957. *Linguistics Across Cultures*. Ann Arbor: University of Michigan Press.

Lakoff, George. 1972. Hedges: a study in meaning criteria and the logic of fuzzy concepts. *Papers from the 8th Regional Meeting*. Chicago: Chicago Linguistic Society.

——— 1987. *Women, Fire, and Dangerous Things: What Categories Reveal about the Mind*. Chicago: University of Chicago Press.

Larsen-Freeman, Diane. 1978. An ESL index of development. *TESOL Quarterly* 12:439–48.

Lass, Roger. 1986. "Irish influence": reflections on "standard" English and its opposites, and the identification of calques. *Studia Anglica Posnaniensia* 18:81–87.

Lazard, Gilbert. 1957. *Grammaire du persan contemporain*. Paris: Klincksieck.

Lazzerini, Lucia. 1982. Aux origines du macaronique. *Revue des langues romanes* 86:11–33.

Lee, W. R. 1968. Thoughts on contrastive linguistics in the context of language teaching. In *Report of the Nineteenth Annual Round Table Meeting on Linguistics and Language Studies*, ed. by James Alatis. Monograph Series on Languages and Linguistics, Georgetown University. Washington, D.C.: Georgetown University Press.

Le Page, Robert, and Andrée Tabouret-Keller. 1985. *Acts of Identity: Creole-Based Approaches to Language and Ethnicity*. Cambridge: Cambridge University Press.

Leslau, Wolf. 1945. The influence of Cushitic on the Semitic languages of Ethiopia. *Word* 1:59–82.

——— 1952. The influence of Sidamo on the Ethiopic languages of Gurage. *Language* 28:63–81.

Leung, K. C. 1978. The Cantonese student in the Mandarin class: some special problems. *Journal of the Chinese Language Teachers Association* 13:51–55.

Levin, Harry, Irene Silverman, and Boyce Ford. 1967. Hesitation in children's speech during explanation and description. *Journal of Verbal Learning and Verbal Behavior* 6:560–64.

Levinson, Stephen. 1983. *Pragmatics*. Cambridge: Cambridge University Press.

Lévi-Strauss, Claude. 1955. The structural study of myth. *Journal of American Folklore* 68:428–44.

Li, Charles. 1984. From verb-medial analytic language to verb-final synthetic language: a case of typological change. In *Proceedings from the Tenth Annual Meeting of the Berkeley Linguistics Society*, ed. by Claudia Brugman and Monica Macaulay. Berkeley: Berkeley Linguistics Society.

Li, Charles, and Sandra Thompson. 1976. Subject and topic: a new typology of language. In *Subject and Topic*, ed. by Charles Li. New York: Academic Press.

Liberman, Alvin, Katherine Harris, Howard Hoffman, and Belver Griffith. 1957. The discrimination of speech sounds within and across phoneme boundaries. *Journal of Experimental Psychology* 54:358–68.

Lightbown, Patsy, and Gary Libben. 1984. The recognition and use of cognates by L2 learners. In *Second Languages: A Cross-Linguistic Perspective*, ed. by Roger Andersen. Rowley, Mass.: Newbury House.

Limper, Louis. 1932. Student knowledge of some French-English cognates. *French Review* 6:37–49.

Linnarud, Moira. 1978. Cohesion and communication in the target language. *Interlanguage Studies Bulletin* 3:23–34.

Littlewood, William. 1973. A comparison of first language acquisition and second language learning. *Praxis des Neusprachlichen Unterrichts* 20:343–48.

1983. Contrastive pragmatics and the foreign language learner's personality. *Applied Linguistics* 4:200–06.

Liu, Lisa Garbern. 1985. Reasoning counterfactually in Chinese: are there any obstacles? *Cognition* 21:239–70.

LoCoco, Veronica. 1975. An analysis of Spanish and German learners' errors. *Working Papers in Bilingualism* 7:96–124.

Long, Michael, and Charlene Sato. 1984. Methodological issues in interlanguage studies: an interactionist perspective. In *Interlanguage*, ed. by Alan Davies, C. Criper, and A.P.R. Howatt. Edinburgh: Edinburgh University Press.

Loveday, Leo. 1982a. Communicative interference: a framework for contrastively analysing L2 communicative competence exemplified with the linguistic behaviour of Japanese performing in English. *IRAL: International Review of Applied Linguistics* 20:1–16.

1982b. *The Sociolinguistics of Learning and Using a Non-Native Language*. Oxford: Pergamon Press.

Lowenberg, Peter. 1986. Non-native varieties of English: nativization, norms, and implications. *Studies in Second Language Acquisition* 8:1–18.

Luján, Marta, Liliana Minaya, and David Sankoff. 1984. The universal consistency hypothesis and the prediction of word order acquisition stages in the speech of bilingual children. *Language* 60:343–71.

Lukatela, G., M. D. Savić, P. Ognjenović, and M. T. Turvey. 1978. On the relation between processing the Roman and the Cyrillic alphabets. *Language and Speech* 21:113–73.

Lyons, John. 1977. *Semantics*. Cambridge: Cambridge University Press.

Maddieson, Ian. 1984. *Patterns of Sounds*. Cambridge: Cambridge University Press.

Major, Roy. 1986. Paragoge and degree of foreign accent in Brazilian English. *Second Language Research* 2:53–71.

1987. A model for interlanguage phonology. In *Interlanguage Phonology*, ed. by Georgette Ioup and Steven Weinberger. Rowley, Mass.: Newbury House.

Mandler, Jean, Sylvia Scribner, Michael Cole, and Marsha DeForest. 1980. Cross-cultural invariance in story recall. *Child Development* 51:19–26.

Mann, Virginia. 1986. Distinguishing universal and language-dependent levels of speech perception: evidence from Japanese learners' perception of English "l" and "r." *Cognition* 24:169–96.

Marckwardt, Albert. 1946. Phonemic structure and aural perception. *American Speech* 21:106–11.

Masny, Diana, and Alison d'Anglejan. 1985. Language, cognition, and second language grammaticality judgments. *Journal of Psycholinguistic Research* 14:175–97.

McLaughlin, Barry. 1978. *Second Language Acquisition in Childhood*. Hillsdale, N.J.: Lawrence Erlbaum.

1981. Differences and similarities between first- and second-language learning. In *Native Language and Foreign Language Acquisition*, ed. by Harris Winitz. Annals of the New York Academy of Sciences, Volume 379. New York: New York Academy of Sciences.

McLaughlin, Barry, Tammi Rossman, and Beverly McLeod. 1983. Second language learning: an information-processing perspective. *Language Learning* 33:135–58.

Meillet, Antoine. 1948. *Linguistique historique et linguistique générale*. Paris: Société Linguistique de Paris.

Meisel, Jürgen. 1983. Strategies of second language acquisition: more than one kind of simplification. In *Pidginization and Creolization as Language Acquisition*, ed. by Roger Andersen. Rowley, Mass.: Newbury House.

Meisel, Jürgen, Harald Clahsen, and Manfred Pienemann. 1981. On determining developmental stages in natural second language acquisition. *Studies in Second Language Acquisition* 3:109–35.

Meo Zilio, Giovanni. 1959. Una serie di morfemi italiani con funzione stilistica nello spagnolo nell'Uruguay. *Lingua Nostra* 20:49–54.

1964. El "Cocoliche" Rioplatense. *Boletín de Filología* 16:61–119.

Mervis, Carolyn, and Emilie Roth. 1981. The internal structure of basic and non-basic color categories. *Language* 57:384–405.

Mohan, Bernard, and Winnie Au-Yeung Lo. 1985. Academic writing and Chinese students: transfer and developmental factors. *TESOL Quarterly* 19:515–34.

Moravcsik, Edith, and Jessica Wirth. 1986. Markedness – an overview. In *Markedness*, ed. by Fred Eckman, Edith Moravcsik, and Jessica Wirth. New York: Plenum Press.

Moulton, William. 1962a. Toward a classification of pronunciation errors. *Modern Language Journal* 46:101–09.

1962b. *The Sounds of English and German*. Chicago: University of Chicago Press.

Mühlhäusler, Peter. 1986. *Pidgin and Creole Linguistics*. Oxford: Basil Blackwell.

Müller, Max. 1861/1965. *Lectures on the Science of Language*. New Delhi: Munshi Ram Manohar Lal.

Muysken, Pieter. 1984. The Spanish that Quechua speakers learn. In *Second Languages: A Cross-Linguistic Perspective*, ed. by Roger Andersen. Rowley, Mass.: Newbury House.

Muysken, Pieter, and Norval Smith, eds. 1986. *Substrata Versus Universals in Creole Genesis*. Amsterdam: John Benjamins.

Nagara, Susumu. 1972. *Japanese Pidgin English in Hawaii: A Bilingual Description*. Honolulu: University Press of Hawaii.

Nelson, Katherine. 1974. Concept, word and sentence: interrelations in acquisition and development. *Psychological Review* 81:276–85.

Neufeld, Gerald. 1978. On the acquisition of prosodic and articulatory features in adult language learning. *Canadian Modern Language Review* 34:163–74.

188   *References*

Obilade, Tony. 1984. Mother tongue influence on polite communication in a second language. *Language and Communication* 4:295–99.
Odlin, Terence. 1986. On the nature and use of explicit knowledge. *IRAL: International Review of Applied Linguistics* 24:123–44.
1987. Word order transfer and metalinguistic awareness. Presented at the University of Illinois Conference on Second Language Acquisition and Foreign Language Learning, Champaign, Ill.
1988. Divil a lie: semantic transparency and language transfer. Presented at the Second Language Research Forum, University of Hawaii at Manoa.
Oller, John, and Elcho Redding. 1971. Article usage and other language skills. *Language Learning* 21/1:85–95.
Oller, John, and Seid Ziahosseiny. 1970. The contrastive analysis hypothesis and spelling errors. *Language Learning* 20:183–89.
Olshtain, Elite. 1983. Sociocultural competence and language transfer: the case of apology. In *Language Transfer in Language Learning*, ed. by Susan Gass and Larry Selinker. Rowley, Mass.: Newbury House.
Olson, Linda, and S. Jay Samuels. 1973. The relationship between age and accuracy of foreign language pronunciation. *Journal of Educational Research* 66:263–67.
Ong, Walter. 1982. *Orality and Literacy*. New York: Methuen.
Orth, John. 1982. University undergraduate evaluational reactions to the speech of foreign teaching assistants. Unpublished Ph.D. dissertation, University of Texas at Austin.
Osgood, Charles, William May, and Murray Miron. 1975. *Cross-cultural Universals of Affective Meaning*. Urbana, Ill.: University of Illinois Press.
Oxford, Rebecca, and Nancy Rhodes. 1988. U.S. foreign language instruction: assessing needs and creating an action plan. *ERIC/CLL News Bulletin* 11:1, 6–8.
Oyama, Susan. 1976. A sensitive period for the acquisition of a nonnative phonological system. *Journal of Psycholinguistic Research* 5:261–85.
Palmer, Harold. 1917. *The Scientific Study and Teaching of Languages*. Yonkers-on-Hudson, N.Y.: World Book Company.
Pandharipande, Rajeshwari. 1983. Linguistics and written discourse in particular contrastive studies: English and Marathi. In *Annual Review of Applied Linguistics, 1982*, ed. by Robert Kaplan. Rowley, Mass.: Newbury House.
Paulston, Christina. 1978. Biculturalism: some reflections and speculations. *TESOL Quarterly* 12:369–80.
Pavlovitch, Milivoie. 1920. *Le langage enfantin: acquisition du serbe et du français par un enfant serbe*. Paris: Champion.
Peck, Sabrina. 1978. Child–child discourse in second language acquisition. In *Second Language Acquisition: A Book of Readings*, ed. by Evelyn Hatch. Rowley, Mass.: Newbury House.
Penn, Julia. 1972. *Linguistic Relativity Versus Innate Ideas*. The Hague: Mouton.
Pica, Teresa. 1984. L1 transfer and L2 complexity as factors in syllabus design. *TESOL Quarterly* 18:689–704.
Pienemann, Manfred. 1981. *Der Zweitspracherwerb ausländischer Arbeiterkinder*. Bonn: Bouvier Verlag Herbert Grundmann.
1984. Psychological constraints on the teachability of languages. *Studies in Second Language Acquisition* 6:186–214.

Pike, Eunice. 1959. A test for predicting phonetic ability. *Language Learning* 9:35–41.

Pike, Kenneth. 1954. *Language in Relation to a Unified Theory of the Structure of Human Behavior*. Glendale, Calif.: Summer Institute of Linguistics.

Platt, John, Heidi Weber, and Ho Mian Lian. 1984. *The New Englishes*. London: Routledge, Kegan, and Paul.

Poplack, Shana. 1980. Sometimes I'll start a conversation in Spanish Y TERMINO EN ESPANOL: toward a typology of code-switching. *Linguistics* 18:581–616.

Propp, Vladimir. 1968. *Morphology of the Folktale*. Austin: University of Texas Press.

Purcell, Edward, and Richard Suter. 1980. Predictors of pronunciation accuracy: a reexamination. *Language Learning* 30:271–87.

Pürschel, Heiner. 1975. *Pause und Kadenz: Interferenzerscheinungen bei der englischen Intonation deutscher Sprecher*. Tübingen: Max Niemeyer.

Purves, Alan. 1986. Rhetorical communities, the international student, and basic writing. *Journal of Basic Writing* 5:38–51.

Rao, Raja. 1963. *Kanthapura*. New York: New Directions.

Ravem, Roar. 1968. Language acquisition in a second language environment. *IRAL: International Review of Applied Linguistics* 6:175–85.

Redlinger, Wendy, and Tschange-zin Park. 1980. Language mixing in young bilinguals. *Journal of Child Language* 7:337–52.

Reisman, Karl. 1974. Contrapuntal conversations in an Antiguan village. In *Explorations in the Ethnography of Speaking*, ed. by Richard Bauman and Joel Sherzer. London: Cambridge University Press.

Richards, Jack. 1971. A noncontrastive approach to error analysis. *English Language Teaching* 25:204–19.

——— 1979. Rhetorical and communicative styles in the new varieties of English. *Language Learning* 29:1–25.

——— 1980. Conversation. *TESOL Quarterly* 14:413–32.

Richards, Jack, and Mayuri Sukwiwat. 1983. Cross-cultural aspects of conversational competence. *Applied Linguistics* 4:113–25.

Ringbom, Håkan. 1976. What differences are there between Finns and Swedish-speaking Finns learning English? In *Errors Made by Finns and Swedish-Speaking Finns in the Learning of English*, ed. by Håkan Ringbom and Rolf Palmberg. Abo, Finland: Department of English, Abo Akademi. ERIC Report ED 122628.

——— 1986. Crosslinguistic influence and the foreign language learning process. In *Crosslinguistic Influence in Second Language Acquisition*, ed. by Eric Kellerman and Michael Sharwood Smith. New York: Pergamon Press.

——— 1987. *The Role of the First Language in Foreign Language Learning*. Clevedon, U.K.: Multilingual Matters.

Ringbom, Håkan, and Rolf Palmberg, eds. 1976. *Errors Made by Finns and Swedish-Speaking Finns in the Learning of English*. Abo, Finland: Department of English, Abo Akademi. ERIC Report ED 122628.

Rintell, Ellen. 1979. Getting your speech act together: the pragmatic ability of second language learners. *Working Papers in Bilingualism* 17:97–106.

——— 1984. But how did you FEEL about that? The learner's perception of emotion in speech. *Applied Linguistics* 5:255–64.

Robins, Robert. 1979. *A Short History of Linguistics*. London: Longman.

Rona, José. 1965. *El Dialecto "Fronterizo" del Norte del Uruguay*. Montevideo: Adolfo Linardi.

Ronjat, Jules. 1913. *Le développement du langage observé chez un enfant bilingue*. Paris: Champion.

Rosansky, Ellen. 1976. Methods and morphemes in second language acquisition. *Language Learning* 26:409–25.

Rosch, Eleanor. 1973. On the internal structure of perceptual and semantic categories. In *Cognitive Development and the Acquisition of Language*, ed. by Timothy Moore. New York: Academic Press.

    1974. Linguistic relativity. In *Human Communication: Theoretical Explorations*, ed. by Albert Silverstein. Hillsdale, N.J.: Lawrence Erlbaum.

Rutherford, William. 1983. Language typology and language transfer. In *Language Transfer in Language Learning*, ed. by Susan Gass and Larry Selinker. Rowley, Mass.: Newbury House.

Ryan, Ellen, Miguel Carranza, and Robert Moffie. 1977. Reactions toward varying degrees of accentedness in the speech of Spanish-English bilinguals. *Language and Speech* 20:267–73.

Sacks, Harvey, Emanuel Schegloff, and Gail Jefferson. 1974. A simplest systematics for the organization of turn-taking in conversation. *Language* 50:696–735.

Sajavaara, Kari, and Jaakko Lehtonen. 1981. A bibliography of applied contrastive studies. In *Contrastive Linguistics and the Language Teacher*, ed. by Jacek Fisiak. Oxford: Pergamon Press.

Sampson, Geoffrey. 1985. *Writing Systems*. London: Hutchinson.

Sandfeld, Kristien. 1930. *Linguistique balkanique*. Paris: Champion.

Sanford, A. J., and S. C. Garrod. 1981. *Understanding Written Language*. Chichester, U.K.: John Wiley.

Sato, Charlene. 1984. Phonological processes in second language acquisition: another look at interlanguage syllable structure. *Language Learning* 34:43–57.

Scarcella, Robin. 1979. On speaking politely in a second language. In *On TESOL '79*, ed. by Carlos Yorio, Kyle Perkins, and Jacquelyn Schachter. Washington, D.C.: TESOL.

    1984. How writers orient their readers in expository essays: a comparative study of native and non-native English writers. *TESOL Quarterly* 18:671–88.

Schachter, Jacquelyn. 1974. An error in error analysis. *Language Learning* 24:205–14.

    1986. In search of systematicity in interlanguage production. *Studies in Second Language Acquisition* 8:119–33.

    In Press. Second language acquisition and its relationship to Universal Grammar. To appear in *Applied Linguistics*.

Schachter, Jacquelyn, and Marianne Celce-Murcia. 1977. Some reservations concerning error analysis. *TESOL Quarterly* 11:441–51.

Schachter, Jacquelyn, and Beverly Hart. 1979. An analysis of learner production of English structures. *Georgetown University Papers on Languages and Linguistics* 15:18–75.

Schachter, Jacquelyn, and William Rutherford. 1979. Discourse function and language transfer. *Working Papers in Bilingualism* 19:1–12.

Schane, Sanford. 1973. *Generative Phonology*. Englewood Cliffs, N.J.: Prentice-Hall.

Schmidt, Annette. 1985. *Young People's Dyirbal*. Cambridge: Cambridge University Press.

Schmidt, Richard. 1987. Sociolinguistic variation and language transfer in phonology. In *Interlanguage Phonology*, ed. by Georgette Ioup and Steven Weinberger. Rowley, Mass.: Newbury House.

—— 1988. The role of consciousness in second language learning. Presented at the Second Language Research Forum, University of Hawaii at Manoa.

Scholes, Robert. 1968. Phonemic interference as a perceptual phenomenon. *Language and Speech* 11:86–103.

Schuchardt, Hugo. 1883a. Kreolische Studien III. Über das Indoportugiesische von Diu. *Sitzungberichte der kaiserlichen Akademie der Wissenschaften zu Wien* (philosophisch-historische Klasse) 103:3–17.

—— 1883b. Kreolische Studien IV. Über das Malaiospanische der Philippinen. *Sitzungberichte der kaiserlichen Akademie der Wissenschaften zu Wien* (philosophisch-historische Klasse) 105:111–50.

—— 1884/1971. *Slawo-deutsches und Slawo-italienisches*. Munich: Wilhelm Fink.

—— 1891/1980. Indo-English. In *Pidgin and Creole Languages: Selected Essays by Hugo Schuchardt*, ed. by Glenn Gilbert. London: Cambridge University Press.

—— 1909/1980. The lingua franca. In *Pidgin and Creole Languages: Selected Essays by Hugo Schuchardt*, ed. by Glenn Gilbert. London: Cambridge University Press.

Schumann, John. 1978. *The Pidginization Process: A Model for Second Language Acquisition*. Rowley, Mass.: Newbury House.

—— 1979. The acquisition of English negation by speakers of Spanish: a review of the literature. In *The Acquisition and Use of Spanish and English as First Languages*, ed. by Roger Andersen. Washington, D.C.: TESOL.

—— 1984. Nonsyntactic speech in the Spanish-English basilang. In *Second Languages: A Cross-Linguistic Perspective*, ed. by Roger Andersen. Rowley, Mass.: Newbury House.

—— 1986. Locative and directional expressions in basilang speech. *Language Learning* 36:277–94.

Scollon, Ron, and Suzanne Scollon. 1981. *Narrative, Literacy, and Face in Interethnic Communication*. Norwood, N.J.: Ablex.

Scovel, Thomas. 1969. Foreign accent, language acquisition, and cerebral dominance. *Language Learning* 19:245–54.

Scribner, Sylvia, and Michael Cole. 1981. *The Psychology of Literacy*. Cambridge, Mass.: Harvard University Press.

Sebeok, Thomas, ed. 1960. *Style in Language.*Cambridge: Mass.: MIT Press.

Seliger, Herbert, Stephen Krashen, and Peter Ladefoged. 1975. Maturational constraints in the acquisition of second languages. *Language Sciences* 38:20–22.

Selinker, Larry. 1969. Language transfer. *General Linguistics* 9:67–92.

—— 1972. Interlanguage. *IRAL: International Review of Applied Linguistics* 10:209–31.

Selinker, Larry, Merrill Swain, and Guy Dumas. 1975. The interlanguage hypothesis extended to children. *Language Learning* 25:139–52.

Sey, K. A. 1973. *Ghanaian English: An Exploratory Survey*. London: Macmillan.

Shapira, Rina. 1978. The non-learning of English: case study of an adult. In *Second Language Acquisition: A Book of Readings*, ed. by Evelyn Hatch. Rowley, Mass.: Newbury House.

Sharwood Smith, Michael. 1986. The competence/control model, crosslinguistic influence, and the creation of new grammars. In *Crosslinguistic Influence in Second Language Acquisition*, ed. by Eric Kellerman and Michael Sharwood Smith. New York: Pergamon Press.

Shaughnessy, Mina. 1977. *Errors and Expectations*. New York: Oxford University Press.

Shaw, Willard. 1981. Asian student attitudes towards English. In *English for Cross-Cultural Communication*, ed. by Larry Smith. New York: St. Martin's Press.

Sheldon, Amy. 1977. The acquisition of relative clauses in French and English: implications for language-learning universals. In *Current Themes in Linguistics*, ed. by Fred Eckman. New York: John Wiley.

Sherzer, Joel. 1974. Namakke, Sunmakke, Kormakke: three types of Cuna speech event. In *Explorations in the Ethnography of Speaking*, ed. by Richard Bauman and Joel Sherzer. London: Cambridge University Press.

Shuman, Amy. 1986. *Storytelling Rights: The Uses of Oral and Written Texts by Urban Adolescents*. Cambridge: Cambridge University Press.

Silvestri, Domenico. 1977. *La Teoria del Sostrato: Metodi e Miraggi*. Naples: Gaetano Macchiaroli.

Singler, John. 1988. The homogeneity of the substrate as a factor in pidgin/creole genesis. *Language* 64:27–51.

Singleton, David. 1987. Mother and other tongue influence on learner French. *Studies in Second Language Acquisition* 9:327–45.

Singleton, David, and David Little. 1984. A first encounter with Dutch: perceived language distance and language transfer as factors in comprehension. In *Language Across Cultures*, ed. by Liam MacMathuna and David Singleton. Dublin: Irish Association for Applied Linguistics.

Sjöholm, Kaj. 1976. A comparison of the test results in grammar and vocabulary between Finnish- and Swedish-speaking applicants for English. In *Errors Made by Finns and Swedish-Speaking Finns in the Learning of English*, ed. by Hakan Ringbom and Rolf Palmberg. Abo, Finland: Department of English, Abo Akademi. ERIC Report ED 122628.

Slobin, Dan. 1977. Language change in childhood and history. In *Language Learning and Thought*, ed. by John MacNamara. New York: Academic Press.

———. 1982. Universal and particular in acquisition. In *Language Acquisition: The State of the Art*, ed. by Eric Wanner and Lila Gleitman. Cambridge: Cambridge University Press.

———. 1985. The child as a linguistic icon-maker. In *Iconicity in Syntax*, ed. by John Haiman. Amsterdam: John Benjamins.

Smith, Larry, and John Bisazza. 1982. The comprehensibility of three varieties of English for college students in seven countries. *Language Learning* 32:259–69.

Smith, Larry, and Khalilullah Rafiqzad. 1979. English for cross-cultural communication: the question of intelligibility. *TESOL Quarterly* 13:371–80.

Snow, Catherine. 1981. English speakers' acquisition of Dutch syntax. In *Annals of the New York Academy of Sciences*, ed. by Harris Winitz. New York: New York Academy of Sciences.

Snow, Catherine, and Marian Hoefnagel-Höhle. 1977. Age differences in the pronunciation of foreign sounds. *Language and Speech* 20:357–75.

Sohn, Ho-Min. 1980. Syntactic and semantic interference for Korean adult English learners. In *Bilingual Education for Asian Americans*, ed. by John Koo and Robert St. Clair. Hiroshima: Bunka Hyoron.

Sorenson, A. P. 1967. Multilingualism in the northwest Amazon. *American Anthropologist* 69:670–84.

Sridhar, S. N. 1981. Contrastive analysis, error analysis, and interlanguage: three phases of one goal. In *Contrastive Analysis and the Language Teacher*, ed. by Jacek Fisiak. Oxford: Pergamon Press.

Stauble, Ann-Marie. 1984. A comparison of a Spanish-English and a Japanese-English second language continuum. In *Second Languages: A Cross-Linguistic Perspective*, ed. by Roger Andersen. Rowley, Mass.: Newbury House.

Steffensen, Margaret, Chitra Joag-Dev, and Richard Anderson. 1979. A cross-cultural perspective on reading comprehension. *Reading Research Quarterly* 15:10–29.

Stendahl, Cristina. 1972. A note on the relative proficiency in Swedish and English as shown by Swedish university students of English. *Moderna Språk* 66/2:117–23.

Stenson, Nancy. 1974. Induced errors. In *New Frontiers of Second Language Learning*, ed. by John Schumann and Nancy Stenson. Rowley, Mass.: Newbury House.

1981. *Studies in Irish Syntax*. Tübingen: Gunter Narr.

Stockwell, Robert, J. Donald Bowen, and John Martin. 1965. *The Grammatical Structures of English and Spanish*. Chicago: University of Chicago Press.

Strick, Gregory. 1980. A hypothesis for semantic development in a second language. *Language Learning* 30:155–76.

Sullivan, James. 1980. The validity of literary dialect: evidence from the portrayal of Hiberno-English features. *Language in Society* 9:195–219.

Suter, Richard. 1976. Predictors of pronunciation accuracy in second language learning. *Language Learning* 26:233–53.

Swan, Michael, and Bernard Smith, eds. 1987. *Learner English: A Teacher's Guide to Interference and Other Problems*. Cambridge: Cambridge University Press.

Sweet, Henry. 1899/1972. *The Practical Study of Languages*. London: Oxford University Press.

Taeschner, Traute. 1983. *The Sun Is Feminine: A Study on Language Acquisition in Bilingual Children*. Berlin: Springer-Verlag.

Tannen, Deborah. 1981. Indirectness in discourse: ethnicity as conversational style. *Discourse Processes* 4:221–38.

1984. Spoken and written narrative in English and Greek. In *Coherence in Spoken and Written Discourse*, ed. by Deborah Tannen. Advances in Discourse Processes, Volume 12, ed. by Roy Freedle. Norwood, N.J.: Ablex.

Tannen, Deborah, and Piyale Öztek. 1981. Health to our mouths: formulaic expressions in Turkish and Greek. In *Conversation Routine*, ed. by Florian Coulmas. The Hague: Mouton.

Tarallo, Fernando, and John Myhill. 1983. Interference and natural language in second language acquisition. *Language Learning* 33:55–76.

Tarone, Elaine. 1979. Interlanguage as chameleon. *Language Learning* 29:181–91.

1980. Some influences on the syllable structure of interlanguage phonology. *IRAL: International Review of Applied Linguistics* 18:139–52.

Taylor, Archer. 1962. *The Proverb*. Hatboro, Pa.: Folklore Associates.

Taylor, Barry. 1975. The use of overgeneralization and transfer learning strategies by elementary and intermediate students of ESL. *Language Learning* 25:73–107.

Taylor, Linda, Alexander Guiora, John Catford, and Harlan Lane. 1969. The role of personality variables in second language behavior. *Comprehensive Psychiatry* 10:463–74.

Thomas, Jenny. 1983. Cross-cultural pragmatic failure. *Applied Linguistics* 4:91–112.

Thomason, Sarah. 1981. Are there linguistic prerequisites for contact-induced language change? Paper presented at the 10th Annual University of Wisconsin-Milwaukee Linguistics Symposium. ERIC Report ED 205054.

Thomason, Sarah, and Terrence Kaufman. 1988. *Language Contact, Creolization, and Genetic Linguistics*. Berkeley: University of California Press.

Thompson, Sandra. 1978. Modern English from a typological point of view. *Linguistische Berichte* 54:19–35.

Thorndyke, Perry. 1977. Cognitive structures in comprehension and memory of narrative discourse. *Cognitive Psychology* 9:77–110.

Tiffin, Brian. 1974. The intelligibility of Nigerian English. Unpublished Ph.D. dissertation, University of London.

Todd, Loreto. 1983. English in West Africa. In *English as a World Language*, ed. by Richard Bailey and Manfred Görlach. Ann Arbor: University of Michigan Press.

Traugott, Elizabeth, and Mary Pratt. 1980. *Linguistics for Students of Literature*. New York: Harcourt, Brace and Jovanovich.

Trévise, Anne. 1986. Is it transferable, topicalization? In *Crosslinguistic Influence in Second Language Acquisition*, ed. by Eric Kellerman and Michael Sharwood Smith. New York: Pergamon Press.

Trudgill, Peter. 1984. *On Dialect*. New York: New York University Press.

1986. *Dialects in Contact*. Oxford: Basil Blackwell.

Upshur, John. 1962. Language proficiency testing and the contrastive analysis dilemma. *Language Learning* 12:123–27.

Vachek, Josef. 1964. Written language and printed language. In *A Prague School Reader in Linguistics*, ed. by Josef Vachek. Bloomington: Indiana University Press.

Van Els, Theo, and Kees De Bot. 1987. The role of intonation in foreign accent. *Modern Language Journal* 71:147–55.

Van Patten, Bill. 1984. Processing strategies and morpheme acquisition. In *Universals of Second Language Acquisition*, ed. by Fred Eckman, Lawrence Bell, and Diane Nelson. Rowley, Mass.: Newbury House.

Varadi, Tamas. 1983. Strategies of target language learners: message adjustment. In *Strategies in Interlanguage Communication*, ed. by Claus Faerch and Gabriele Kasper. London: Longman.

Veronique, Daniel. 1984. The acquisition and use of French morphosyntax by native speakers of Arabic dialects. In *Second Languages: A Cross-Linguistic Perspective*, ed. by Roger Andersen. Rowley, Mass.: Newbury House.

Vihman, Marilyn. 1985. Language differentiation by the bilingual infant. *Journal of Child Language* 12:297–324.

Vildomec, Veroboj. 1963. *Multilingualism*. Leyden: A. W. Sythoff.

Walters, Joel. 1979a. Strategies for requesting in Spanish and English – structural similarities and pragmatic differences. *Language Learning* 29:277–93.

1979b. The perception of politeness in English and Spanish. In *On TESOL '79*, ed. by Carlos Yorio, Kyle Perkins, and Jacquelyn Schachter. Washington, D.C.: TESOL.

Wardhaugh, Ronald. 1970. The contrastive analysis hypothesis. *TESOL Quarterly* 4:123–30.

Weinreich, Max. 1980. *A History of the Yiddish Language*. Chicago: University of Chicago Press.

Weinreich, Uriel. 1953/1968. *Languages in Contact*. The Hague: Mouton.

Wexler, Kenneth, and Peter Culicover. 1980. *Formal Principles of Language Acquisition*. Cambridge, Mass.: MIT Press.

White, Lydia. 1985. The "pro-drop" parameter in adult second language acquisition. *Language Learning* 35:47–62.

1987. Markedness and second language acquisition: the question of transfer. *Studies in Second Language Acquisition* 9:261–85.

Whitman, Randall, and Kenneth Jackson. 1972. The unpredictability of contrastive analysis. *Language Learning* 22:29–42.

Whitney, William. 1881. On mixture in language. *Transactions of the American Philological Association* 12:5–26.

Whorf, Benjamin. 1956. *Language, Thought, and Reality*. Cambridge, Mass.: MIT Press.

Willems, Nico. 1982. *English Intonation from a Dutch Point of View*. Dordrecht: Foris Publications.

Winfield, Fairlie, and Barnes-Felfeli, Paula. 1982. The effects of familiar and unfamiliar cultural context on foreign language composition. *Modern Language Journal* 66:373–78.

Wode, Henning. 1978. Developmental sequences in naturalistic L2 acquisition. In *Second Language Acquisition*, ed. by Evelyn Hatch. Rowley, Mass.: Newbury House.

1981. *Learning a Second Language: An Integrated View of Language Acquisition*. Tübingen: Gunter Narr.

1983a. Four early stages in the development of L1 negation. In *Papers on Language Acquisition, Language Learning, and Language Teaching*, ed. by Henning Wode. Heidelberg: Julius Groos.

1983b. On the systematicity of L1 transfer in L2 acquisition. In *Papers on Language Acquisition, Language Learning, and Language Teaching*, ed. by Henning Wode. Heidelberg: Julius Groos.

1983c. Language acquisition, pidgins, and language typology. In *Papers on Language Acquisition, Language Learning, and Language Teaching*, ed. by Henning Wode. Heidelberg: Julius Groos.

Wolfram, Walt. 1978. Contrastive linguistics and social lectology. *Language Learning* 28:1–28.

Wolfson, Nessa. 1981. Compliments in cross-cultural perspective. *TESOL Quarterly* 15:117–24.

Wright, Joseph. 1898. *The English Dialect Dictionary*. London: Oxford University Press.

Young, D. I. 1974. The acquisition of English syntax by three Spanish-speaking children. Unpublished M.A. thesis, University of California at Los Angeles.

Zobl, Helmut. 1980. The formal and developmental selectivity of L1 influence on L2 acquisition. *Language Learning* 30:43–57.

1982. A direction for contrastive analysis: the comparative study of developmental sequences. *TESOL Quarterly* 16:169–83.

1983. L1 acquisition, age of L2 acquisition, and the learning of word order. In *Language Transfer in Language Learning*, ed. by Susan Gass and Larry Selinker. Rowley, Mass.: Newbury House.

1984. The wave model of linguistic change and the naturalness of interlanguage. *Studies in Second Language Acquisition* 6:160–85.

1986. Word order typology, lexical government, and the prediction of multiple, graded effects in L2 word order. *Language Learning* 36:159–83.

Language index

Since references to English occur on almost every page of the text, only specific varieties of English (e.g., Nigerian English) are indexed here.

Author index

In all cases of work involving co-authors, only the name of the first author of the work appears in this index.

Subject index